Centennial Essays
for Robinson Jeffers

Centennial Essays
for Robinson Jeffers

Edited by Robert Zaller

DELAWARE
Newark: University of Delaware Press
London and Toronto: Associated University Presses

Associated University Presses
440 Forsgate Drive
Cranbury, NJ 08512

Associated University Presses
25 Sicilian Avenue
London WC1A 2QH, England

Associated University Presses
P.O. Box 39, Clarkson Pstl. Stn.
Mississauga, Ontario,
L5J 3X9 Canada

The paper used in this publication meets the requirements of the American National Standard for Permanence of Paper for Printed Library Materials Z39.48-1984.

Library of Congress Cataloging-in-Publication Data

Centennial essays for Robinson Jeffers / edited by Robert Zaller.
    p.   cm.
  Includes bibliographical references.
  ISBN 0-87413-414-5 (alk. paper)
  1. Jeffers, Robinson, 1887–1962—Criticism and interpretation.
  I. Jeffers, Robinson, 1887–1962.   II. Zaller, Robert.
PS3519.E27Z576   1991
811'.52—dc20   90-50542
                                                              CIP

PRINTED IN THE UNITED STATES OF AMERICA

Contents

Acknowledgments   7

Introduction
ROBERT ZALLER   9

Poet without Critics: A Note on Robinson Jeffers
HORACE GREGORY   15

Robinson Jeffers, American Poetry, and a Thousand Years
ROBERT ZALLER   29

Robinson Jeffers: Poet of Controversy
ALEX A. VARDAMIS   44

A Sovereign Voice: The Poetry of Robinson Jeffers
ROBERT BOYERS   68

The Problematic Nature of *Tamar and Other Poems*
TIM HUNT   85

Reading Robinson Jeffers: Formalism, Poststructuralism,
and the Inhumanist Turn
DAVID COPLAND MORRIS   107

Robinson Jeffers' Ordeal of Emergence
WILLIAM EVERSON   123

"Something New Is Made": *Bricolage* and Jeffers' Narrative
Poems of the 1920s
ARTHUR B. COFFIN   186

Loving to Death: A Consideration of "The Loving
Shepherdess"
R. W. (HERBIE) BUTTERFIELD   200

The Emasculation Syndrome among Jeffers' Protagonists
ROBERT J. BROPHY   214

Jeffers' Artistry of Line
DELL HYMES   226

The Verbal Magnificence of Robinson Jeffers
  FREDERIC I. CARPENTER   248

The Politics of Robinson Jeffers
  EDWARD A. NICKERSON   254

Robinson Jeffers
  CZESLAW MIŁOSZ   268

Contributors   274

Index   277

Acknowledgments

This book is most indebted to the late George L. White, who urged it on me. To the contributors who have made it possible, my thanks for generous diversity of insight and patience with their editor. There are many roads to Jeffers; each has riches to yield.

Jean Ritter-Murray, John Hicks, Hadley Osborn, and many others have made my visits to Tor House and Carmel deeply rewarding; my thanks for their encouragement and support. Stanley Burnshaw provided, as always, wise counsel and penetrating criticism. Peter Dale and Herbie Butterfield, warm friends of Jeffers in England, have offered both critical and personal hospitality; to both, many thanks are due. Pria Jha typed a preliminary manuscript.

As always, my deepest debt is to Lili. To paraphrase Jeffers himself, let it only be said that we have spent the night well.

Introduction

Robert Zaller

This volume was prepared in commemoration of the centenary year of Robinson Jeffers' birth.[1] It is the first critical collection devoted exclusively to Jeffers, and contains, in addition to nine commissioned essays, a selection of important essays published in the past four decades.

John Robinson Jeffers was born in Sewickley, a suburb of Pittsburgh, Pennsylvania, on 10 January 1887. His father was a professor of theology, and ambitious for his son. Jeffers was educated at private schools in Zurich, Lausanne, Leipzig, and Geneva. He was fluent in French and German—even the Swiss dialect of Romansch appears in his verse drama "The Alpine Christ"—and was drilled in Latin and Greek. Jeffers never aspired to be a critic, but his erudition and range of reference was as wide as that of anyone in his generation.

Jeffers graduated from Occidental College in Los Angeles, where the family had settled in 1903, and did graduate work at the University of Southern California and the University of Washington. After some years of drift, three events suddenly locked Jeffers' life into place. He came into a modest legacy that enabled him to devote himself to a literary career; he was freed to marry the woman he had courted for seven years, Una Call Kuster, by the latter's divorce; and, kept from settling in England by the outbreak of the First World War, he found in the little town of Carmel-by-the-Sea what was to be his home for nearly fifty years and in the grandeur of the central California coast the permanent subject of his poetry.

Jeffers' romantic isolation in Carmel has been exaggerated. The town was a thriving artist's colony whose residents at one time or another included George Sterling, Jack London, Sinclair Lewis, Mary Austin, and Lincoln Steffens. If Jeffers was aloof by nature, Una was intensely sociable, and her letters record an active round of dining and partying. Twin sons, Donnan and Garth, were born to them in 1916, and two years later Jeffers bought property two miles outside the town and began to build his house.

Jeffers harbored large ambitions and produced diligent quantities of verse in his first years at Carmel. Occasional gleams of genuine talent appeared in them, but for the most part they were, as he himself commented, imitations of "dead men's music." A volume published by Macmillan, *Californians,* drew modestly favorable reviews; a second manuscript, offered to the same publisher, was rejected.

In the five years after the end of World War I, in ways still imperfectly understood, Jeffers found his mature voice. Robert Boyers has called it "sovereign" and William Everson has likened the force of its impact on him to a religious conversion. When it first reached a wider public in *Roan Stallion, Tamar and Other Poems* (1925), it left sober critics groping for comparison with the greatest figures of classical literature. For a decade Jeffers sustained this initial impression in the narratives and shorter poems of *The Women at Point Sur* (1927), *Cawdor* (1928), *Dear Judas* (1929), *Descent to the Dead* (1931), *Thurso's Landing* (1932), *Give Your Heart to the Hawks* (1933), and *Solstice* (1935). In the 1940s he extended his reputation to the theater with an adaptation of Euripides' *Medea* that enjoyed a successful Broadway run, and in the 1950s the honors of an elder poet came his way. But poetic fashion was already passing him by in the 1930s, when modernism and its critical votaries began to entrench themselves in the academy and progressive social ideology to demand its due. By the end of World War II, poets unaffiliated with the academy were rapidly becoming the exception rather than the rule, and Jeffers' political isolationism was even more out of step with the times than had been his earlier aversion to the New Deal. His rhetoric as well seemed hollow and grandiloquent to a generation bred on tight ironies, measured stanzas, and recondite allusions. When Roethke, Lowell, and Berryman opened up a new terrain in the 1950s, it remained one whose intense privatism offered no purchase for Jeffers. Ironically, the one poet writing most nearly in Jeffers' vein of long narrative and meditative lyric, Kenneth Rexroth, was the most publicly hostile to his work. Most others were content simply to ignore him. By the time of his death in 1962, he was largely a forgotten figure.

A full generation has passed since then, and Jeffers' place in American literature remains unsettled. Small claims have never been made for him, and there is little middle ground. For his admirers he is one of the greatest American poets of the twentieth century, if not the greatest; to his detractors he is an embarrassing reminder of the literary provincialism that once promoted Vachel Lindsay and Carl Sandburg as major figures. It may be, as critics such as Tim Hunt suggest, that with the passing of the wars of modernism, a greater degree of consensus will emerge.

The essays in this volume all assume Jeffers' permanent value but differ in assessing it. For some, his principal achievement is in the long narratives with which his name is chiefly associated; for others, in the shorter lyrics where his feeling for natural beauty emerges most directly. Again, some find in his work a coherent philosophical position, while others see him as fundamentally eclectic in the manner of Eliot or Pound, experimentally using the cultural materials his epoch furnished to hand. Several essays concentrate on the problematics of Jeffers' literary reputation and career. Tim Hunt and William Everson focus on the critical period of his apprenticeship and first maturity. Everson's pathbreaking essays on the early work, themselves journeys of personal exploration, are reprinted in full, while Hunt's lucid study of the postwar poems represents the finest close analysis we have had of the subtle but decisive shifts of attitude and style that ushered in the major work. Both Hunt and David Copland Morris address the vexed question of Jeffers' relation to modernism, and, in Morris's essay, poststructuralism. Arthur B. Coffin finds an affinity between Jeffers and Lévi-Strauss, and it may be remarked that the poet's notion of temporal recurrence has (perhaps through Nietzsche) a close analogue in the French anthropologist as well.[2]

Jeffers' relation to anthropological symbol is discussed by Robert Brophy, who offers an extension of the thesis argued in his important *Robinson Jeffers: Myth, Ritual and Symbol in His Narrative Poems*, while Dell Hymes provides the most detailed examination of Jeffers' metric in twenty years. Brophy, Coffin, and R. W. (Herbie) Butterfield concentrate particularly on the major narratives of the 1920s, with Butterfield presenting a sensitive reading of one of the most accessible and affecting of the longer poems, "The Loving Shepherdess."

Two of the essays in this volume allude directly in their titles to the quality of "voice" in Jeffers, and Frederic I. Carpenter's is boldly titled, "The Verbal Magnificence of Robinson Jeffers." Many others have attested to a sense of almost physical presence in reading Jeffers. Everson has spoken of a "giant hand"; and not only critics, but an entire generation of American poets, including Robert Hass, Adrienne Rich, William Pitt Root, Gary Snyder,

James Tate, Diane Wakoski, and Alan Williamson have borne witness to his remarkable and continuing presence in American letters.[3] But perhaps the most striking testimony is offered by Czeslaw Miłosz, whose essay is both a tribute to a peer and a frank acknowledgment of difference, even antagonism. One can reject, as Miłosz does, almost every value, even every experience in Jeffers, and still be left, as Miłosz is, with the sense of challenge that signifies greatness in a poet. It is that sense, shared in different ways by each contributor to this book, that is the reason for its existence.

NOTES

1. The year was marked as well by the publication of the first two general selections of Jeffers' work since 1965, *Rock and Hawk: A Selection of Shorter Poems by Robinson Jeffers,* compiled and edited by Robert Hass (New York: Random House), and *Robinson Jeffers: Selected Poems,* edited by Colin Falck (Manchester: Carcanet Press). Selections were also published in German and Japanese translations by Piper in Munich (Eva Hesse) and Kokubun-Sha in Tokyo (Tony Miura). Beginning in 1988, Stanford University Press issued a four-volume *Collected Poetry,* edited by Tim Hunt, and published a new critical study by William Everson, *The Excesses of God: Robinson Jeffers as a Religious Figure.* A new biography, James Karman's *Robinson Jeffers: Poet of California* (San Francisco: Chronicle Books), also appeared in 1987, and special Jeffers issues were published by *American Poetry Magazine* and *The Library Chronicle.* For a general listing of the centenary publications and activities, see the *Robinson Jeffers Newsletter,* 71 (January 1988).
2. Cf. the comments in György Markus, *Language and Production: A Critique of the Paradigms* (Dordrecht: D. Reidel, 1986), 22.
3. See Robert Zaller, ed., *The Tribute of His Peers: Elegies for Robinson Jeffers* (Carmel: Tor House Press, 1989).

Centennial Essays
for Robinson Jeffers

Poet without Critics: A Note on Robinson Jeffers

Horace Gregory

1

At the moment there are good reasons for rereading the poetry of Robinson Jeffers. First of all, the poet himself is a singular figure in American letters and he occupies the rare position in this country of being a "poet" in the European sense of the word. He insists upon holding to a world view as well as his own handful of currently unpopular opinions. He has become a master of a style without nervous reference to recent fashions in literary criticism. "I can tell lies in prose," he once wrote, which means that his primary concern is with the statement of a few essential poetic truths. Today it is obvious that he is willing to leave a final judgment of what he has written to the decision of posterity.

To reread him is to step aside from the classroom discussions and shoptalk of poetry that flood the rear sections of literary quarterlies where his name is seldom mentioned at all. He is well removed from the kind of company where poetry is "taught" so as to be understood, where critics and reviewers are known to be instructors of literature in colleges and universities. But he is also at some distance from the time when his Californian narratives in verse, "Roan Stallion" and "Tamar," swept through the furnished rooms and studios of Greenwich Village with the force of an unpredicted hurricane. That was thirty years ago. Today as Jeffers is reread there is no danger of being smothered by the heavily breathing presence of a deep-throated, bare-thighed-and-breasted Jeffers–D. H. Lawrence cult, which had read Freud not wisely but with artless ardor and spent vacations in New Mexico.

Writers like Lawrence and Jeffers who are worshiped by cults

Reprinted from *The Dying Gladiator and Other Essays* by Horace Gregory (New York: Grove Press, 1961), 3–20.

frequently inspire the more violent forms of academic snobbery. Neither came from the "right" prep school, college, or university; neither Oxford or Cambridge could claim Lawrence, nor could the Ivy League universities and colleges in the United States gather their share of glory from Jeffers' reputation. Both Lawrence and Jeffers have outlived their cults; and Lawrence, safely dead and of British origin, no longer irritates the thin, tightly stretched surface of academic temper in the United States. This phenomenon, which is not without its trace of envy, partly explains the neglect, in quarterly reviews, of Jeffers' later writings. It can be said that in recent years Jeffers has been a poet without critics, but this does not mean that his name has been forgotten, his books unread, or his plays in verse neglected on the stage. A few years ago his *Medea* had a respectable run on Broadway, and an off-Broadway theater in New York found audiences for his new play, *The Cretan Woman.*

The initial advantage of rereading Jeffers' poetry now is that it can be approached without the formulas of critical fashions ringing in one's ears. Since 1925 he has published more than fifteen books of verse—a quantity of poetry which resembles the production of his ancestors, the romantic poets of nineteenth-century Britain. Rereading his poems, one finds them falling into three divisions: the southwestern narratives with their richness of California sea-sky-and-landscape; the shorter poems which are largely conversation pieces—for Jeffers is not a lyric poet—and a fine group of elegies, his *Descent to the Dead,* the result of a visit in 1929 to the British Isles; and the semidramatic poems inspired by Greek themes and overlaid with Nietzschean and twentieth-century philosophies.

2

It is best to begin when and where Jeffers' earlier reputation began; the time was 1925 and the place was New York; and credit for the publication of *Roan Stallion, Tamar and Other Poems* should be given to James Rorty, a writer who met Jeffers during a stay in California and with selfless enthusiasm persuaded New York friends to read "Tamar," to write about it, to make the presence of Jeffers known to New York publishers. Although Jeffers never shared the excitements and diversions of literary circles on the Atlantic Coast, the moment was prepared to receive his semi-biblical, semi-Sophoclean American southwestern narratives. Discussions of Steinach operations for restoring sexual vitality were in the air, and so were questions from Krafft-Ebing, Freud, and Jung; D. H. Lawrence's *The Rainbow* was in print as well as Sherwood Anderson's *Dark Laughter*. If a post-World War I urban generation had not discovered sex, it had learned to talk loudly and almost endlessly about it. Nothing was easier than to apply cocktail conversations to Jeffers' "Tamar" and "Roan Stallion," which at first reading—and particularly to those who lived in cities—held the same attractions as an invitation to a nudist colony on the Pacific Coast.

Yet it was not without self-critical discernment that Jeffers gave first place to "Tamar" when he prepared his *Selected Poetry* in 1937. For whatever reasons his public had accepted it twelve years earlier, at a time when he had passed the age of thirty-five, the poem has all the merits of a style that he had made his own. As early as 1912 he had paid for the printing of a first book, *Flagons and Apples;* in 1916 a second book, *Californians*, had been published by Macmillan; and neither, aside from the praise of a small group of friends, had received encouragement. His friendships, which included the long-sustained devotion of his wife, Una Call, also embraced the good will of George Sterling, who had known Ambrose Bierce, Joaquin Miller, and Jack London, and who was one of the few to see promise in Jeffers' early books of poems. Like Jeffers, who had been born in Pittsburgh in 1887, Sterling, a native of New York State, had become a converted Californian. Sterling's own verse had been inspired by the pages of *The Savoy* and *The Yellow Book* as well as by readings in Oscar Wilde and Ernest Dowson. "Poetry. . . ," he said, "must . . . cherish all the past embodiments of visionary beauty, such as the beings of classical mythology." Sterling's last work, shortly before his suicide in 1926, was a pamphlet written in praise of Jeffers. No doubt Jeffers had been made aware of the presence of evil through his wide readings, but it was through the loyal patronage of Sterling that he became an heir of "Bitter" Bierce. To the general reader, however, Jeffers' first two books offered little more than glimpses of a belated debt to Dante Gabriel Rossetti in *Flagons and Apples*, and a Wordsworthian manner, which included hints of pantheism, in *Californians*.

Before Jeffers met his wife and Sterling, he had an unusual education. He was the precocious son of a teacher of theology at Western Theological Seminary in Pittsburgh. His father taught him Greek, Latin, and Hebrew, and when the boy was five and six, took him on trips to Europe. For three years, between the ages of twelve and fifteen, his father sent him to boarding schools in Switzerland and Germany; and at fifteen, Jeffers entered the University of Western Pennsylvania. The next four years were spent in Occidental College and the Universities of Zurich and Southern California, and these years included studies in medicine and forestry. All this would be of no importance if it did not throw light on the individual ranges of Jeffers' poetry, his familiarity with Greek and Roman and biblical themes, with German philosophy, with medical terms and semiscientific details, and—since he read French with facility—his possible knowledge of the writings of Sade. Certainly his education[1] provided reasons for an affinity with Sterling, whose idea of poetry embraces, however vaguely, "beings of classical mythology." At the very least, Jeffers is a writer whose early years had prepared him for more than a regional view of the world and its affairs.

A second reading of "Tamar" reveals it as a biblical story in Californian undress. Characters in Jeffers' southwestern narratives, from "Tamar" to "The Loving Shepherdess," from "Give Your Heart to the Hawks" to "Hungerfield," are often lightly clothed and are subject to the wind, sun, and rain of California climate. Chapter 13 of the second book of Samuel is one source of Jeffers' parable,[2] which contains the story of Amnon's love for his sister, Tamar. Other associations taken from the two books of Samuel permeate the poem, for the sons of Samuel "walked not in his ways, but turned aside after lucre and took bribes, and perverted judgment," a statement which is appropriate to Jeffers' view of America and Western civilization. As a parable the poem acquires the force of a Calvinist sermon from an American pulpit, yet it also carries within it echoes of Nietzsche's speech of Silenus, "What is best of all is beyond your reach forever: not to be born, not to *be*, to be *nothing*," and behind these words Sophocles' remark, "Not to be born is best for man." In Tamar's words the echoes are clearly heard: "O God, I wish / I too had been born too soon and died with the eyes unopened. . . ." Jeffers also puts into the mouth of Tamar a remark which has its origins in the doctrines of Sade: "we must keep sin pure / Or it will poison us, the grain of goodness in a sin is poison. / Old man, you have no conception / of the freedom of purity." And as Tamar speaks she has given herself over to unchecked forces of evil. In Sade's novel *Justine,* his heroine is tortured because she fails to purge her taint of goodness; as the poem nears its end, the whipping of Tamar by her brother is the last love scene between them.

This is not to say that Jeffers by voicing echoes of Sade's doc-

trines had advanced them as examples for Californians to follow;
it is rather that he has given the forces of evil a well-established
voice of authority, but in doing so he has succeeded with such
vehemence that he might be misunderstood by a careless reader.
Even at this risk, he has also succeeded in giving the unleashed
forces of hell refreshed reality. In his poem, the house of David,
Tamar's father—and Tamar is the daughter of King David in the
second book of Samuel—is destroyed by fire that in its first association creates a literal image of hell and, in its second, of the
funeral pyres of the Romans.

So far I have mentioned only the principal elements of
"Tamar," its Californian setting, one of the sources of its story, and
a few of the concepts that are made relevant to the retelling of the
story—but these do not complete the list of associations that the
poem brings to mind, for "Tamar," beneath the surface of a swiftly
moving plot, has a richness of detail that rivals the complex fabric
of Elizabethan dramatic verse. In the biblical story the seduction
of Tamar by Amnon is scarcely more than an invitation to come to
bed; in Jeffers' version the seduction scene has an Ovidian ring; a
hidden stream, a pool tempts brother and sister; naked, they
enter it and one recalls Ovid's stories of Narcissus and Echo,
Hermaphroditus and Salmacis, and by association there is a particularly Roman touch, a glimpse of Phoebus' chariot wheel, from
a window of David's house overlooking the Pacific:

> It was twilight in the
> room, the shiny side of the wheel
> Dipping toward Asia; and the year dipping toward
> winter encrimsoned the grave spokes of sundown. . . .

It is this kind of richness that places "Tamar" among the major
accomplishments in twentieth-century poetry. And what of the
ghosts that haunt the house of David in "Tamar"? They are very
like the images of guilt that invade the darkened walls of Macbeth's castle. An idiot sets fire to David's house, and one thinks of
the line ". . . a tale told by an idiot, full of sound and fury." In this
instance, an idiot hastens the end of sound and fury.[3]

How deliberate Jeffers was in making a highly individual combination of Californian locale, biblical and Græco-Roman themes,
Elizabethan richness of detail, plus Nietzschean ethics and Calvinist denouements, it is impossible to say. The great probability is
that, having a deeply felt desire to warn the world of the dangers
of its involvements in world wars, Jeffers brought all the re-

sources, conscious or hidden, of his imagination into play. To
Jeffers, World War I was a warning of weaknesses inherent in a
civilization that permitted mass murders and a situation that approached total war. War, by example, creates a precedent for
violent action; and in "Tamar" that conclusion is shown by the
desire of Tamar's brother to leave his father's house to go to war,
not merely to escape the consequences of evil at home, but to
plunge himself into scenes of mass destruction. Private violence
and public warfare are mutually influential—and the essential sin
was not to walk in the ways of Samuel.

Whatever else may be said of Jeffers' beliefs and opinions as
they appear with marked consistency throughout the various
poems he has written, he has gone to war in the cause of peace;
and it should also be said that Jeffers' emotional fervor, his hon-
esty, and his lack of personal vanity strongly resemble the evan-
gelical passion of his Protestant heritage: his image of Christ is
always divine. His poem to America, his "Shine, Perishing Republic," has that fervor, its eloquence, its nobility, its protest
against earthly tyrants:

> And boys, be in nothing so moderate as in love of man, a clever
>   servant, insufferable master.
> There is in the trap that catches noblest spirits, that caught—they
>   say—God, when he walked on earth.

But before one considers the merits of Jeffers' best writings,
one should spare breath for certain of their failures, for Jeffers is
a poet of large flaws and no weaknesses—and the flaws are often
easier to see than his larger merits. In the great army of characters
that his poems present to us, one has yet to discover a wholly
admirable or completely rounded human being—the nearest approach, and her virtue is one of courage, is the heroine of "Give
Your Heart to the Hawks," a woman who attempts to save her
husband from suicide and fails. An impatient reader of Jeffers,
overwhelmed, yet half attracted, and then repelled by the scenes
of overt Lesbianism in "The Women at Point Sur" and by the sight
of a mother offering herself, half-naked, to her son in "Such
Counsels You Gave to Me," would conclude that the poet kept bad
company and was himself "immoral." The same reader would also
find difficulties in fully accepting Jeffers' beautiful pastoral, "The
Loving Shepherdess," which may have been written with a memory of the Elizabethan John Fletcher's *The Faithful Shepherdess* in

mind.⁴ The witless little shepherdess, dressed in the fewest of rags, is open to all men, young and old; and it is as though she had obeyed Sade's instructions to little girls. Whenever in Jeffers' poetry one finds a possible echo of Sade's doctrines, the mind, if not the blood, runs cooler. Even Robespierre and Bonaparte, worldly men enough at the sight of blood, and who welcomed Sade as a forthright critic of elder institutions, were shocked and grew chilled when they read Sade's manifestoes in the cause of sexual freedom; they were not prudes, but they concluded that Sade's remarks were too much of a good thing. And truly enough Sade implied too much deliberation in the pursuits of his particular happiness; his logic created a law for sexual lawlessness that all institutions, ancient or modern, have been forced to reject. Jeffers' desire to deal solely with elemental passions tends to mislead the reader into the colder regions of hell that are a paradox of romantic agony: the reader is repelled.⁵

Another reader, equally impatient, finds something ridiculous in Jeffers' scenes of sexual violence; since no comic relief is given to the reader in Jeffers' Californian narratives, the reader is forced to supply that missing element in the progress of the story—and sex viewed from a point outside the scene itself always has a touch of the ridiculous in it; if it did not there would be no moments of relaxation in the stories that used to be told in smoking cars. It is almost gratuitous to say that Jeffers' characters lack humor, which is a flaw that Jeffers shares with Wordsworth; and in the progress of his more violent scenes of action, a need is felt for a drunken porter to cross the stage as in *Macbeth*. This does not mean, however, that Jeffers lacks ability to write of drunkenness; few scenes in contemporary fiction can equal the vividness of the drunken party which is prelude to the story of "Give Your Heart to the Hawks"; in poetry, and in its own grim fashion, its veracity equals the mild, half-melancholy scene of E. A. Robinson's "Mr. Flood's Party." (Robinson, by the way, is one of the few elder American poets for whom Jeffers has expressed firm admiration.) "Such Counsels You Gave to Me" must be counted as one of Jeffers' more conspicuous failures: the bare bones of the "Oedipus complex" shine too brightly through it. As the story opens one knows only too well that the weak son is fated to poison his red-faced, hard-drinking father; since 1900 this situation has been the stock property of countless novels and plays; a sinister yet charming hero-villain disposes of a father who is overweight or a rich aunt who spikes her tea with whisky. But in Jeffers' case these flaws are not those of a small-minded writer or a minor poet.

3

Jeffers' merits as a poet are less well known that the flaws which I have just enumerated. From "Roan Stallion" and "Tamar" onward, Jeffers' technical contribution to twentieth-century poetry has been the mastery of alternate ten and five stress lines in narrative verse; in some of his shorter poems and in passages of some of his dramatic sequences, he employs a five and three stress variation of his narrative line. In this particular art no living poet has equaled him, and no other poet in America, from Philip Freneau to E. A. Robinson, has developed a narrative style of greater force, brilliance, and variety than his. While reading one of Jeffers' poems one never falls asleep; although there are times when his moral fervor is overweighted and has results which seem far from his stated intentions, he has never committed the greatest of all literary crimes—dullness. Among his shorter poems, his conversation pieces have contained prophecies which at the moment of publication seemed wrongheaded, probably mad, or willfully truculent. Time has proved Jeffers right more frequently than his adverse readers had thought possible; although the poem is too long for quotation here, the thoughtful reader cannot fail to be impressed by his "Woodrow Wilson (February 1924)" today. Wilson, the nearly tragic American hero, has been and still is the most difficult of all public figures to write about, yet Jeffers has succeeded in doing so. The poem's last lines, words spoken as if from Wilson's lips, indicate, however briefly, the nature of Wilson's failure:

    "This is my last
Worst pain, the bitter enlightenment that buys peace."

Jeffers' opinions (which are less political than colored by his hatred of war, his adaptation of Nietzschean ethics, and non-churchgoing Christianity) occasioned his publishers, in a recent book of his poems, *The Double Axe,* to disclaim responsibility for them. Jeffers had strange things to say of World War II and its aftermath, which he had predicted long before they arrived; he was much too familiar with the scene to be tactful; in another ten years he will probably be found less far from the truth than the majority of his contemporaries. There has been considerable misunderstanding of Jeffers' portrait of Hitler, which he included in *Be Angry at the Sun* in 1941; his Hitler was a figure not unlike Macbeth, a Macbeth who had also become the hero of a Wag-

nerian opera; his doom was accurately foretold; yet at the time
Jeffers' poem appeared many thought that Jeffers had praised
Hitler, or at least had made him seem too powerful. There is less
doubt today that Jeffers' portrait needs no retouching to give it
greater veracity.

Of the shorter poems, his volume *Descent to the Dead* is among
his masterpieces; it includes his lines on "Shakespeare's Grave,"
"In the Hill at New Grange," "Ghosts in England," "Iona: The
Graves of the Kings"—all memorable poems. It is impossible for
an anthologist to make a neat selection of Jeffers' poems and then
bind them shrewdly between the poems written by his contemporaries. It so happens that Jeffers has never written an "anthology
poem";[6] he is best represented by his *Selected Poetry*, which shows
the range of his narratives tempered by his elegies, self-critical
comments, and occasional observations; many of them may be
read as footnotes to his longer poems. Selections of his shorter
poems by anthologists distort the essential qualities of his poetry.

A few quotations from Jeffers' shorter poems do show, however, how he has shocked people of rigidly fixed political opinions; from "Blind Horses" one may take the lines:

> Lenin has served the revolution,
> Stalin presently begins to betray it. Why? For the sake of
> power, the Party's power, the state's
> Power, armed power, Stalin's power, Caesarean power.

And these were printed in 1937 when many people throughout
Europe and some in the United States thought differently or
would have feared to make their opinions known at all. And from
"Thebaid" the observation:

> How many turn back toward dreams and magic, how many children
> Run home to Mother Church, Father State.

This is a statement which, like other elements in Jeffers' poetry,
many may find easy to read but difficult to take; and yet it defines
with Jeffers' insight and discernment a symptom of the times
through which he has lived. Of the same temper are these lines
from "Ave Caesar":

> We are easy to manage, a gregarious people,
> Full of sentiment, clever at mechanics, and we love our luxuries.

Something of the force of Jeffers' sense of the past may be glimpsed at in these lines from "Ghosts in England":

> There was also a
> ghost of a king, his cheeks hollow as the brows
> Of an old horse, was paddling his hands in the reeds of Dozmare
> Pool, in the shallow, in the rainy twilight,
> Feeling for the hilt of a ruinous and rusted sword. But they said
> "Be patient a little, you king of shadows,
> But only wait, they will waste like snow." Then Arthur left hunting
> for the lost sword, he grinned and stood up
> Gaunt as a wolf; but soon resumed the old labor, shaking the reeds
> with his hands.

It is scarcely necessary to add that this image of King Arthur searching for Excalibur and his early moment of glory has the character of major verse. And the style in which it is written also reveals Jeffers' interlinear art of writing verse.

4

Jeffers' success in reviving Greek themes through Nietzschean and even Wagnerian interpretation has also been a source of annoyance to those who hope to read their classics in "pure" translations. The "pure" translation of Græco-Roman classics does not and cannot exist in English; and it is a truism that absolute translations of poetry from one language into another cannot be made. The best that can be hoped for is that the translator has a more than literal understanding of the poetry he translates and that he has the genius to convert his original sources into poetry in English. Jeffers' re-creations of ancient stories, particularly the plays of Euripides into English dramatic verse, have never pretended to be more than adaptations of situations, scenes, and characters. Actually, his performances are as far removed from their original sources as Shakespeare's adaptations from Plutarch's *Lives* in *Julius Caesar* and *Antony and Cleopatra*, as far as Jeffers' "Tamar" is from the second book of Samuel in the Old Testament. In his own way he has applied to ancient writings Ezra Pound's rule, "make it new." Like W. B. Yeats, Jeffers was not "a born dramatist"; as Yeats was essentially a lyric poet, so Jeffers has been a distinguished writer of contemplative and narrative verse. As Yeats's adaptation of *Oedipus at Colonus* reflects Irish seascape in a Dublin accent, so Jeffers' adaptations from the Greek are never far from the climate of the California Pacific Coast.

If Jeffers, even more than Yeats, is not a professional dramatist and is far removed from those who can be called "men of the theater," there are times when his poetry reaches high levels of dramatic power. This has long been evident in his variation of the Orestes cycle in "The Tower Beyond Tragedy"; and its concluding statement of how Orestes "climbed the tower beyond time, consciously, and cast humanity, entered the earlier fountain" (walked then, as Nietzsche would say, beyond good and evil) places the poem among the major accomplishments of our time. The same power enters his poem "At the Fall of an Age," with its story of the death of Helen on the island of Rhodes where she was worshiped as a tree-goddess, twenty years after the fall of Troy. The two speeches of Achilles' Myrmidons, risen from the dead, have all the accents of living yet timeless verse; the second speech runs as follows:

Is there any stir in the house?
Listen: or a cry?
Farm-boys with spears, you sparrows
Playing hawk, be silent.
Splendid was life
In the time of the heroes, the sun went helmeted, the moon was
    maiden,
When glory gathered on Troy, the picketed horses
Neighed in the morning, and long live ships
Ran on the wave like eagle-shadows on the slope of mountains.
Then men were equal to things, the earth was beautiful, the crests of
    heroes
Waved as tall as the trees.
Now all is decayed, all corrupted, all gone down,
Men move like mice under the shadows of the trees,
And the shadows of the tall dead.
The brightness of fire is dulled,
The heroes are gone.
In naked shame Agamemnon
Died of a woman.
The sun is crusted and the moon tarnished,
And Achilles has chosen peace.
Tell me, you island spearmen, you plowboy warriors,
Has anyone cried out in the dark door?
Not yet. The earth darkens.

There is nothing in poetry written during the twentieth century
that is quite like this speech; few poets have written as well and the
authority of the speech is unmistakable. Jean Cocteau once wrote
that a true poet writes to be believed, not praised, and in these
lines Jeffers' art of persuading the reader is unquestionable. Nor
is he less convincing in the writing of Aphrodite's speech in his
recent play, *The Cretan Woman,* a play inspired by and not a
translation of Euripides:

> . . . So I have come down to this place,
> And will work my will. I am not the least clever of the powers of
>   heaven . . .
>   I am the goddess
>   the Greeks call Aphrodite; and the Romans will call me Venus; the
>   Goddess of Love. I make the orchard-trees
> Flower, and bear their sweet fruit. I make the joyful birds to mate in
>   the branches, I make the man
> Lean to the woman. I make the huge blue tides of the ocean follow
>   the moon; I make the multitude
> Of the stars in the sky to love each other, and love the earth. Without
>   my saving power
> They would fly apart into the horror of the night. And even the
>   atoms of things, the hot whirling atoms,
> Would split apart: the whole world would burst apart into smoking
>   dust, chaos and darkness; all life
> Would gasp and perish. But love supports and preserves them: my
>   saving power.
>   This is my altar,
> Where men worship me. Sometimes I grant the prayers of those that
>   worship me: but those who reject me
> I will certainly punish.

The quality of this speech equals the speeches in the plays of the
Greek dramatists, but it is also singularly modern poetry; the
quality of its language is direct and unstrained—no irrelevant
effort at meaning is forced into it; the poetic nature of the speech
is *there,* and for its purpose cannot be said in any other way; it is
evidence enough of the genius of the man who wrote it. *The Cretan
Woman* is a far more successful play to read than Jeffers' *Medea;*
for his *Medea* opens with a flood of emotional speeches that
cannot be sustained throughout the first act, therefore the play is
top-heavy, and his readers as well as his audiences are likely to be
exhausted long before the final curtain falls. Jeffers' version of
Euripides' *Hippolytus* reserves its strength for the last scene and
agony of Theseus; and at this conclusion, one believes that Jeffers

has lost none of the mastery that he acquired thirty years ago, rather he has set himself the further task of transforming his narrative genius into writing verse for the stage, or perhaps television.

Robinson Jeffers' accomplishments and the modesty of his private life, now saddened by the death of his wife, should serve as an example to the present as well as the next generation of writers. Within the last thirty years he has made no compromise with the changing fashions of the day. For some readers Jeffers' attitude, which is not unlike the positions held by William Faulkner and W. B. Yeats, has always seemed too aristocratic. Even now I can hear someone saying, "Jeffers loves nothing but rocks and stones; I love mankind." But those who love abstract mankind too feverishly deny the rights of individual distinction and all the choices between men of good and bad, and by implication they also deny the right of the artist to be himself. Jeffers has re-established the position of the poet as one of singular dignity and courage. He is neither voiceless nor without his readers; and he is not without wisdom in seeming to await the verdict of posterity.

NOTES

1. Jeffers' education was of a kind familiar to well-to-do European gentry of the nineteenth century, but considerably less so to young Americans of the same period. Exceptions in the United States were Henry James's early travels with his father, and the continued educations after college of Longfellow, Trumbull Stickney, George Cabot Lodge, and Henry Adams. Jeffers' development as a narrative poet also follows the precedent of many major nineteenth-century poets; Jeffers and his writings are "in the tradition."

2. For biographical information concerning Jeffers, as well as the fact that one of the sources of "Tamar" may be found in the second book of Samuel, I am indebted to Lawrence Clark Powell's *Robinson Jeffers: The Man and His Work.*

3. In Jeffers' short poem "Self-Criticism in February," there are the following lines which describe the nature of his ghosts, his romanticism, his unchurched belief in God:

It is certain you have loved the beauty of storm disproportionately.
But the present time is not pastoral, but founded
On violence, pointed for more massive violence: perhaps it is not
Perversity but need that perceives the storm-beauty.
Well, bite on this: your poems are too full of ghosts and demons,
And people like phantoms—how often life's are—

. . . .
    you have never mistaken
Demon nor passion nor idealism for the real God.
Then what is most disliked in those verses
Remains most true.

4. This supposition is not so fantastic as it may seem: John Fletcher's lyrical *The Faithful Shepherdess* was far too static in movement to be a successful play; it is, however, an excellent poem. Its plot closely resembles Jeffers' poem with this difference: Fletcher's shepherdess is deceived into being promiscuous through magic worked by a sullen shepherd and she is at last rescued and absolved by a river god.

5. In a footnote to the pamphlet called "Frenchmen! A further effort is needed if you would be republicans!" in his *La Philosophie dans le Boudoir* (1795), Sade wrote: "The first stirring of desire that a girl feels is the moment that Nature means her to prostitute herself, and with no other consideration in mind, she should obey Nature's voice; she outrages Her laws if she resists them."

6. The perfect "anthology poem" is a showpiece of which Poe's "The Raven" and Tennyson's "May Queen" and "Crossing the Bar" were valiant examples; many minor poets seem to write for anthologies alone; and indeed, some poets like A. E. Housman are at their best when a small selection of their poems are reprinted in anthologies. With more wit and, incidentally, more truth than tact, Laura Riding and Robert Graves reviewed the practice of editing anthologies in their book, *A Pamphlet Against Anthologies*.

Robinson Jeffers, American Poetry, and a Thousand Years

Robert Zaller

Few American writers have been subject to more conflicting evaluations than Robinson Jeffers; few reputations have suffered more fluctuating fortunes. Critics such as Mark Van Doren and Babette Deutsch greeted the appearance of "Tamar" and "Roan Stallion" in the 1920s with comparisons to Shakespeare and the Greeks, and more than forty years later, Van Doren concluded his introduction to Jeffers' *Selected Letters* by saying, "Homer and Shakespeare. In what more fitting company can we leave him?" Jeffers remained a commanding figure on the American literary scene down to the Second World War, and even in the late 1940s, when his reputation was clearly in decline, Selden Rodman could still hail him as "the closest thing to a major poet we have."[1]

The very éclat of Jeffers' debut mitigated against a more lasting success. Shakespeare and Homer set a difficult standard. Nor did Jeffers, in part by choice, enjoy the benefits of a coterie. He remained on the West Coast, a place where no national reputation in this country has yet been made, and, though hospitable to visitors, he did not encourage them. There was thus no network of friendship and obligation to keep Jeffers in circulation, to tide him over the lulls that befall every career, and to cushion the blow when the New Critics began to find him irrelevant. It was not so much that he was a target of the New Criticism as that he became gradually invisible to it, and posthumous long before he died. Even the few official marks of recognition that came his way in the 1950s smacked more of the faint praise accorded an honorable longevity than of the honors heaped on those being readied for the pantheon. His death in 1962 occasioned chiefly the surprise that he had still been living. He dwindled into the anthologies, where one can still encounter shorter poems such as "Hurt Hawks" and "Shine, Perishing Republic," and scan in the bio-

Reprinted from *Agenda* 24–25 (Winter 1986–Spring 1987): 89–104.

graphical notes the titles of some of the long ones that few people now read. Of all the major poets of the period, he is the last to have had a scholarly Collected Poems,[2] and a full-dress biography remains to be written.[3]

The picture should not be overstated. Scholarly interest in Jeffers has never died out, and the Tor House Foundation continues to promote interest in his work. If he has been largely ignored by the current critical consensus, he remains a potent symbolic figure for many of the younger generation of American poets.[4] Nonetheless it is clear that, whatever his influence, he is far from being the kind of acknowledged figure who, like Pound, Eliot, or Stevens, compels a continuing dialogue within the larger literary community.

For Jeffers' detractors, there is no particular mystery in this. It merely reflects the natural corrective supplied over time to a grossly inflated reputation, and if anything requires explanation it is the existence of that reputation in the first place. One need not share such a view to find the question it propounds worth addressing. Why did Jeffers make such a sudden and dramatic impact on the twenties? How did this affect his own artistic responses? And why, after a time, did he begin to slip into the relative obscurity in which we find him today?

It is often overlooked that although Jeffers' success was sudden, it was far from facile. More than a decade of slow and painful maturation lay behind the enraptured notices that greeted the appearance of *Roan Stallion, Tamar and Other Poems* in 1925.[5] Jeffers' first published work, *Flagons and Apples* (1912), is chiefly valuable in reminding us how unformed his talent still was at the age of twenty-five. It may only have been sometime between his marriage to Una Call Kuster in August 1913 and his settlement in Carmel in the autumn of 1914 that his sense of vocation clearly crystallized. Before he was still a bohemian poet and casual litterateur. Thereafter he devoted himself steadily to the production of verse on a scale of grandeur and ambition rivaled only by Pound's *Cantos*.

In later life Jeffers claimed that he was incapable of writing prose, though as any reader of his letters and occasional pieces knows, he was a masterly stylist. What he meant was that he had eschewed prose as a medium of expression, intending, with a singularity of commitment unique in modern letters, to address his public in verse alone. When we recall his observation in the foreword to his *Selected Poetry* that he had meant to recapture for poetry the energies it had lost to prose and consider too his manifest gifts for narrative and drama, it is clear that he could easily have chosen the novel or the theater as a means of expression. His commitment, therefore, was not merely a choice among skills, but a programmatic decision.

At the same time Jeffers had decided as early as 1914 to reject the dominant poetic trends of his time, symbolism and imagism, though he lacked as yet the sense of his own voice and could only, as he put it, go on imitating "dead men's music."[6] Wordsworth, Shelley, Tennyson, and Hardy all served him as models, and World War I was his theme. The Great War was in many ways the decisive experience of Jeffers' adult life. Like Pound, Eliot, and Frost, he was drawn to Europe in the formative stages of his career; in the spring of 1914, he and Una had planned to take up residence in England. The war intervened, stranding him six thousand miles away. We can only speculate on how Jeffers' development might have been affected by an extended stay abroad. As it was, he remained to puzzle out his future on the Pacific coast, a Puritan solitary fashioning his own Eden. But Europe, and the war, obsessed him by their very inaccessibility. As the war's scope and tragedy became apparent, he attempted to grapple with it in a dramatic poem of epic proportions, "The Alpine Christ." Jeffers finally abandoned and later repudiated it as a failure. One would not quarrel with this judgment, but, if a failure, "The Alpine Christ" is a fascinating and sometimes a noble one. Its recent rediscovery—it was presumed lost for many years—compels a sweeping reassessment not only of Jeffers' early development but of his conflicted relationship to the legacy of European culture in general and his stance as an "American" poet.

What Jeffers published during these years was not the huge, unfinished torso of "The Alpine Christ," however, but the far less ambitious poetry of *Californians*, which contained his first narratives of the Pacific coast region. The publisher was a prestigious commercial house, Macmillan; the verse, though still apprentice work, was at least respectable; and the reviews were decent.

No doubt Jeffers was encouraged by this first sign of success in the great world. Despite marital difficulties and serious psychological stress arising from his still-unresolved feelings about the war (he was rejected for active service), he plunged ahead with new work, as well as the building of a permanent residence, Tor House. By 1920 he had a new collection ready for his publisher, including "The Coast-Range Christ" and other of the poems gathered by William Everson into the posthumous volume of *Brides of the South Wind*.[8]

Macmillan's reply was a classic example of the second-book rejection letter. Jeffers saw his new manuscript as an advance in his personal development and a milestone in his career. Macmillan saw an unwelcome solicitation from a long-since remaindered first author whose book had achieved neither sale nor scandal. The effect on Jeffers was traumatic. He withdrew deeper into isolation and ceased to send out even individual poems for publication.

The next four years are the most interesting and at the same time the most obscure of Jeffers' career. Before the Macmillan rejection, Jeffers might still think of himself as a young writer, already noticed, with his prospects yet before him. Afterward the facts looked very different. He was thirty-three years old, with a wife and two children, and no profession except the one he had apparently failed at. He had a small private income that would keep him from penury, but not, perhaps, from indolence. What poet's gifts had not declared themselves by the age of thirty-three? Keats and Shelley were already dead by that time, a fact Jeffers had reflected on painfully. The very routine of his days must have mocked him. The poems he wrote in the morning no one wanted, and the stones he laid for Tor House in the afternoon were building not a refuge but a tomb.

We have much to learn about the circumstances of those dark years and about the genesis of the extraordinary works—"Tamar," "The Tower Beyond Tragedy," and "Roan Stallion"—that emerged from them, and made Jeffers' fame. Those years formed his persona as well, the face he turned to (and sometimes from) the public that had so unexpectedly become his.

It takes effort now to remember how stunning Jeffers' first success was. Babette Deutsch's comment in the *New Republic* is perhaps most summary: "This reviewer, reading Jeffers, felt somewhat as Keats professed to feel, on looking into Chapman's Homer." The *New York Times'* reviewer, in a remark deliberately aimed at Eliot and Pound, questioned "whether there is another poet writing in America today—or in England for that matter—" who could "write in so indelible a fashion." The *Argonaut* declared flatly that "Robinson Jeffers is one of the very few poets of the early Twentieth Century that the Twenty-First will read." And *Time* Magazine, putting its imprimatur on all the rest, stated that "The significance of Robinson Jeffers as a poet is, by critical consensus, that of one to rank with the greatest poets of all generations."[9]

Discounting the hyperbole, it is clear that Jeffers made an

extraordinary impression on his first public. Literary merit or novelty cannot explain it alone. Jeffers was an original voice, but not a poetic innovator. He wrote an unfashionable line, even an awkward one. His stories concerned obscure people in an obscure place. One must seek elsewhere to comprehend the nature of his success.

American literature before Jeffers was still in many ways shackled to the conventions of the nineteenth century. Literary naturalism as practiced by Frank Norris, Theodore Dreiser, and Upton Sinclair had opened up some of the seamier sides of American life, without however breaking through the fundamental prudery of our tradition. Walt Whitman aside—and he was still, at this point, very much aside—it might well be said that as of 1920 the deepest and frankest exploration of sexuality in our literature was still *The Scarlet Letter*. But the new social mores derived from the large-scale entry of women into the workforce, the first victories of feminism, the currents from Europe that had culminated in the research of Freud, and the libidinal aftershock of World War I that so deeply affected Jeffers himself,[10] had made sexuality both an issue and a theme—the great, unexpressed theme of postwar culture. In their very different ways, the most gifted writers of the epoch had taken up this theme: James Joyce in Ireland, D. H. Lawrence in England, Robert Musil in Austria. Of these three, it was Lawrence with whom Jeffers had the closest affinity. Lawrence was also the only one of the three whose mature works were available to Jeffers in the early 1920s.

Like the earlier Lawrence, Jeffers was preoccupied with the destructive and apocalyptic side of human sexuality. For Jeffers, as for Lawrence, sexuality was a fundamentally anarchic force, capable of overturning all convention and law. With the Nietzschean cast of their thought, both men identified it at bottom with the will. The result was the exploration of the roots of incest in "Tamar" and "The Tower Beyond Tragedy," and of bestiality in "Roan Stallion." These works marked the first imaginative conquest of the Freudian revolution in America. Jeffers' triumph in them was to make their subject matter available to American literature in a manner that gave no excuse for censorship. He was fully explicit without being in the least salacious; he laid bare the power of the impulse, not the inconsequentiality of the act. The vague consensus that still identifies Jeffers with "Tamar" and "Roan Stallion" is not misplaced, for these were the works that revolutionized the literature of the twenties. The force to which

the critics of the period responded was not merely the quality of
the verse, but the sense of possibility opened up by the terrain
Jeffers had conquered.

This terrain was rapidly exploited by the two major figures who
emerged in Jeffers' wake, William Faulkner and Eugene O'Neill.
It is surprising that no critic except John T. Irwin appears to have
pointed out the influence of Jeffers on Faulkner.[11] Even more
obvious is the debt of O'Neill in his reworkings of Greek tragedy
and his preoccupation with incest and family decadence. Both of
these men, as artists of stature in their own right, developed the
Jeffersian themes of inversion, generational conflict, and temporal succession in their own ways. But both followed in the path
that Jeffers had laid out.

Jeffers' own response to celebrity was to forge ahead with a
major new work, more ambitious in size and scope than anything
he had hitherto attempted. This was "The Women at Point Sur,"
which he hoped, as he confided in a rare moment of afflatus, would
be the *Faust* of his generation.[12] Clearly, Jeffers planned to consoli-
date his reputation with it and to place himself at that level of
unarguable stature that Eliot, for example, had achieved in *The
Waste Land*. And without question, to fashion *The Women at Point
Sur* out of the false starts and disparate drafts he had accumulated
ever since he had begun to explore the subject that lay deepest
within him, his relationship to his father, he worked harder and
more intensely than at any other time in his life.

"The Women at Point Sur" was not an immediate failure. The level
of public expectation alone tided it past the disappointment of
many critics, and it won at least deferential praise from others.
Jeffers continued to defend it, despite acknowledging "grave
faults." Certainly it is an extraordinary work. Jeffers put much of
his deepest insight into it, and no American poet since, except
Pound, has even attempted a work of comparable significance.
But it did not clinch his reputation; rather, it gravely undermined
it. When, ten years later, he chose the volume of his *Selected Poetry*,
he included only a single one of its 175 pages, explaining tersely
that he had omitted it because it was "least understood and least
liked."[13] But "The Bird with the Dark Plumes," a poem written
shortly after the failure of "Point Sur" had become clear, expressed
his feelings more directly:

> The bird with the dark plumes in my blood,
> That never for one moment however I patched my truces
> Consented to make peace with the people,

It is pitiful now to watch her pleasure in a breath of tempest
Breaking the sad promise of spring.
Are these that morose hawk's wings, vaulting, a mere mad swallow's,
The snow-shed peak, the violent precipice?
Poor outlaw that would not value their praise do you prize their
    blame?
"Their liking" she said, "was a long creance,
But let them be kind enough to hate me, that opens the sky."
It is almost as foolish my poor falcon
To want hatred as to want love; and harder to win.

(CP 1:402)

"The Bird with the Dark Plumes" might easily be read as an early example of Jeffers' supposed misanthropy. It is better seen, I think, as an attempt to right his balance, not only in the aftermath of "Point Sur's" reception, but in the wider context of the fame that had so suddenly and in many ways disturbingly descended on him. Jeffers' sense of himself as a man at odds with his time, nurtured in his long season of adversity, was central to his self-conception as a poet. The notoriety that had all but made a cult figure of him was therefore profoundly suspect. "The Women at Point Sur," with its compression of utterance, ellipsis of plot, and absence of any sympathetic character, was precisely a rejection of such notoriety and a demand for recognition at the highest and most uncompromising level. Its failure, however painful, was thus at the same time a confirmation of his "difficult" destiny. The plumed falcon was, as Jeffers recognized, the pride in him that craved wounding, the sense of isolation that his art had formed itself against. A more extreme example of this attitude is evident in another poem of the same period, "An Artist," in which Jeffers depicts himself in the thinly veiled guise of a sculptor who, forsaking his public at the height of his renown, carves monstrous titans in the solitude of the mountains. But this impulse is negated by the rational and ultimately controlling speaker of "The Bird with the Dark Plumes," who rejects the terms of approbation ("love" and "hatred") as such in favor of an austerer dialogue. The terms of that dialogue—the relation, as Jeffers saw it, between the poet and the tribe—were worked out in the three major meditative poems of the late twenties, "Apology for Bad Dreams," "Meditation on Saviors," and "The Broken Balance."[14] But it was not until the approach of another world war became apparent in the thirties that Jeffers began to act deliberately upon this new conception.

While thus reassessing his career, Jeffers plunged into the composition of another narrative, "Cawdor," and his productivity did not flag until after the midthirties. In many ways, these middle-period narratives represent the prime of Jeffers' achievement. Their formal mastery is more secure, the handling of mythological and anthropological elements more assured, the development of plot and character firmer and more consistent. What they no longer possess in sheer dynamism of impulse they make up in finer craft, and, while melodrama has been purged, there is no lack of passion. The nature of that passion, however, and certainly Jeffers' attitude toward it, has changed. Here once again, a comparison with Lawrence may be useful. If both men shared a common perception of the enormous potential of sexuality for renewal or destruction, and a sense of the urgency of this theme for the postwar situation of the West, their views diverged sharply after the midtwenties, though Jeffers never lost his appreciation for Lawrence's achievement. Lawrence's later work celebrated sexuality as the key to cultural renewal, while Jeffers reached, in "Point Sur," the opposite conclusion: that the loosening of sexual mores was a symptom of cultural degeneracy rather than its cure. This should have come as no surprise to readers of "Tamar" and "The Tower Beyond Tragedy," where sexual temptation leads, in the one case to apocalyptic destruction, and in the other to passionate renunciation. But Jeffers' view of sexuality became progressively more negative after "Point Sur," and it may be said narrower too, culminating in the description of love in "Thurso's Landing" (1932) as the "furious longing to join the sewers of two bodies" (*CP* 2:252)

Jeffers could not of course have rewritten "Tamar" even if he had wished to, any more than Lawrence could have rewritten *Women in Love*. Moreover, once the novelty, and in a more superficial sense the scandal of his early work had worn off, readers and critics were left to confront a sensibility that, while thoroughly modern, was clearly at odds with that particular strain that had identified itself as modernist. The heart of the modernist credo was the primacy and at least implicitly the redemptive potential of the aesthetic act, a notion best expressed in Nietzsche's dictum, "We possess art lest we perish of truth." This was the stance of the early Eliot and Pound, and it became the root principle of the New Critics, with their insistence on the sovereignty and independence of the aesthetic object. Jeffers too was concerned with literary permanence, and relatively indifferent to the social context of works of art. But he utterly rejected the idea that they could possess independent, let alone transcendent value. For

Jeffers, human beauty was derived from natural beauty, grounded in it, comprehended by it; one could only, as he said in one of the numerous poems of the thirties devoted to the subject, "Love the wild swan." But this did not merely make human artifacts inferior to natural grandeur. It meant that such artifacts derived whatever worth they possessed from their grounding in natural process. It meant a rejection of any concept of a realm of independent aesthetic value. Man perished not from truth but from its absence, and his works—including works of art—were in that absence as ugly, Jeffers said, as "a severed hand":

> A severed hand
> Is an ugly thing, and man dissevered from the earth and stars and
>   his history . . . for contemplation or in fact . . .
> Often appears atrociously ugly. Integrity is wholeness, the greatest
>   beauty is
> Organic wholeness, the wholeness of life and things, the divine
>   beauty of the universe. Love that, not man
> Apart. . . .
>
> ("The Answer," *CP* 2:536)

Jeffers was equally at odds with the political populism of the thirties. Social justice mattered to him, and human suffering mattered a good deal, but he believed in none of the remedies being offered for either. At a time when Eliot was embracing Anglo-royalism and Pound beginning his disastrous flirtation with fascism, Jeffers scoffed at both as "Mother Church" and "Father State" ("Thebaid," *CP* 2:532). Communism seemed an even less desirable alternative, combining the worst features of both. As writers came under increasing pressure to take sides, Jeffers declared his own function to be "truth-bound, the neutral / Detested by all the dreaming factions" ("The Great Sunset," *CP* 2:534). In a more sardonic vein, he responded in "Self-Criticism in February" (*CP* 2:561) to the suggestion that he "sing / That God is love, or perhaps that social / Justice will soon prevail" with a tart: "I can tell lies in prose."

Such an attitude could not but appear callous, even cavalier in the climate of the thirties. There can hardly be found in any of Jeffers' narratives of the period the least suggestion that his country was in the throes of a great depression. Much the same, of course, may be said of Faulkner, and for much the same reason: both men took for their subject rural communities that were already chronically depressed. But in Faulkner's case, those who

wished to could at least point to the social relevance of his treatment of the "Negro question." There seemed to be no political
dimension to Jeffers' narratives at all. His position on international affairs was equally unsatisfactory. Asked to comment on the
Spanish civil war, he replied that he would put his hand in a fire to
stop the suffering, but would not give a flick of his little finger to
help either side win.[15]

Jeffers' refusal of partisan commitment was nonetheless entirely consonant with the view he had evolved of the poet's role in
society. His early rejection of symbolist and postsymbolist movements was based on his perception that a closed and self-referen-
tial aestheticism was doomed to irrelevance and ultimate triviality.
But the symbolist aesthetic itself seemed to him merely the symptom of a wider anxiety and disorder in the world. His examination
of incest in "Tamar" and "The Tower Beyond Tragedy" had implicitly addressed this problem; in "The Women at Point Sur" the
relation between sexual and social disorder became explicit, even
programmatic.

As I have suggested, Jeffers' poetic persona took its final shape
in the late twenties. In "Apology for Bad Dreams," he explored the
relation between personal trauma and poetic vocation. In "Meditation on Saviors," he weighed and rejected the role of prophet-
savior that Pound was so misguidedly to assume in the thirties. In
the verse drama "Dear Judas," he examined the impulse to mar-
tyrdom in the "poet" Jesus.[16] Yet at the same time he knew that the
poet's task was inextricably bound up with prophecy and that any
attempt to evade it, whether by submission to ideology or an
assumption of superiority or indifference, could lead only to
sterility or irrelevance:

> I pledged myself awhile ago not to seek refuge, neither in death nor
>   in a walled garden,
> In lies nor gated loyalties, nor in the gates of contempt, that easily
>   lock the world out of doors.
>   . . . .
> This people as much as the sea-granite is part of the God from
>   whom I desire not to be fugitive.
>   ("Meditation on Saviors," CP 1 : 396, 398)

The final crystallization of Jeffers' attitude resulted from his
trip to England, Scotland, and Ireland in the summer of 1929.
This was the trip he and Una had planned fifteen years earlier on
the eve of World War I, but both he and Europe had changed in

the interim. Jeffers was no longer a pilgrim but a tourist, his life
and art firmly rooted at home. What he found in postwar Europe
and described in a cycle of sixteen poems, "Descent to the Dead"
(*CP* 2:107–30), was a dying civilization that had exhausted the
very soil it stood upon:

> . . . a uterine country, soft
> and wet and worn out, like an old womb
>
> ("Ossian's Grave")
>
> Worn and weak with too much humanity . . .
>
> ("Subjected Earth")
>
> The rags of lost races and beaten clans . . .
>
> ("Ghosts in England")

Jeffers' response to the Old World was far from simple rejection.[17] He had a profound sense of the continuity of the West's
civilization, and between the late twenties and the midthirties he
devoted much of his time to systematically exploring its foundation in Hebraic, Hellenic, and Germanic myth.[18] America, he
knew, was the product of its values—"we are one", he wrote in
"Shine, Republic" (*SP* 568), "and Washington, Luther, Tacitus,
Aeschylus, one kind of man"—and hence was inextricably bound
up with its fate as well. But it appeared to him that the processes of
decay that afflicted the West as a whole were more advanced in
Europe than in America. Washington, the most recent of his
culture heroes—the valuers of freedom—had still been within the
living memory of his own grandfather; but it was impossible to
imagine such a man again in Europe. The best the Old World
could now produce was someone like Clemenceau ("The Dead to
Clemenceau: November 1929," *CP* 2:127), the cynical servant of
historic inevitability, and the new European prototype was Napo-
leon, whose even uglier avatars, Stalin, Mussolini, Hitler, were
already visible. If America could not ultimately avoid Europe's
fate, it could at least delay it. As Jeffers offered a counsel of wise
detachment to those who sought personal wholeness and integrity
in a period of decline, so the logic of his perspective led him to
suggest a political detachment from the affairs of Europe as the
onset of a new war became increasingly apparent.

Thus Jeffers was led to prophesy, and yet more futilely to
preach. Prophecy, in the sense of intuiting the larger truths of
one's time and memorably communicating them, was integral, as
we have seen, to Jeffers' mature conception of the poet's task. But

the function of the poet-prophet was to state, not to persuade. If
any were to heed him, well and good; but the imagination of the
majority could be arrested only by the sacrificial act of the savior:
"*This* people has not outgrown blood-sacrifice, one must writhe on
the high / cross to catch at their memories" ("Meditation on Saviors"). But as the savior's impulse to self-sacrifice generated his
original vision, so it clouded and eventually consumed it. To see or
to act: one could choose either, but not both.

As war drew closer in the thirties, however, and with it the
prospect of American involvement, Jeffers found it difficult and
finally impossible to keep his distance from events. Caught "Between news-cast and work-desk," he was often reduced to topical
commentary, and declared defensively that it was "right that a
man's views be expressed, though the poetry suffer for it."[19] The
poetry did suffer, both in *Be Angry at the Sun* (1941) and its
successor, *The Double Axe* (1948). The latter volume, appearing at
the beginning of the Cold War, was particularly unpropitious. As
Jeffers had opposed America's participation in World War II, so
now he warned against the "corrupting burden" of empire it was
about to assume. Liberal critics read him as a mere isolationist;
conservatives saw him as indifferent to the Communist menace. If
Jeffers' historical pessimism still had a certain cachet in the thirties
among the generation reared on Spengler, his views had no place
in the imperial consensus that took shape after the Second World
War.

None of this could have surprised Jeffers, who had long fore-
seen his eventual isolation, and more than half courted it. "If one
should tell them what's clearly seen," he wrote in a poem of the
early thirties, "They'd not understand; if they understood they
would not believe; / If they understood and believed they'd say, /
'Hater of men . . .'" ("Crumbs or the Loaf," *CP* 2:281). Another
poem of the period begins with an even more frontal disclaimer:
"I am not well civilized, really alien here: trust me not" ("The
Trap," *CP* 2:415). In "The Tower Beyond Tragedy," Jeffers had
meditated on Cassandra as the archetype of the prophet; a
quarter of a century later, in the poem entitled "Cassandra," he
likened himself directly to the prophetess cursed by unbelief, "to
men / And gods disgusting."[20]

The persona of the rejected prophet was both a device to shock
Jeffers' public into listening to him and a mask to protect himself
against the ultimate certainty that it would not. Despite his refusal
of a more active role, however, he chafed at the passivity of his
situation. "I agree with you," he addresses an imaginary inter-

locutor in a wartime poem, "It is a foolish / business to see the future and screech at it" ("So Many Blood-Lakes," *DA* 132). Nor could he accept, he wrote in "The Blood-Guilt" (*DA* 161), the satisfaction of the "justified prophet":

                                                    If you had not
    been beaten beforehand, hopelessly fatalist,
You might have spoken louder and perhaps been heard, and
    prevented something.
                                    I? Have you never heard
That who'd lead must not see?
                                    You saw it, you despaired
    of preventing it, you share the blood-guilt.
                                                            Yes.

Jeffers' dialogue with his public was a complex interaction of value, temperament, and circumstance. He had never considered it the function of poetry to address issues. The poet's job, he wrote, was to "praise life" and to "awake dangerous images" (*CP* 2:415, 309). The praise of life was the breath of poetry, the aesthetic response as such. The dangerous images were those of tragedy, the tale of the tribe; and within tragedy lay prophecy, the impersonal truth at the heart of action. That prophecy had assumed a more overt and didactic role in his own poetry was circumstantial. The time, he felt, called for plainer speaking; the truth had become too urgent for parable. But even at his most hortatory, he clung to a larger perspective and never succumbed (as did Pound) to the claims of history.

Jeffers' most comprehensive statement of his poetic was in his late essay, "Poetry, Gongorism and a Thousand Years." In it he tries to imagine what a great poet in his time might be like:

> . . . this hypothetical great poet would break sharply away from the directions that are fashionable in contemporary poetic literature. He would understand that Rimbaud was a young man of startling genius but not to be imitated; and that "The Waste Land," though one of the finest poems of this century and surely the most influential, marks the close of a literary dynasty, not the beginning. . . . Our supposed poet, being distinctly separate from his time, would be able to see it and to see around it. And I do not think he would give much attention to its merely superficial aspects, the neon lights and toothpaste advertising of this urban civilization. . . . these things change out of recognition, but great poetry is pointed at the future. Its author, whether consciously or not, intends to be understood a thousand years from now; therefore he chooses the more permanent aspect of things, and sub-

jects that will remain valid. . . . If the present time overhears him, and listens too—all the better. But let him not be distracted by the present; his business is with the future.[21]

Is this the prescription for a great poet, or the actual portrait of one? Jeffers' boyhood fantasies of mastery were powerful enough to be recalled in adulthood and to form a recurrent theme in his verse.[22] The reader who has come this far will require no further evidence of Jeffers' identification with great figures, whether political or religious. What he had sublimated into the "second-best" career of a poet[23] was an ambition that measured itself by the highest standard. The praise of his first critics, with their direct comparisons to Shakespeare and the Greeks, must have confirmed his sense of destiny. The reversals after *The Women at Point Sur* did not shake it. "I also make a remembered name," he wrote in the meditation on Ossian that forms part of "Descent to the Dead" (*CP* 2 : 108). Later in the same cycle, the poem "Inscription for a Gravestone"—clearly intended to be Jeffers' own—is printed on facing pages with "Shakespeare's Grave" (*SP* 480–81). Was it mere accident that set these two graves side by side?[24]

We cannot know, of course, how Jeffers finally regarded his achievement. But the issue of greatness, first posed by the critics and, more subtly, by the poet himself, has laid a corrupting burden of its own on his readers today—a burden because it implies so colossal a prejudgment of the work and our reaction to it, and corrupting because we cannot, whatever our response to Jeffers may be, pass on it. Is it at least in part for this reason that academic criticism has given him such a wide berth? But we are not Jeffers' public of a thousand years hence, nor need we be to address the task that is properly ours, to integrate this difficult, in many ways intractable, but surely towering figure into the American literary tradition.

NOTES

1. Ann N. Ridgeway, ed., *The Selected Letters of Robinson Jeffers 1887–1962* (Baltimore: Johns Hopkins University Press, 1968), ix; henceforth cited as *SL*. Selden Rodman, review of *The Double Axe and Other Poems*, *Saturday Review*, 31 July 1948, 13–14.

2. *The Collected Poetry of Robinson Jeffers*, Tim Hunt, ed., 4 vols. (Stanford: Stanford University Press, 1988–   ); henceforth cited as *CP*.

3. Melba Berry Bennett's *The Stone Mason of Tor House: The Life and Work of Robinson Jeffers* (Los Angeles: Ward Ritchie Press, 1966), is now corrected and

supplemented by James Karman, *Robinson Jeffers: Poet of California* (San Francisco: Chronicle Books, 1987).

4. James Tate, Robert Hass, William Pitt Root, and Alan Williamson are among the younger poets who have addressed poems to Jeffers. See my *The Tribute of His Peers: Elegies for Robinson Jeffers* (Carmel, Calif.: Tor House Press, 1989).

5. This period in Jeffers' life is still obscure. See my *The Cliffs of Solitude: A Reading of Robinson Jeffers* (New York: Cambridge University Press, 1983), esp. chaps. 1 and 2, and the essays by William Everson and Tim Hunt in this volume.

6. *Roan Stallion, Tamar and Other Poems* (New York: Modern Library, 1935), x.

7. See William Everson's introduction to his edition of *The Alpine Christ and Other Poems* (Cayucos, Calif.: Cayucos Press, 1974), reprinted in this volume. Jeffers had reported the poem lost to his earliest bibliographer, S. S. Alberts.

8. Caycuos, Calif.: Cayucos Press, 1974.

9. These encomia are quoted on the dust jacket of the third edition of *The Women at Point Sur* (New York: Liveright, 1929).

10. See *The Cliffs of Solitude*, chap. 2 and *passim.*, for commentary on this subject.

11. In *Doubling and Incest/Repetition and Revenge: A Speculative Reading of Faulkner* (Baltimore: Johns Hopkins University Press, 1975).

12. *SL* 105.

13. *The Selected Poetry of Robinson Jeffers* (New York: Random House, 1959), xiii; henceforth cited as *SP*.

14. For a fuller discussion, see *The Cliffs of Solitude*, 210ff.

15. *SL* 266. Cf. the lines in the poem "Rearmament" (*CP* 2:515): "I would burn my right hand in a slow fire / To change the future . . . I should do foolishly."

16. Jesus is so described by Jeffers in "Theory of Truth" (*CP* 2:608).

17. The theme of Europe in Jeffers' work awaits analysis. In "The Alpine Christ," the Swiss mountain scenery of Jeffers' boyhood schooling is strongly identified with his father. In "Descent to the Dead," the images are powerfully (and negatively) maternal. Cf. the even more negative feminine imagery in Jeffers' late narrative, "The Double Axe."

18. In the dramatic poems "Dear Judas," "At the Fall of an Age," and "At the Birth of an Age" (*CP* 2:5–44; 284–305; 420–84).

19. Prefatory note to *Be Angry at the Sun* (New York: Random House, 1941), unpaginated.

20. *The Double Axe and Other Poems* (New York: Liveright, 1977), 117; henceforth cited as *DA*.

21. *New York Times Magazine*, 18 January 1948, sec. 6.16.

22. *SL* 281. Jeffers' most overt contemplation of power is in "Meditation on Saviors" (*CP* 1:396–401). The fantasy elements in the early drafts of "The Women at Point Sur," however, are in many ways even more revealing.

23. Cf. the poem of that title (*CP* 2:132).

24. Jeffers does offer a near-disclaimer in his essay: "there has been a great poet in our time—*must I say comparatively great?*—an Irishman named Yeats . . ." (emphasis added). The question, one might suggest, belies the assertion, though Jeffers' admiration for Yeats was undoubted. Cf. also the reference to Dante in the title poem of *Be Angry at the Sun.*

Robinson Jeffers: Poet of Controversy

Alex A. Vardamis

Since Robinson Jeffers first appeared in print in 1912, his critical reputation has undergone radical fluctuations. Idolized in the nineteen-twenties, vilified in the forties, overlooked in the fifties, in the sixties and seventies his philosophic stance helped to inspire a social movement while, ironically, his poetry was largely ignored. Accused of fascism, communism, anarchism, pacifism, isolationism, sadism, misanthropy, and atheism, he remains a poet of great power who has seldom been judged on the merits of his poetry. To trace the ebb and flow of his fame is in many ways to explore the history of American thought in the past seven decades.

Significant critical recognition of Robinson Jeffers began with the appearance in 1924 of *Tamar and Other Poems.* The volume went unnoticed until Jeffers sent a copy to his friend, the California poet and bohemian, George Sterling. Sterling, deeply impressed, sent *Tamar* to James Rorty, a professional journalist, who in turn introduced it to Mark Van Doren and Babette Deutsch. Sterling called the title piece, "Tamar," the "strongest and most dreadful poem" he had ever read and judged that it stood "among the unforgettable dreams of art."[1] Rorty, writing in the *New York Herald and Tribune,* called *Tamar* "a magnificent tour de force. . . . Nothing as good of its kind has been written in America."[2] Van Doren, in the *Nation,* wrote that "few [volumes] are as rich with the beauty and strength which belongs to genius alone."[3] In the *New Republic,* Deutsch found "thinking in these lyrics which lifts them . . . on to the plane of great writing." She compared reading Jeffers' poetry to what Keats felt looking into Chapman's Homer.[4] Influenced by these highly favorable reviews, others agreed that a poetic genius had arrived on the American scene. James Daly, writing in *Poetry,* said that "Jeffers is unsurpassed by any other poet writing in English,"[5] and *Time,* finding Jeffers "unmistakably powerful," compared him to Whitman.[6]

The following year, Boni and Liveright published *Roan Stallion,*

Tamar and Other Poems which, in addition to "Tamar," presented two new long narratives, "Roan Stallion" and "The Tower Beyond Tragedy," and several short poems. This volume, a best-seller, created a sensation. With this single book of poetry Jeffers achieved fame. Reviews appeared in many respected literary publications. The *New Republic* ranked him "with the foremost American poets not only of his generation, but of all the generations that preceded him."[7] In the *New York Times Book Review,* Percy Hutchinson called him a genius comparable to the Greeks and praised parts of the new volume as "equaled only by the very great."[8] Edwin Seaver, in the *Saturday Review of Literature,* found "'Roan Stallion'. . . a magnificent achievement."[9] H. L. Mencken, in the *American Mercury,* saw "a fine and stately dignity in him, and the rare virtue of simplicity."[10]

Praise was not restricted to the literary journals. The *Los Angeles Times* declared Jeffers "a major poet and one of the greatest America has yet produced."[11] The *Salt Lake City Telegram* saw in "the emergence of Robinson Jeffers . . . the outstanding literary event in years."[12] The *Omaha World Herald* praised the elemental quality of the poetry,[13] and the *Brooklyn Eagle* proclaimed Jeffers a genius.[14] Without a doubt, Jeffers was the most popular serious poet in America in the twenties and early thirties.

The appearance of each new volume of Jeffers' poetry became an occasion for his admirers to renew their praise. In 1932, with the publication of *Thurso's Landing and Other Poems,* his sixth volume since *Tamar,* Jeffers' popularity crested. He appeared on the cover of *Time* magazine.[15] Benjamin De Casseres, who, in 1929, found in Jeffers "The tragic terror of Aeschylus, the supreme artistic aloofness and impersonality of Shakespeare . . . and, beyond all, the defiant and aurealed wickedness of Nietzsche's Antichrist and Superman,"[16] returned to predict that "in 50 years only two living Americans will be read, Robinson Jeffers and James Branch Cabell."[17] Mabel Dodge Luhan dedicated her book on her association with D. H. Lawrence, *Lorenzo in Taos,* to Jeffers. Lawrence Clark Powell published his doctoral dissertation, *An Introduction to Robinson Jeffers.* Although Jeffers failed to win the Pulitzer Prize in 1932 (he was never to receive it), Henry Seidel Canby reflected general critical opinion when he declared that Jeffers should have received the award because he was "among the few poets of unquestioned eminence writing in America."[18] Several influential critics accorded him highest praise that year. Granville Hicks, a Marxist, wrote that *Thurso's Landing* swept "forward on the wings of an imagery even nobler than that we have known."[19] Percy Hutchinson, in the *New York Times Book Review,* found the new book Jeffers' "crowning achievement to date."[20] In 1933, only eight years after *Tamar,* S. S. Alberts's *A Bibliography of the Works of Robinson Jeffers* was published. In 1935 Niven Busch noted, in assessing Jeffers' literary success, that Jeffers had not "in the last nine years, written anything which sold less than six editions, [while] *Roan Stallion, Tamar and Other Poems* zoomed through fourteen, and this month received the accolade of inclusion in the Modern Library."[21]

But the early thirties also witnessed the beginning of a precipitous decline in Jeffers' critical reputation. The wild enthusiasm of the twenties often reversed itself in the thirties. Jeffers' detractors heaped scorn upon the poet who had been judged a new Whitman. Occasionally the criticism extended to *ad hominem* attacks. Yvor Winters, concluding a scathing review, suggested that rather than force any more of his poetry on America, Jeffers should consider suicide.[22] Winters, who was loosely connected with the New Critics and philosophically a humanist, would conduct an almost personal vendetta against his fellow Californian. Condemning *Dear Judas* as revolting and maudlin, he found no quotable lines in the poem "save perhaps three," and those "heavy with dross."[23] In a review of *Thurso's Landing,* he stated his case more succinctly: "The book is composed almost wholly of trash."[24] Winters was perhaps the most vituperative of the critics who were increasingly hostile to Jeffers in the thirties and forties.

What caused this abrupt reversal? Why was Jeffers displaced so abruptly from the ranks of the major American poets? Factors other than the quality of the poetry itself contributed to his decline. To examine the curve of Jeffers' critical reputation is to measure the literary, political, and historical pulse of America in the thirties and forties.

First of all, the Depression and the widespread poverty it brought to America in the thirties influenced literary critics, who, caught up in the excitement of the New Deal, demanded socially and politically conscious literature. Jeffers did not satisfy their demands. Ruth Lechlitner, writing in the *New Republic* in 1936, mirrored the disgust that critics directed at the poet who seemed content to predict doom when everyone's efforts were needed to improve society. She chastised Jeffers for being above politics, saying that the "plain annihilation of humankind (followed by peace) will do Mr. Jeffers nicely. Provided . . . that he can sit in his stone tower, surrounded by California scenery, while the whole disgusting business is going on, and dash off a last poem or two before peace gathers him to her bosom."[25] Several other reviewers criticized Jeffers' pessimism and his lack of constructive social criticism. An early admirer, James Rorty, wrote in 1932 that he expressed "the death wish of a spent civilization," while "a new literature is emerging, the work of poets ardently partisan to human life and the conquests of human consciousness. Their ardors," he concluded, "are just as valid as Jeffers' enthusiasm for basalt and grave maggots."[26] In a 1938 review in *Poetry* of *Such Counsels You Gave To me*, Eda Lou Walton attacked what she took as Jeffers' antisocial anarchism, and saw him as one who has "removed himself too far from his own age to be seriously listened to as a prophet."[27] The critics of the decade found, as Delmore Schwartz said in 1939, that Jeffers' poetry, because it rejected humanity, was "without interest and without value."[28] Popular opinion reflected that judgment.

Jeffers' pronouncements concerning the Second World War further damaged his reputation. Jeffers was gravely distracted by the onset of the war, a preoccupation reflected in *Be Angry at the Sun* (1941). His prefatory remarks to the volume served warning that the themes of his poetry were changing: "I wish to lament the obsession with contemporary history that pins many of these pieces to the calendar, like butterflies on cardboard. Yet it is right that a man's views be expressed, though the poetry should suffer for it." In *Be Angry at the Sun* Jeffers issued a passionate plea for the United States to avoid entanglement in another European war. War, as he saw it, was the absolute human folly. His ensuing isolationism was as unpopular in the forties as was his lack of social commitment in the thirties. Stanley Kunitz, a sympathetic critic, warned Jeffers that if he did not "accept moral obligations and human values," he would "range himself on the side of the destroyers."[29]

The Double Axe and Other Poems, published in 1948, contained political views that Random House found sufficiently embarrassing to disclaim responsibility in a preface it added to the book. The first of its narratives, "The Love and the Hate," deals with a dead soldier who returns home to find his father spouting empty patriotic slogans. In some of the shorter poems, Churchill, Hitler, Roosevelt, and Stalin are equated as warlords. Not surprisingly, in the immediate postwar years Jeffers' views were almost universally condemned. The *St. Louis Post-Dispatch* declared that "only the most devout followers of the right-wing nationalists, the lunatic fringe, and the most ardent of Roosevelt haters could, after reading *The Double Axe*, welcome the return of Robinson

Jeffers."[30] *Time* Magazine condemned his isolationist stance and his implication "that no human kindness or decency would survive modern warfare."[31] The *Library Journal* found *The Double Axe* a "hateful book . . . a gospel of isolationism carried beyond geography, faith and hope."[32] The politics of the book, rather than its poetry, engaged the critics. Jeffers' political invective thus seriously damaged his literary reputation.

Because Jeffers was an isolationist at a time when the war against fascism took on aspects of a holy crusade, he was occasionally suspected of being himself a fascist. The accusation first appeared in a review of *Solstice* in 1935 in which Philip Blair Rice said that Jeffers' ideas resembled "good fascism."[33] Babette Deutsch, in the *Virginia Quarterly Review* in 1942, felt that *Be Angry at the Sun* gave color to the suspicion that Jeffers had fascist sympathies.[34] The accusation lingered. As late as 1971, in the *Saturday Review*, John Hughes called Jeffers a "monomaniacal proto-fascist."[35]

Two volumes that appeared in the seventies renewed the argument. In 1976 James Shebl's *In This Wild Water: The Suppressed Poems of Robinson Jeffers* was published. It offered to the public, for the first time, the poems that Random House had found to be politically most objectionable and had asked Jeffers to omit from the original version of *The Double Axe*. In 1977 Liveright reissued *The Double Axe and Other Poems*, containing the full text of Jeffers' original manuscript. The reaction to these two publications demonstrated that the controversy about United States participation in the Second World War was still alive.

Vernon Young, in *Parnassus*, may have expressed the most extreme response to the new edition. He found that the suppressed poems "are so degradingly inept as poems and as political thought, so unbelievably crude as polemic, of historical or philosophic credence so devoid, that any previous admirer of Jeffers should be grateful to Commins [Saxe Commins, Jeffers' editor at Random House] for having tried to spare reader and poet alike the embarrassment of publication; [but] less than grateful to Ward Ritchie [publisher of the Shebl book] and Liveright for now exposing to the air the wolverine stench of these sick fulminations." Young saw "unmistakably pro-fascist sympathies" in the poems, that "vomit[ed] cosmic . . . generalizations which no educated mind would accept. . . ." Later in the article, Young decided that the only explanation for the incongruity between "the majestic integrity" of the poetry Jeffers had written between 1925 and 1935, "which vindicated claims for him to be recognized as America's greatest poet," and his later verse had to be that "Jeffers' mind was unravelling."[36] The change of insanity to explain a writer's opinion has been employed before, both in the East and in the West. Ezra Pound and Knut Hamsun come to mind.

Other critics had high praise for the reappearance of *The Double Axe and Other Poems*. In 1978, William Nolte felt that "*The Double Axe* was probably the most incendiary volume of verse ever printed on these shores; it was and is certainly the most scathing indictment of war and war-mongers ever composed by an American."[37] C. J. Fox, writing in 1980, stated that "*The Double Axe* leaves one with the sense of a writer who, far from trying to be 'poetic,' is communicating in totally unvarnished fashion quite uncanny insights and premonitions, all the more remarkable for having emerged from an age sodden with propaganda." Fox ranked *The Double Axe* "as one of the most challenging books to come out of World War II. . . ." He compared the fierce indignation that the book aroused among reviewers with the "abuse heaped on Pasternak and Solzhenitsyn by the Moscow press[,]" noting "that Jeffers had touched a very sensitive nerve indeed."[38]

The antiwar poems that appeared in *Be Angry at the Sun* (1941) and *The Double Axe* (1948) played a pivotal role in defining Jeffers' reputation. Political opinion, inevitably, colored the reviewers' judgments. If a critic were able to view World War II in a wider perspective of human history, and not simply as a crusade against a unique evil, an objective reading of these poems might be possible. Not enough time has gone by, perhaps, to permit such equanimity. Until then, Jeffers' critical reputation will, to some extent, be influenced by the political and historical perspective of the reviewers.

The reasons for Jeffers' objection to American participation in World War II were in fact unambiguous. In "Shine Empire," published shortly before the outbreak of the war, he argued that America "Powerful and armed / neutral in the midst of madness / . . . might have held the whole world's balance / and stood / Like a mountain in the wind. We were misled and took sides." Let the insanity of war rage abroad, he declared: "All Europe was hardly worth the precarious freedom of / one of our states: what will her ashes fetch?" Jeffers' views were consistent. He deplored as well America's involvement in the other two wars in his adult lifetime: World War I and the Korean War. Few Americans of this century have so long and so vehemently spoken out against war. Whatever cause the nation hid behind, the sword's reality was, for Jeffers, "Loathsome / disfigurements, blindness, mutilation, locked / lips

of boys / Too proud to scream" ("Contemplation of the Sword").
Such views were not the way to win admirers in a nation at war. It
was difficult for those involved in the war effort to sympathize
with an isolationist sitting safely above the beach at Carmel.

Although politics played a significant role in his fall from grace,
detractors had vehemently objected to what they perceived as a
glorification of immorality and violence from Jeffers' first appearance in print. Religious conservatives criticized Jeffers' "Dear
Judas" for its unorthodox interpretation of Jesus. Yvor Winters
found that "Mr. Jeffers' mouthpiece and hero, Jesus, is a little
short of revolting as he whips reflexively from didactic passion to
malice, self-justification, and vengeance."[39] Harriet Monroe, editor of *Poetry,* censured "Roan Stallion" for its concern with "abnor-
mal passions."[40] In 1929 Robert Hillyer, although acknowledging
Jeffers' poetic skill, judged his material "revolting."[41] Howard
Mumford Jones, in a review of *The Women at Point Sur,* found in it
an excess of sex, insanity, and perversity,[42] and Babette Deutsch
saw "irrelevant sordidness" in the volume.[43] In a grass-roots reaction to Jeffers' poetry in *Carnegie Magazine* in 1928, the reviewer
complained of the moral perversion in his long poems, and
warned the public not to read Jeffers aloud in family circles.[44]

For all those who condemned what they considered immorality
in Jeffers' poetry, others were attracted by its passionate iconoclasm. Many bohemians of his era shared with Jeffers a general
philosophical attitude that was radically antiestablishment. His
warmest admirers, George Sterling, Edna St. Vincent Millay, and
others, lived the sexual revolution four and five decades before
the media discovered it. To many of the avant-garde, the poetry of
Jeffers, shocking, radical, and Nietzschean, seemed the quintessential expression of their own passions. De Casseres commended
in Jeffers "the satanic joy in the hideous of Baudelaire."[45] Sterling
likened Jeffers' poetry to "great serpents coiled around high and
translucent jars of poison, gleaming with a thousand hues of
witch-fire."[46] Arthur Davison Ficke, the bohemian poet and man
of letters, praised the poet's "nightmare sex designs," believing
that his purpose was "to blast the human universe apart."[47] With
an ironic smile, Robert Frost sees Jeffers, along with Eugene
O'Neill, busily stoking the fires of Hell.[48] When Mabel Dodge
Luhan tried to entice Jeffers to her colony in Taos in the early
1930s, it was because she saw in him the potential messiah of a
new ethic. At the beginning of his career, Jeffers undoubtedly did
attract an audience because of his unconventional attitudes, but as
the early critics grew older what seemed radical became com-

monplace. Beyond mere shock effect, it was Jeffers' apparent insistence on human insignificance that was unacceptable to some who originally had been his most ardent admirers.

The humanist critics, in general, found little to honor in Jeffers. Those who, like Irving Babbitt, Paul Elmer More, and Norman Foerster, refused to accept the animal component in human nature and believed that a poem should be judged in terms of its advancement of human morality, would understandably be unreceptive to the philosophical content of Jeffers' Inhumanism, which argues for a rational acceptance of the fact that humanity is neither central nor important in the universe. Small wonder that More condemned modern literature's degeneration into "the clever futilities of an Aldous Huxley or the obscene rigamarole of a James Joyce, or seeking to escape the curse of impotence, into the sadism of a Robinson Jeffers."[49] Critics who believed in the rational perfectibility of human beings reacted negatively to Jeffers. More often than not, they ignored him.

Marxist critics, writing in journals such as the *New Masses* and the *Nation*, were among the first to pay Jeffers serious attention, despite their reservations about his politics. Horace Gregory, expressing a typical Marxist ambivalence towards Jeffers, praised him in 1934 as a "superlative nature poet . . . who made us see the underside of a vast dream called American prosperity. . . ."[50] Rolfe Humphries, on the other hand, condemned Jeffers in 1935 for making "no effort to show that the present horrible frustrations, deformations and agonies of men are due to the fact that they are for the most part still living under the degenerating capitalism of the twentieth century," adding that Jeffers "served a very useful purpose to the governing class" by telling humanity that it is futile to protest against its hard, inevitable lot.[51] Alan Swallow wrote in 1937 that Jeffers' failures could be traced to the fact that he "works so completely within the bourgeois culture."[52] Victor Francis Calverton declared that Jeffers' tragedies are a "reflection of the violent, toppling ruins of a dying civilization."[53] Gregory remained a persistent admirer who, as late as 1955, judged "Tamar" to be "one of the major accomplishments of twentieth-century poetry."[54] Even in the Soviet Union the poet was noticed. In 1934, *International Literature* contained a major review of Jeffers' work, finding it typically decadent but at the same time calling him "A great American writer, class-conscious and courageous enough to express it."[55] Although the Marxists sometimes condemned Jeffers, they seldom ignored him.

Nor was Jeffers ignored by most of his fellow writers. Many of the important literary personalities of the twenties and thirties praised him. Robert Frost, who maintained a lifelong respect for Jeffers, counted himself "an admirer," not least because Jeffers "kept California as a base" and did not "run out to New York."[56] Sinclair Lewis, in accepting the Nobel Prize in 1930, complained that the American Academy of Arts did not include original and vital poets such as Edna St. Vincent Millay, Carl Sandburg, and Jeffers. Millay, a personal friend of Jeffers and his family, repeatedly praised his work, calling herself "his most enthusiastic admirer,"[57] and saying that he wrote "the most tragic, marvelous stuff."[58] Sandburg appreciated him as a second Balboa who had opened America's eyes to the magnificence of the Pacific Ocean.[59] Edgar Lee Masters, a constant admirer, said that "The Women at Point Sur" was the greatest poem that had been produced in America in many years, containing among its virtues "the intensity of Sophocles."[60] He judged that the "success which Jeffers may achieve is beyond prediction."[61] T. S. Eliot lamented in 1962 that Jeffers had never been adequately appreciated.[62] Selden Rodman believed that Jeffers belonged "in the ranks of Dryden and Byron," and that, as the "best of all poets writing in English today," he remained "as close to a major poet as we have."[63] Sara Teasdale compared "Tamar" with Milton's "Samson Agonistes."[64] James Dickey, writing in 1964, had high praise: "As obviously flawed as he is, Jeffers is cast in a large mold; he fills a position in this country that would simply have been an empty gap without him: that of the poet as prophet, as large scale philosopher, as doctrine giver. . . . One cannot shake off Jeffers' vision as one can the carefully prepared surprises of many of the neatly packaged stanzas we call 'good poems.' . . . Few visions have been more desperate, and few lives organized around such austere principles. It seems to me that we must honor these things."[65] In 1970 Richard Eberhart commented that Jeffers "does not make poetry which depends upon symbol, innuendo, or any kind of double-talk. Of its kind there has been nothing successfully like it since Whitman. It is direct. It is a man speaking. Granted there are other graces and enviable ways for poetry, this way can be uniquely powerful in the hands of a great talent."[66]

Not all of Jeffers' literary contemporaries, however, agreed with these assessments. It was the New Critics, many themselves poets, who damaged Jeffers most severely. Unlike other detractors, they did not object specifically to Jeffers' subject matter or philosophy, but rather to his poetic style and technique. They particularly valued imagery, wit, irony, paradox, and ambiguity, and stressed close textual reading of tight, concentrated, shorter poems. Almost without exception they rejected Jeffers' verse, calling attention to its "looseness of rhythms" and the absence, as Robert Penn Warren noted in 1937, of the "concentration of interest in detail that gives a short poem its power." Warren judged the short poems in *Solstice* to be "turgid and feeble."[67] The judgments of this influential group ranged from Yvor Winters' savage attacks to Allen Tate's moderate defense, in which he conceded occasional "fine restraint and modulation of tone in [Jeffers'] short poems."[68] R. P. Blackmur, writing in the *Kenyon Review* in 1952, castigated ". . . the flannel-mouthed inflation in the metric of Robinson Jeffers with his rugged rock-garden violence."[69] Randall Jarrell wrote in 1963: "Jeffers' poems do not have the exactness and concision of the best poetry; his style and temperament, his whole world view, are to a surprising extent a matter of simple exaggeration."[70] In 1941, John Crowe Ransom wondered why critics bothered with Jeffers at all,[71] and, in 1951, when he compiled an anthology of the major and minor poets of the first fifty years of the century, Jeffers was omitted. The disdain of the New Critics in the period of their dominance from the 1930s to the 1960s resulted in the removal of Jeffers from consideration as a poet of the first rank by many.

Jeffers' death in 1962 received front-page notice in only a handful of newspapers, and even in Carmel, coverage of the final day of the Pebble Beach Golf Tournament overshadowed the passing of the poet who had helped make the central California coast famous. Reflecting general opinion, the *San Francisco Chronicle* noted, two days after his death, that "the greatest thing that Jeffers did for American poetry was to learn Greek."[72] Indeed, at the time of his death, Jeffers was best known not for his poetry, but for his adaptation of Euripides' *Medea*, which opened in 1947 to favorable reviews from the New York theater critics and enjoyed a successful run. Jeffers' version was praised for its "beauty of language"[73] and its sense of theater. Brooks Atkinson, in his review of *Medea* in the *New York Times*, opined that its "literary style is terse, idiomatic and sparing. The imagery is austere and brilliant."[74]

Jeffers' last poems were published posthumously in 1963. The reviews of *The Beginning and the End* frequently provided a retrospective evaluation of the poet. Despite the fact that Jeffers' reputation was in eclipse, he retained an important following, and his admirers were convinced that he would eventually rejoin the ranks of the major poets of the century. *Time* Magazine, while oddly claiming that Jeffers had never been very popular (apparently its reviewer had failed to check the magazine's backfile), asserted that Jeffers was "one of the greatest American poets."[75] William Everson (Brother Antoninus) noted the "undeviating capacity to say what is meant without equivocation," and found that "great enough for any man to go out on."[76] A reviewer in *Fiddlehead* claimed that "as time goes by he will have to be placed among the major American poets of this century."[77] William Turner Levy, in the *New York Times Book Review*, found that although "Jeffers' answer will not be ours . . . he instructs us how our minds might be exalted in beauty—and so share in the divine quality and fabric of all creation."[78] The poet Stephen Spender found "these last poems of Jeffers . . . extremely moving" and added that they "may well be his best poetry."[79] Winfield Townley Scott summarized Jeffers' career as "far more important in American poetry than the critics in latter years have supposed." He concluded that although Jeffers may have been overrated at his zenith, there was no question that he "has been underrated in recent decades."[80] Although Jeffers still had detractors who found that these last poems "added up to a failure . . . a waste of time to write or read,"[81] a number of influential critics still insisted that Jeffers was a major poet.

In the quarter century since Jeffers' death, a devoted circle of scholars have continued to write thoughtful studies of his works. Their assessments range from qualified praise to adulation of the type expressed by Bill Hotchkiss when he declared that "Robinson Jeffers is the single greatest American poet of this century; and within the entire American tradition, Walt Whitman stands as his single peer. Indeed, from Homer to the present, there are precious few whose works seem equally the works of giants."[82] At times, the faith of these scholars in the inevitability of a Jeffers revival has been almost religious in intensity. In 1976, William Nolte claimed that "After a sharp decline in popularity just before, during, and after World War II, Jeffers' stock has in recent years been on the rise again both at home and abroad."[83] Another admirer, Robert Ian Scott, noted in 1979 that "despite decades of academic ignorance and hostility, Jeffers' books have kept selling whenever available."[84] Hotchkiss saw a "Jeffers renaissance, now well underway."[85] Writing in the *Antigonish Review* in 1980, C. J. Fox also found that "A Jeffers revival now seems well underway in literary America. . . . Books and articles now drop steadily from academic and other presses. . . ."[86]

Objectivity must be maintained in evaluating Jeffers' current literary reputation. To judge whether or not a significant revival is underway one should, as much as possible, turn to verifiable data, examining, as well, what lies behind the possible renewal of interest. With that caveat in mind, there is no doubt that Jeffers' reputation has risen from the low levels it reached in the late 1930s and the 1940s, and that indeed renewed interest seemed to be most noticeable during the decade from the mid-1960s to the mid-1970s.

Since *Beginning and the End and Other Poems*, several new editions of Jeffers' poetry have appeared. In 1965, Random House issued a Vintage paperback, *Selected Poems*, that included poetry written after the 1938 *Selected Poetry*. The first edition of nine thousand copies sold out within a year and Random House went to press with another five thousand. In the same year, *Not Man Apart: Photographs of the Big Sur Coast*, an illustrated collection of Jeffers' nature poetry, was published by the Sierra Club. The poet was presented, in the words of Loren Eiseley, as the "most powerful embodiment of the untamed Pacific environment."[87] It still remains a popular text. New Directions published a paperback edition of *Cawdor and Medea* in 1970. In 1977 three new editions of Jeffers' poetry were published, in cloth and paperback, by Norton, under the Liveright imprimatur: *The Women at Point Sur and Other Poems*, *Dear Judas and Other Poems*, and *The Double Axe and Other Poems*. *The Double Axe* included, as noted above, eleven poems that had been dropped from the original edition. All three volumes were reissued in 1987, in paper only. The cumulative sales of these 1977 and 1987 editions, as of June 1987, were 17,630.[88] A new printing of the original *Selected Poetry* appeared in 1987. Various other new editions of Jeffers' poetry and prose have been published as well in recent decades. Among these are: *Flagons and Apples* (1970), *Californians* (1971), *The Alpine Christ* (1974), *Brides of the South Wind* (1974), *Poetry, Gongorism and a Thousand Years* (1974), and *Jeffers Country* (1971), with poetry by Robinson Jeffers and photographs by Horace Lyons. In addition, several limited editions of Jeffers texts have appeared. Jeffers' centennial in 1987 was marked by two substantial reprintings of his verse: *Rock and Hawk: A Selection of Shorter Poems* [by Jeffers], edited by Robert Hass, and, in England, a *Selected Poems*, edited by Colin Falck. It is apparent that the publication of Jeffers' books remains a profitable undertaking for publishing houses on both the East and West coasts. In addition, the four-volume *Collected Poetry*, edited by Tim Hunt, is being issued by Stanford University Press.

A further indication of renewed interest in Jeffers since his death can be measured by doctoral dissertations. From 1930 to 1962, no single year saw more than one dissertation on Jeffers, and the total for those 33 years was five. Since then the situation has changed. In 1966 three dissertations on Jeffers appeared, in 1967 five, in 1970 two, in 1971 four, in 1973 three, and in 1976 three. There has been one or more virtually every year since. The number of masters' theses written about Jeffers has followed a similar pattern. Even discounting for the general increase in graduate theses in the past generation, the steady if slow interest in Jeffers' work is undeniable. Among those who wrote dissertations and theses in those years are some who continue to play an important role in Jeffers scholarship: Arthur Coffin, Ann Ridgeway, Edward Nickerson, James Shebl, Bill Hotchkiss, and Robert Brophy.

Perhaps the most diligent and devoted of Jeffers scholars is Robert Brophy. His studies on the poet and his work have been numerous and of high quality. He has edited the quarterly *Robinson Jeffers Newsletter* since 1968, when Melba Bennett, its founder and editor, died. Under Brophy's direction, the *Newsletter,* which began in 1962, has steadily increased in importance and has become a valuable repository for all manner of information about the poet. Containing full-length scholarly articles, bibliographic studies, previously unpublished primary and secondary material, book reviews, personal reminiscences, letters and other biographical material, announcements of forthcoming publications, and other activities of interest to the public and scholar alike, the *Newsletter* has already proved an indispensable source for Jeffers studies. Brophy, in addition to his scholarly contributions in the *Newsletter* and elsewhere, published the monograph *Robinson Jeffers: Myth, Ritual and Symbol in His Narrative Poems* in 1973. In this major work Brophy uses ancient myth and ritual to explain the death and rebirth cycles and the religious significations that underlie five of Jeffers' narrative poems: "Tamar," "Roan Stallion," "The Tower beyond Tragedy," "Cawdor," "At the Birth of an Age," and the lyric poem, "Apology for Bad Dreams." The centerpiece of Brophy's book is, perhaps, his reinterpretation of Jeffers' "Tamar," the narrative poem that helped launch Jeffers' reputation in 1924.

Several other book-length studies of Jeffers' poetry have appeared in the last two decades. William Everson's *Fragments of an Older Fury* (1968) was among the first to offer a careful explication of a Jeffers poem, using the close textual techniques of the New

Critics. Arthur Coffin's *Robinson Jeffers: Poet of Inhumanism* provided a detailed study of the philosophical framework of Jeffers' poetry. In *Rock and Hawk: Robinson Jeffers and the Romantic Agony*, which appeared in 1978, William Nolte redefined Jeffers' Inhumanism within the context of romanticism. Robert Zaller's *The Cliffs of Solitude*, published in 1983, is a comprehensive overview of the entire oeuvre. Combining close textual analysis, biography, and psychoanalytic theory as a means of examining Jeffers' recurring themes of "incest, castration, and parricide," Zaller succeeds in placing the poet within a new context.[89] A second book by Everson, *The Excesses of God* (1988), considers Jeffers as a religious poet. These are but some of the more significant critical studies of Jeffers that have appeared since the poet's death. The variety of their approaches—philosophical, anthropological, psychological, and religious—attests to the breadth of his poetic undertaking.

There have been additional contributions to a fuller understanding of Jeffers. In 1966 appeared the first biography of the poet, Melba Berry Bennett's *The Stone Mason of Tor House*. James Karman's *Robinson Jeffers* (1987) importantly modifies it. *The Selected Letters of Robinson Jeffers*, edited by Ann Ridgeway, was published in 1968. In addition to the many letters of Una Jeffers that have appeared in the *Robinson Jeffers Newsletter*, a limited edition of the love letters of Robin and Una was published under the title *Where Shall I Take You To* in 1987. Jeanetta Boswell's partially annotated bibliography of secondary sources, *Robinson Jeffers and the Critics, 1912–1983*, is a useful updating of Alex Vardamis's 1972 *The Critical Reputation of Robinson Jeffers*. Gradually scholars are creating an impressive body of serious critical studies and apparatus that is contributing to a reevaluation of the poet.

Jeffers' fame has spread, in recent years, beyond the scholarly community. Articles on Jeffers have appeared in publications as diverse as the monthly Pacific Gas and Electric Company inclosure *PG & E Progress, Sunset Magazine*, the *Sierra Club Bulletin*, and *Architectural Digest*. In 1983, Judson Jerome devoted his poetry column in *Writer's Digest* to an intelligent analysis of "Roan Stallion" in which he suggested that neophyte poets could well take a lesson from this "tale that rivets the imagination and brings into haunting presence the dark magic of folklore."[90] A children's novel, *A Heart to the Hawks*, by Don Moser, which deals with a boy's fight against land developers, was published in 1975 by Atheneum. Jeffers was frequently quoted in the 1970s and 1980s in calendars published by the Sierra Club. Political figures, as well, have discovered Jeffers. California's former governor, Edmund

G. Brown, Jr., declared in an April 1975 *Playboy* interview that
Jeffers was one of the few authors important to him. With an
irony Jeffers would no doubt have appreciated, Secretary of Defense James Schlesinger asserted at a NATO Nuclear Planning
Group meeting in Monterey that same year that Jeffers' poem,
"Shine, Republic" reflects the American role in the [NATO] alliance, the meaning of the alliance and what it brings together."[91]

Jeffers has been the subject of a number of celebrations at
various academic institutions, including San Francisco State College in 1969, the University of Kansas in 1974, and Southern
Oregon State in 1975, while Occidental College and San Jose State
University honored him in 1987 at the centenary of his birth. In
1978 Tor House, Jeffers' home, became part of the National
Trust. The Robinson Jeffers Tor House Foundation, which plays
an important role in administering the property and making it
available to scholars and the public, was incorporated in May of
that year. The annual Tor House Festival was first held in Carmel
in the fall of 1979.

Jeffers' plays and dramatic productions of his poetry are frequently staged. Dame Judith Anderson appeared as Medea in
Woodland Hills, California, in 1965, and has given readings
through the years, notably of *Medea* and other poems at the
University of California at Santa Barbara in 1972, and of Jeffers'
letters at Carmel in 1986. In 1983 she played the Nurse and Zoe
Caldwell the title role in a revival of Jeffers' *Medea*. An operatic version premiered in San Diego in 1972, and another
of "Tamar" in 1975. The poem "Joy" was set to music, and the
Beach Boys had a hit record featuring a rock rendition of
"The Beaks of Eagles" in 1974. In 1975, "A.M. America," ABC's
morning show, featured a birthday salute to Jeffers, and in 1981
PBS broadcast "Tor House: Lines from Robinson Jeffers," narrated by Burgess Meredith. A 1963 Steuben Glass exhibition featured a sculpture inspired by Jeffers' "Birds and Fishes." In 1974
Jeffers postcards were sold in St. Paul, Minnesota, and in 1976 a
shop in Pacific Grove featured Robinson Jeffers T-shirts. On a
more enduring plane, the U.S. Post Office issued a stamp honor-
ing the poet on August 13, 1973. Clearly, Jeffers remained a
presence on various levels of American culture, both popular and
serious.[92]

Jeffers is known abroad as well. He has been translated into
French, Spanish, Italian, Czech, German, Arabic, Slovak, Polish,
Japanese, Danish, Greek, Bulgarian, Portuguese, Serbo-Croatian,
and most recently, by Lars Nystroem into Swedish (1984). The
Swedish translation occasioned a major comment on Jeffers' work

in *Sydsvenska Dagbladet.* Niklas Tornlund found that Jeffers' poetry forced the reader to mobilize his inner resources and to counter the poet's challenging pessimism.[93] Jeffers has been produced on the stage or on radio around the world in, among other places, Czechoslovakia, Yugoslavia, West Germany, Great Britain, Australia, and South Africa. In Czechoslovakia, an operatic version of "Hungerfield" has been mounted. Docents at Tor House describe frequent visits of Japanese tourists who come to pay their respects to a favorite American poet. Indeed, Jeffers is perhaps better known in Czechoslovakia, West Germany, and Japan than he is in many parts of America.

It is no accident that Jeffers' recent popularity was at a high point in the late sixties and early seventies. Several factors were at play. Jeffers' death was closely followed by the assassination of President John F. Kennedy. In the decade that followed, America underwent a social and cultural upheaval in which traditional values were challenged or cast aside. In the twenties, Jeffers' iconoclasm had given voice to the radical aspirations of the avant-garde. Similarly, the prophetic Jeffers offered sustenance to the disillusioned and disenchanted youth of the sixties and seventies. The loss of faith in America's leaders and in its system of government, and despair over the seemingly endless war in Vietnam, all echoed Jeffers' chief concerns.

Jeffers' antiwar poems assumed particular relevance for the Vietnam War generation. Some critics, however, found little connection between the poems in *Be Angry at the Sun* and *The Double Axe* and the Vietnam War protest movement. In a hostile review of the reissued *Double Axe* in *Parnassus*, Vernon Young deplored the ready tendency to link opposition to the Vietnam War with Jeffers' denunciation of America's involvement in World War II.[84] Others disagreed. C. J. Fox noted in 1980 that Jeffers' opposition to America's intervention in World War II "brought him, a few years after his death in 1962, more or less perfectly into tune with the anti-interventionist ideas of the New Left in the era of Vietnam." Fox added that the central figure of the long title poem in *The Double Axe* "talks and acts like an angry Vietnam veteran three decades before his time," and concluded that Jeffers would surely have been gratified to know that the opponents of the Vietnam War had harked back to him for their intellectual and emotional underpinning.[95] In 1976, Nolte, discussing Jeffers' rejection of the moral arguments used to justify American intervention in the World Wars, saw "the same reasons touted in support of the ten-year conflict in Asia."[96]

In the years of Vietnam and Watergate, Jeffers' prophecies

seemed relevant to many. James Dickey, writing before the coincidences between Jeffers' poetry and the concerns of the Vietnam generation could be known, wrote: "It is extraordinarily strange how the more aweful and ludicrous aspects of the atomic age have come to resemble Jeffers' poems."[97] C. J. Fox noted that Jeffers predicted "a future generation of youth who would not serve in a new conflict brought on by old gentlemen shouting for war. With disenchantment over Vietnam and America's imperial role spreading, Jeffers—branded, in effect, a hate-mongering reactionary in the forties—would, had he survived, have found the young radicals of the sixties and seventies strangely congenial."[98] Nolte, in "Robinson Jeffers, An Uncanny Prophet," wrote that "Jeffers was our most far-sighted poet; and nearly the whole of his work concerns the values that men hold, usually to their detriment and despair."

Similarly, the ecology movement of that era found encouragement in the poet who repeatedly raised his voice in the battle for a balanced relationship with nature. Those who deplored the urbanization of America and the spreading uniformity of a culture that destroyed its natural beauty responded to the Jeffers who, in poem after poem, struck out against the reckless spoliation of the environment. William White, commenting on the issuance of the Jeffers postage stamp, wrote that "The present-day ecologists should make Jeffers their hero; he was talking in philosophical and poetical terms years ago of the things they are talking about in 1973."[99] In 1977, Kevin Starr pointed out in the *Sierra Club Bulletin* that no other artist had done more than Jeffers to nourish a "new respect of nature on its own terms." He explained that "because of his poetry we are more aware of the otherness of natural things. And in that new respect for otherness in the inanimate, in that fresh and vital respect to the beingness of rocks and rivers and trees, are the sound beginnings of an environmentalism that is so very much more than a program of protection. It is a philosophy of creation itself."[100] Jeffers thus offered a philosophical foundation for the nascent ecology movement.

In sum, Jeffers proved congenial in the 1960s and 1970s to Americans who were committed to peace, to ecological reform, and to new values. As a result, his literary reputation was partially resurrected. The war protesters of that era, the environmentalists, those who distrusted the establishment, all wary of the claims of scientists, tired of the cold war and the nuclear arms race, and yearning for a return to the essential things, found in Jeffers a kindred spirit. Ironically, however, Jeffers' poetry was once again judged for political reasons. Inevitably, as the passionate concerns of the Vietnam era subsided, so, too, did some of the enthusiasm for the poet. The fact remains that Jeffers, in comparison to poets like Robert Frost, T. S. Eliot, Wallace Stevens, William Carlos Williams, Theodore Roethke, and Robert Lowell, has a limited following, particularly in the academy. Jeffers is not generally taught in the American colleges and universities. Robert Ian Scott might find that "university students who have spent weeks wrestling with poetry by Eliot and Wallace Stevens generally greet Jeffers' poems with a grateful 'At last, a poet who writes coherently about the world we live in!'"[101] And it has been true that when students are given the opportunity to read Jeffers, they usually react favorably. As Judson Jerome testified, reading Jeffers in his freshman year at the University of Oklahoma in 1943 was for him "one of the many literary experiences that opened the vista of possibility in poetry, and has caused me to be disappointed in the ways more recent poets have responded to that challenge."[102] Had Jerome been in college in recent years it is not likely that he would have been exposed to Jeffers. Bill Hotchkiss, who came to write his dissertation on Jeffers, tells us that he never read a Jeffers poem as an undergraduate in the fifties at the University of California at Berkeley or as a graduate student at San Francisco State. All he took away from his readings in contemporary criticism was the sense of Jeffers as "an outrageously inferior poet." Not until 1963, when he took a course from William Nolte at the University of Oregon, was he introduced to Jeffers.[103] Jeanetta Boswell, in her 1986 introduction to *Jeffers and the Critics*, admits that she "came to Jeffers with little knowledge and less appreciation." She regretted the years she had "taught American literature and did little or nothing with Jeffers" because she "did not know he was a major poet."[104] Hotchkiss's and Boswell's experiences are not atypical.

In May 1986, in an attempt to discover the extent of current academic interest in Robinson Jeffers in America, I sent questionnaires to a random cross-section of American colleges and universities. Included were religious-affiliated, state, and private institutions. Of the fifty schools responding, only eight said that they taught Jeffers in any course, graduate or undergraduate, for more than one hour a semester. Sixteen more taught Jeffers for an hour or less. "Hurt Hawks" was the poem most often selected for presentation. The remaining institutions responded that they did not teach Jeffers at all. Jeffers, at the time of the survey, was not included in the curriculum of Antioch, Bard, Bowdoin, Bryn

Mawr, Cornell, Mount Holyoke, Ohio Wesleyan, Saint Olaf, Smith, Stanford, Swarthmore, the United States Air Force Academy, Vassar, Williams, and the Universities of Oregon, North Dakota, Wisconsin, and California at both the Berkeley and Los Angeles campuses.

Many of these institutions said that they had last taught Jeffers in the early to midseventies. The chairman of the English department at the University of Pennsylvania reported that Jeffers' appeal is "not as it was 15 years ago." "Robinson Jeffers, alas, has not been taught for some years at Vassar and is not being taught now," was the reply from Poughkeepsie. "Clearly we neglect Jeffers," mused the English chairman at Colby, and added, "I don't know why."

Jeffers' neglect in the academic world has clear consequences for his reputation at large. The makers of critical judgment in America are graduates of schools that are, by and large, influenced by the selections that the New Critics made in the thirties, forties, and fifties. Many of the present educators in today's universities and colleges regard Jeffers primarily as a regional nature poet, or as an example of extreme American romanticism. They tend to see Jeffers as he was described by Randall Jarrell in 1942: "An example too pure and too absurd even for allegory is Robinson Jeffers, who must prefer a hawk to a man, a stone to a hawk, because of an individualism so exaggerated that it contemptuously rejects affections, obligations, relations of any kind whatsoever, and sets up as a nostalgically-awaited goal the war of all against all. Old Rocky Face, perched on his sea crag, is the last of *laissez faire;* Free Economic Man at the end of his rope."[105]

Now, a hundred years after the poet's birth, the critical reception of Robinson Jeffers is at a crossroads. Undeniably, in the sixties and seventies Jeffers regained at least some of the popularity he had enjoyed in the twenties. Environmentalists flocked to the Big Sur country, not least because Jeffers had first painted its splendors. Protestors against the Vietnam War and other American military interventions found confirmation for their convictions in some of his antiwar poetry. It is perhaps significant that *The Double Axe,* upon its reissue in 1977, outsold the other two volumes, *The Women at Point Sur* and *Dear Judas,* which appeared at the same time. Although interest in Jeffers was, to a degree, centered in California, Americans from all parts of the country found that Jeffers spoke to them clearly on relevant issues. Nevertheless, although a continuing number of graduate students write dissertations on him, often with scant encouragement from their mentors, Jeffers was, and is, not generally taught in the schools. Those who ignore him might say that they do so because he is not a major poet and they have little enough time to cover the "indispensable" American poets of the twentieth century. It is often assumed as well that Jeffers' poetry is easily accessible, and hence in no need of the explication lavished on a Pound or Stevens. The recent Jeffers scholars and critics have responded to this argument. Through their detailed, analytical studies, they have demonstrated that Jeffers is not merely a teller of stirring, violent stories or a poet of simple lyrics. They have demonstrated that Jeffers had more to say and often said it more profoundly and beautifully than the apparently more difficult contemporary poets so favored in most English departments. In the development of this solid scholarly foundation lies the way to a permanence based not on fads and fashions, but on an appreciation of Jeffers' stature and his unique contribution to the art of poetry and the development of thought in this century. The trend begun in the past two decades towards a careful critical reevaluation of his canon will eventually demonstrate the hollowness of Jarrell's *ex cathedra* pronouncements.

Jeffers stands ready to fill a void in the intellectual development of this generation. In the literature of a century that has been so often both introspective and egocentric, Jeffers offers a unique vision of the truly essential. He could be an antidote for a world that has, unfortunately, forgotten to judge within a grand context. When the political debates of the thirties and forties, and even of the sixties have passed into history, it will be observed that here is a poet who sees beyond the current flutterings of the age.

NOTES

1. George Sterling, "Rhymes and Reactions," *Overland Monthly* 83 (November 1925): 411.

2. James Rorty, "In Major Mold," *New York Herald and Tribune Books*, 1 March 1925, 1–2.

3. Mark Van Doren, "First Glance," *Nation* 120 (11 March 1925): 268.

4. Babette Deutsch, "Brains and Lyrics," *New Republic* 43 (27 May 1925): 23–24.

5. James Daly, "Roots under the Rocks," *Poetry* 26 (August 1925): 278–85.

6. "Pacific Headlands," *Time* Magazine 5 (30 March 1925): 12.

7. Babette Deutsch, "Bitterness and Beauty," *New Republic* 45 (10 February 1926): 338–39.

8. Percy A. Hutchinson, "An Elder Poet and a Young One Greet the New Year," *New York Times Book Review*, 3 January 1926, 14, 24.

9. Edwin Seaver, "Robinson Jeffers' Poetry," *Saturday Review of Literature* 2 (16 January 1926): 492.

10. Henry Louis Mencken, "Books of Verse," *American Mercury* 8 (June 1926): 251–54.

11. Lillian C. Ford, "New Major Poet Emerges," *Los Angeles Times*, 11 April 1926, sec. 3. 34.

12. "Publication of Poems by Jeffers Creates Strong Demand for More," *Salt Lake City Telegram*, 29 November 1925, magazine, 1.

13. Review of *Roan Stallion, Tamar and Other Poems, Omaha World Herald*, 24 January 1926, magazine, 6.

14. Gremin Zorn, "Books of the Moment Seen Critically by Prospectors in the Literary Mountains," *Brooklyn Eagle*, 16 January 1926, 5.

15. "Harrowed Morrow," *Time* Magazine 19 (4 April 1932).

16. Benjamin DeCasseres, *The Superman in America* (Seattle: University of Washington Bookstore, 1929), 22–25.

17. Benjamin DeCasseres, "Robinson Jeffers," *University of North Carolina Daily Tar Heel* 40 (24 January 1932): 1.

18. Henry Seidel Canby, "The Pulitzer Prizes," *Saturday Review of Literature* 8 (23 April 1932): 677.

19. Granville Hicks, "A Transient Sickness," *Nation* 134 (13 April 1932): 433.

20. Percy Hutchinson, "Robinson Jeffers' Dramatic Poem of Spiritual Tragedy," *New York Times Book Review*, 3 April 1932, 2.

21. Niven Busch, "Duel in a Headland," *Saturday Review of Literature* 11 (9 March 1935): 533.

22. Yvor Winters, "Robinson Jeffers," *Poetry* 35 (February 1930): 279–86.

23. *Ibid.*

24. Yvor Winters, review of *Thurso's Landing and Other Poems, The Hound and the Horn* 5 (July–September 1932): 681, 684–85.

25. Ruth Lechlitner, review of *Solstice and Other Poems, New Republic* 25 (8 January 1936): 262.

26. James Rorty, "Symbolic Melodrama," *New Republic* 71 (18 May 1932): 24–25.

27. Eda Lou Walton, "Beauty of Storm Disproportionately," *Poetry* 51 (January 1938): 209–13.

28. Delmore Schwartz, "Sources of Violence," *Poetry* 55 (October 1939): 30–38.

29. Stanley J. Kunitz, "The Day is a Poem," *Poetry* 59 (December 1941): 148–54.

30. R. I. Brigham, "Bitter and Skillful Treatise in Verse," *St. Louis Post-Dispatch*, 1 August 1948, sec. 6. 4f.

31. "And Buckets o' Blood," *Time* Magazine 52 (2 August 1948): 79.

32. Gerald McDonald, Review of *The Double Axe and Other Poems, Library Journal*, 73 (15 June 1948): 948.

33. Philip Blair Rice, "Jeffers and the Tragic Sense," *Nation* 141 (23 October 1935): 480–82.

34. Babette Deutsch, "Poets and the New Poets," *Virginia Quarterly Review* 8 (Winter 1942): 132–34.

35. John V. Hughes, "Humanism and the Orphic Voice," *Saturday Review* 54 (22 May 1971): 31–33.

36. Vernon Young, "Such Counsels He Gave to Us: Jeffers Revisited," *Parnassus* 6 (1977): 178–97.

37. William H. Nolte, "Robinson Jeffers Redivivus," *Georgia Review* 32 (1978): 429–34.

38. C. J. Fox, "Full Circle: The *Zeitgeist* and Robinson Jeffers," *Antigonish Review* 43 (1980): 91–104.

39. Winters, "Robinson Jeffers."

40. Harriet Monroe, "Pomp and Power," *Poetry* 28 (June 1926): 160–64.

41. Robert Hillyer, "Five American Poets," *New Adelphia* 2 (March–May 1929): 280–82.

42. Howard Mumford Jones, "Dull Naughtiness," *Chicago News*, 3 August 1927, 14.

43. Babette Deutsch, "Or What's a Heaven for? *New Republic* 51 (17 August 1927): 341.

44. Samuel Harden Church, "A Pittsburgh Poet Discovered," *Carnegie Magazine* 2 (November 1928): 180–82.

45. DeCasseres, *The Superman in America.*

46. Sterling, "Rhymes and Reactions," 411.

47. Arthur Davison Ficke, "A Note on the Poetry of Sex," in *Sex in Civilization*, ed. Victor Francis Calverton and Samuel D. Schmalhausen (New York: Macaulay Co., 1929), 666–67.

48. Robert Frost, "A Masque of Mercy," in *The Poetry of Robert Frost*, ed. Edward Connery Lathem (New York: Holt, Rinehart & Winston, 1969), 516.

49. Paul Elmer More, "A Revival of Humanism," *Bookman* 71 (March 1930): 1–11.

50. Horace Gregory, "Suicide in the Jungle," *New Masses* 25 (13 February 1934): 18–19.

51. Rolfe Humphries, "Robinson Jeffers," *Modern Monthly* 8 (January and February 1935): 680–89, 748–53.

52. Alan Swallow, "The Poetry of Robinson Jeffers," *Intermountain Review.* 2 (Fall 1937): 8–9.

53. Victor Francis Calverton, "Pathology in Contemporary Literature," *Thinker* 4 (December 1931): 7–16.

54. Gregory, "Poet without Critics: A Note on Robinson Jeffers," In *New World Writing: Seventh Mentor Selection* (New York: New World Writing, 1955), 40–52; also reprinted in this volume.

55. Leonard Spier, "Notes on Robinson Jeffers: A Critical View of a Noted American Poet," *International Literature* (Moscow) 6 (1934): 112–17, reprinted in the *Robinson Jeffers Newsletter* 33 (December 1979), 36–42.

56. Frost, "A Poet Speaks of Poets," *Los Angeles Times*, 22 May 1958, sec. 3.5.

57. "Four Forgotten Books Win $2,500 Prizes," *New York Times*, 30 January 1937, 15.

58. Heywood Broun, "It Seems to Me," *New York Times*, 30 January 1937, 15.

59. Carl Sandburg, "The Judgment of his Peers," *Carmelite: Robinson Jeffers Supplement* 1 (12 December 1928): 5.

60. "A New Chant of Despair by Robinson Jeffers," *New York Sun*, 1 July 1927, p. 10.

61. Edgar Lee Masters, "The Poetry Revival of 1914," *American Mercury* 26 (July 1932): 272–80.

62. Quoted in Robert Brophy, "T. S. Eliot and Robinson Jeffers: A Note," *Robinson Jeffers Newsletter* 38 (April 1974): 4, 5.

63. Selden Rodman, "Transhuman Magnificence," *Saturday Review of Literature* 31 (31 July 1948): 13–14.

64. Quoted in a letter of 8 August 1925 from Robinson Jeffers to Sara Teasdale, in *Selected Letters of Robinson Jeffers, 1897–1962*, ed. Ann N. Ridgeway (Baltimore: Johns Hopkins Press, 1968), 43.

65. James Dickey, "First and Last Things," *Poetry* 103 (February 1964): 320–21.

66. Richard Eberhart, "The Poetry of Robinson Jeffers, Read by Judith Anderson," Record Cover, Caedmon Records, TC 1297 (1970).

67. Robert Penn Warren, "Jeffers on the Age," *Poetry* 49 (February 1937): 279–82.

68. Allen Tate, *Sixty American Poets, 1894–1944* (Washington, D.C.: Library of Congress, 1945), 55–59.

69. R. P. Blackmur, "Lord Tennyson's Scissors: 1912–1950," *Kenyon Review* 14 (Winter 1952): 1–20.

70. Randall Jarrell, "Fifty Years of American Poetry," *Prairie Schooner* 37 (Spring 1963): 1–27.

71. John Crowe Ransom, *The New Criticism* (Norfolk, Conn.: New Directions, 1941), 216, 236–37.

72. "Robinson Jeffers," *San Francisco Chronicle*, 23 January 1962, 34.

73. Ward Morehouse, "The New Play: 'Medea' a Harrowing Drama, Magnificently Played by Judith Anderson," *New York Sun*, 21 October 1947, 24.

74. Brooks Atkinson, "Medea for Moderns," *New York Times*, 26 October 1947, sec. 11.1.

75. "Homesick for Death," *Time* 81 (3 May 1963): 114.

76. William Oliver Everson (Brother Antoninus), review of *The Beginning and the End and Other Poems, Ramparts* 2 (Christmas 1963): 95–96.

77. Lauriat Lane, Jr., "The Greatness of Robinson Jeffers," *Fiddlehead* 58 (Fall 1963): 67–68.

78. William Turner Levy, "The Theme is Always Man," *New York Times Book Review*, 5 May 1963, 5.

79. Stephen Spender, "Rugged Poetry Imbued with Spirit of the Hawk," *Chicago Sunday Tribune Magazine of Books*, 12 May 1963, 3.

80. Winfield Townley Scott, "The Undeserved Neglect," *New York Herald Tribune Books*, 16 June 1963, 10.

81. Gervase Toelle, "Familiar Lament," *Spirit* 30 (September 1963): 115.

82. R. W. Hotchkiss, *Jeffers: The Sivaistic Vision* (Auburn, Calif.: Blue Oak Press, 1975), 17–18.

83. William Nolte, "Robinson Jeffers, An Uncanny Prophet," *The Alternative: An American Spectator* 10 (May 1976): 11–15.

84. Robert Ian Scott, "The Ends of Tragedy: Robinson Jeffers' Satires on Human Self-Importance," *Canadian Review of American Studies* 10 (1979): 231–41.

85. Hotchkiss, *Jeffers: The Sivaistic Vision*, 16.

86. Fox, "Full Circle."

87. Loren Eiseley, foreword to *Not Man Apart: Lines from Robinson Jeffers*, ed. David Ross Brower (San Francisco: Sierra Club, 1965; New York: Ballantine Books, 1969), 23.

88. Sales figures provided by Liveright on 5 June 1987: *The Women at Point Sur:* 1977 cloth—835, 1977 paper—4259; 1987 paper—1,188. *Dear Judas and Other Poems:* 1977 cloth—1,095, 1977 paper—2,889; 1987 paper—867. *The Double Axe:* 1977 cloth—1,164, 1977 paper—4,271; 1987 paper—1,062.

89. Robert Zaller, *The Cliffs of Solitude: A Reading of Robinson Jeffers* (New York: Cambridge University Press, 1983).

90. Judson Jerome, "Roan Stallion," *Writers Digest*, April 1983, 52–55.

91. James Schlesinger, quoted in the *Robinson Jeffers Newsletter* 42 (August 1975): 1, 2.

92. The information in the preceding three paragraphs constitutes a random sampling of items included, for the most part, in the "News and Notes" column of the *Robinson Jeffers Newsletter* between 1965 and 1987.

93. Niklas Tornlund, "Tre Amerikanska Poeter Paa Svenska," *Sydsvenska Dagbladet*, 16 April 1985, 4.

94. Young, "Such Counsels He Gave to Us."

95. Fox, "Full Circle."

96. Nolte, "Robinson Jeffers Redivivus."

97. Dickey, "First and Last Things."

98. Fox, "Full Circle."

99. William White, "Robinson Jeffers on a Postage Stamp," *American Book Collector* 24 (1974): 30.

100. Kevin Starr, "Robinson Jeffers and the Integrity of Nature," *Sierra Club Bulletin* 62 (May 1977): 36–40.

101. Scott, "The Ends of Tragedy."

102. Jerome, "Roan Stallion."

103. Hotchkiss, *Jeffers: The Sivaistic Vision*, 37, 38.

104. Jeanetta Boswell, *Robinson Jeffers and the Critics, 1912–1983* (Metuchen, N.J.: Scarecrow Press, 1986), viii.

105. Randall Jarrell, "The End of the Line," *Nation* 154 (21 February 1942): 222–28.

A Sovereign Voice:
The Poetry of Robinson Jeffers

Robert Boyers

A generation of critics and observers has agreed to bestow upon
Robinson Jeffers the gravest sentence the critical imagination can
conceive, the conclusion of ultimate irrelevance for both his life
and work. And though Jeffers, dead now since 1962, never gave a
damn about either criticism or the critical imagination, nor for
that matter about responses to his own poetry, those of us who
continue to find in Jeffers a good deal to study and admire ought
a little to speak out in his behalf from time to time. The pro-
pitiatory ritual need not always be wholly gratuitous after all, and
one has reason to fear that the inevitable decline in Jeffers' reputation may not contain within it the seeds of some future revival.

Already the figure of Jeffers as a kind of gloomy apparition
haunting the parapets of the stone tower he built and lived in has
come to assume nearly mythical dimensions, and his isolation
from the movements, whether artistic or political, of his time has
been too easily attributed to savage intemperance or to idiotic
philosophic ideologies relating to the doctrine of inhumanism.
Indeed, more than any other poet of the modernist or postmod-
ernist periods, Jeffers has served as a whipping boy to a variety of
well-placed poets and critics who have found it stimulating to deal
with him exclusively on their terms, though never on his. Thus,
for Yvor Winters, Jeffers' poetry presented a simple spectacle of
"unmastered and self-inflicted hysteria" working upon concerns
that were "essentially trivial." For Randall Jarrell, an infinitely
more gifted and judicious writer than Winters, Jeffers' poetry
demonstrated that "the excesses of modernist poetry are the necessary concomitants of the excesses of late-capitalist society," and,
what is more, set up "as a nostalgically awaited goal the war of all

Reprinted from *Modern American Poetry: Essays in Criticism,* ed. Jerome Mazzaro
(New York: McKay, 1970), 183–204.

against all." For Kenneth Rexroth, whose championing of the most defiantly mediocre talents on the west coast is notorious and might at least have extended to a major talent like Jeffers', Jeffers' poetry is "shoddy and pretentious," with "high-flown statements indulged in for their melodrama alone."

There is no single source for such misstatements and half-truths, and it would seem clear that any correctives would lie in the direction of Jeffers' verse itself, illuminated in part by the interesting documents that have been recently brought to light. And in turning to Jeffers and his work it is also useful to acknowledge that distinctions must be made and retained in discussing what is fine and what is not, for Jeffers wrote a great deal in the course of a professional career that spanned fifty years, and he was not always a meticulous or especially prudent craftsman. Clearly he did not linger over brief passages to the degree Ezra Pound might have urged him to, and he felt none of the urgency to revise and refine his work that is characteristic of modern poets as diverse as T. S. Eliot and Marianne Moore. Not that Jeffers is crude or simple-minded, for he is not. Jeffers knew his gift and trusted his ability to give it adequate expression. As to whether that expression were sometimes more than adequate, he would leave it to others more anxious about such questions than he to decide.

In fact, the ferocity of the critical reaction against Jeffers that really began to set in after the end of World War II is in certain respects explicable in terms of the adulatory sympathies his earlier verse inspired in a number of people who might have been expected to know better. One of Jeffers' most consistent admirers, Mark Van Doren, in the foreword to Jeffers' *Selected Letters*, concludes with the line: "Homer and Shakespeare. In what more fitting company could we leave him?" Such conjunctions are not likely to sit well with more balanced observers of our poetry, and there is no doubt that Jeffers was frequently embarrassed by attempts to claim more for his achievement than it could realistically support. No doubt there is in Jeffers' best work a peculiarly sovereign quality—peculiar in our time, at least: an ability to make large statements on large questions with little of the customary qualification and caution we have come to accept as almost obligatory in our serious literature. Only Jeffers' concerns are so much less varied than Shakespeare's, the range of his poetic devices so limited by contrast with not only Shakespeare's but Eliot's and Yeats's and Auden's, the generosity of his commitments so restricted by his fear of excessive involvement with other

human beings as reflected in his poetry and in personal documents. Even in the case of Jeffers' characters in the long narratives, which would seem to confer some degree of similitude
with Homeric figures, Jeffers' creations do not really warrant such
a comparison, for the memorable characters are largely maniacal,
gripped by obsessions that never really evoked what Jeffers
thought they would: unable clearly to distinguish his own views
from those of his characters in ambitious works like "The Women
at Point Sur," perhaps because he never fully considered the long-
range implications of his sentiments and avowals, Jeffers could do
no more than "look grim" when confronted by articulate critics of
his narratives "and assure them that my hero was crazy but I am
not." The Homeric perspective can by no means be equated with
such a muddle.

In a way it is unfortunate that Jeffers wrote any long narratives
at all, for none succeeds, and for reasons that need hardly be
elaborated in detail. Structurally, they are sound enough, but the
texture of these poems is swollen by effusions of philosophizing
and by attempts to impose representative signification on charac-
ters·and actions that are so extraordinary as to be either ludicrous
or simply shocking. Not that any serious reader is going to rush
shrieking from the room at the mention of a little incest at a time
when every perversion has been relieved by repetition and familiarity of its capacity to extract from readers even a bit of a chill.
What is shocking in Jeffers' narratives, from "Tamar" through the
later poems, is the author's contentions of symptomatic and representative status for the perverse obsessions of his characters. Obviously the single-mindedness of Jeffers' pursuit of his themes in
the long poems ought to dispel any notion that he indulged his
fantasies in the interests of melodrama alone, as Rexroth claimed.
Jeffers simply thought he had hit upon a fruitful means for
engaging the most profound problem he could imagine: the relationship of the individual to his time, and the uses and limitations
of human freedom. Jeffers was mistaken in that his means were
not adequate to the task he set himself. Never a good judge of the
work of other poets, Jeffers really was incapable of criticizing his
own poetry, even after a period of years had gone by to provide a
measure of detachment. Attempts to justify the narratives on
philosophical grounds held but mild interest for Jeffers, who
could barely force himself to breeze through books written on his
work, and none of these succeed in justifying the narratives as
poetry in terms that Jeffers himself could have admired. The
bravest attempt we have had is the chapter on "Point Sur" by

Brother Antoninus in *Robinson Jeffers*, his book-length defense of the poet, but I do not imagine that most readers of poetry will any longer find the poem tolerable, if ever they did.

Only "Roan Stallion" among Jeffers' narratives would seem to provide the consistently varied texture that is requisite in a long poem, but even here one finds it difficult to accept Jeffers at his own estimate and in the terms of his advocates. While the entire poem is powerful and not at all absurd, as some have claimed, the whole fails to sustain particular elements in the imagery. The magnificent evocation of the roan stallion as a symbol of male potency is quite as fine in its way as D. H. Lawrence's comparable use of horses in his novel *The Rainbow*, published ten years before Jeffers' poem. But the eroticism in these passages of "Roan Stallion" is not clearly related to the basic thrust of the poem, which cannot be taken to be an indictment of male potency in general. If, as Jeffers wrote in a letter, "the woman fell in love with the stallion because there was no one else she could fall in love with," why is her attraction to the horse evoked in literally sexual terms? Unabashed sexuality the woman had had a good deal of, and there was no reason for her to be drawn to the horse for more of the same. Familiarity with Jeffers' universe, with the universe created by his many poems, suggests that the stallion was to call to mind qualities quite distinct from pure sexuality, though related, and yet these qualities are never sufficiently identified. The figure refuses to yield its latent connotations and is distinguished by an opacity that characterizes the image rather than the symbol. In this respect Jeffers' failure has a good deal in common with much of the narrative poetry produced in the romantic period. In each there is a strong lyrical element which calls into question the poet's center of interest and the consequent interest of readers. While the structure of the work naturally tends to focus attention on the unfolding of events in the phenomenal world, the poet's interest seems always elsewhere, in the emotions that give rise to action, and in abstract conceptions of fate and will. Poets find themselves more immediately and intimately involved in their characters than they ought to be in narrative poems, unable to decide where their creations begin and they leave off. W. H. Auden has lately described Byron's failure in poems like *Childe Harold* in such terms, and postromantic critics like Bradley have been similarly concerned with these matters.

In short, then, for a number of reasons, Jeffers devoted a great deal of his time and energy to the cultivation of a subgenre—narrative poetry—to which his gifts were not especially adaptable.

What is also distressing, though, is that the attention Jeffers has received has been so disproportionately weighted in the direction of these failed narratives and that his stock has fallen so badly as a result. What more signal instance have we of the capitulation of criticism to what is most gross and obvious in a man's work, and in a generation that has had the temerity to exhume and to sanctify an Emily Dickinson, a body of work at once fragile, restrictive, and yet upon examination singularly exotic and intense both in formal and human qualities? It is as though there had been a tacit agreement among all influential parties that Jeffers' shorter poems should be looked upon as nothing more than an adjunct to the narratives, perhaps even as something less, as filler for the volumes his publishers issued with remarkable regularity for so many years. As it is, Jeffers' short poems, many of them rather lengthy by standards of the conventional lyric, will fill an enormous volume when they are collected, and an impressive volume it will be; for at his best Jeffers could blend passion and restraint, image and statement, contempt and admiration, as few poets of any time have been able to, and often with a music so ripe and easy that it is able to impress itself upon our senses without our ever remarking its grace and majesty, its sureness of touch. How better to know what we mean when we speak of such qualities than to locate them in those poems whose perfection of form and control of tone set them apart from the rest of the poet's work? I would select the following as representative of Jeffers at his best, in an order I might recommend to a skeptical and rather hard-nosed student whom I especially wanted Jeffers to reach: "Ossian's Grave," "The Broadstone," "The Low Sky," "Antrim," "A Little Scraping," "November Surf," "Hurt Hawks," "Fire on the Hills," "Ante Mortem," "Post Mortem," "Credo," "Rearmament," "Haunted Country," "Return," "The Treasure," "Practical People," "The Maid's Thought," "To the Stone-Cutters," "The Cruel Falcon."

No doubt I have neglected someone's favorites in drawing such a list, but consensus is not what matters here. I am sure that responsible arguments might be made for poems like "The Purse Seine" and "Shine, Perishing Republic," which have been frequently anthologized, or for a sobering longer poem like "Hellenistics," so earnestly extolled by Brother Antoninus; but each of these has a ponderousness that is somehow too reminiscent of the longer poems, an indulgence of the explicit statement that runs against the grain of the hard, oblique quality we are given to demand of the poetry we admire. Of course, there are many fine things in many of the poems I have rejected, if we may use so strong a word: one thinks of the weaving of exclamations in and out of "The Purse-Seine," the parallelisms binding the otherwise loosely flowing open-ended line structures, the colorful images sheathed in the poet's wonder, quietly unfolding a vision of entrapment that is to stand in analogy to our own:

> I cannot tell you
> How beautiful the scene is, and a little terrible, then, when the
>   crowded fish
> Know they are caught, and wildly beat from one wall to the other of
>   their closing destiny the phosphorescent
> Water to a pool of flame, each beautiful slender body sheeted with
>   flame, like a live rocket
> A comet's tail wake of clear yellow flame; while outside the
>   narrowing
> Floats and cordage of the net great sea-lions come up to watch,
> Sighing in the dark; the vast walls of night
> Stand erect to the stars.

How starkly these fine lines contrast with Jeffers' attempts to draw his analogy, with the crude simplifications of a political and social reality that leads to confusion and a blunting of those energies the poem had quietly released: "I cannot tell you how beautiful the city appeared, and a little terrible. / I thought, we have geared the machines and locked all together into interdependence; we have built the great cities; now / There is no escape. We have gathered vast populations incapable of free survival, insulated / From the strong earth." What one can say to all this as poetry, except that it is disastrous to use inflated rhetorical expressions of the sort represented in this sampling without some sense of irony, of the disparity between the more poetic language one familiarly relies upon and the gross sociologisms Jeffers would permit to roughen the texture of the verse.

There is, we have been given to understand, a certain ignominy readily to be associated with the use of the term "poetic language," and it ought perhaps to be justified in connection with a poet like Jeffers, who has been accused of shoddy versifications and pretentious inflation of imagery and rhetoric. Clearly, it would seem, what is shoddy can never be poetic, since what is poetic is always to some degree conscious, restrained, elegant, and delivers up its meanings in terms that are pleasurable wholly apart from what is being delivered or represented. The experienced reader of poetry will usually have little difficulty in distinguishing what is shoddy from what is not. In the matter of pretension, there may be a good deal of difficulty that will be less securely resolved. Pretension, after all, has to do with qualities that may be largely extrinsic to the poetry itself, with an attitude or pose that may be justly or unjustly presumed to have dictated not only the broad contours of a poem but its particular words and images. Often, one may safely predict, the presumption of general attitudes by readers will have little to do with what actually inheres in a given body of work, but will be used to explain or to justify an antipathy which may have more to do with the limitations of a reader than with the failings of a poet. Surely Yvor Winters' abstract identification of mysticism with muddle is fundamentally responsible for his inability to achieve even an elementary understanding of Jeffers, whose poetry evinces a materialism that is distinctly removed from the kind of mysticism to which Winters so objected. Given his constitutional incapacity to apprehend as genuine any perspective on human life other than his own, Winters found in Jeffers' work a muddle, and it was inevitable that he should then seek to wither his adversary by the positing of mysticism as the source of his defection from authenticity.

But as to the question of what does and does not constitute poetic language, one may concede that critics of Jeffers have on occasion found fruitful grounds for argument. There is a good deal of pretension in the narratives, where prophetic rant frequently mounts to a kind of hysteria that has very little to do with the appeal poetry is to make to our senses. John Crowe Ransom has written that "the poetic consideration of the ethical situation is our contemplation and not our exercise of will, and therefore qualitatively a very different experience: knowledge without desire." I am not certain that I like the Aristotelian antithesis between *knowledge* and desire, but Ransom's formularization will do for our purposes. What is pretentious in the work of art, Ransom's statement suggests, is its attempt to be more than it can be, to *do* where its function is primarily to be. Which is not to say that a work of art, in particular the poem, cannot represent a position, take sides, for obviously it can; but if it does, it must do so almost in spite of itself. What is important about it is the metamorphic flexibility which facilitates the passage of our imagination into and out of a number of conditions of being, for without such passage, and without real variety, there will be no tension and no intensity of concern on our part. One thinks of Keats's famous letter in which he describes the poetical character: "it is not itself—it has no self—it is everything and nothing." That is to say, the poet is conceived in terms of a neutrality that permits him to assume qualities of the objects he contemplates.

What does such speculation lead us to conclude about those elements in Jeffers' work which have been vigorously assailed? Again, distinctions must be kept in mind. In what sense can Jeffers' work be said to suffer from pretension? It is pretentious when it ceases to control those elements of will that stand behind any creative act—elements which for the most part cannot be permitted to govern the nature of intensity of the poet's expression. Only the precise materials the poet uses can legitimately determine the intensity of expression and the poet's posture, for in its own terms the poem posits a world of its own, a word-world, if you will, which stands not so much in imitation of the phenomenal world we inhabit as merely in analogy to it. Given such a relationship, degrees of intensity and tonal qualities of a poem cannot be said to issue legitimately from contemplation of a reality that is not that poem's authentic reality. We take for examination a brief poem from Jeffers' final volume, entitled "Unnatural Powers":

> For fifty thousand years man has been dreaming of powers
> Unnatural to him: to fly like the eagles—this groundling!—to
>   breathe under the seas, to voyage to the moon,
> To launch like the sky-god intolerable thunder-bolts: now he has got
>   them.
> How little he looks, how desperately scared and excited, like a
>   poisonous insect, and no God pities him.

The poem has the merit of focusing in brief compass what may be said of Jeffers' failures in a great many short poems. The poet here stands not within his poem, as Keats would have had him, not dissolved in the terms of his saying; nor does he stand beside his materials gently or fiercely ordering, arranging them as Wallace Stevens would characteristically reveal himself handling the creatures of his own imagination; nor even does Jeffers stand here above his materials, for to stand above would be to retain some manner of relation. Jeffers here stands without the substance of his poem, not above or aloof, but apart. The words are connected by a will that is in no way implicated in the words themselves, so that the ordering, the structuring of sentiments cannot be judged except by reference to that will, which we can have no way of knowing. The poem calls neither for understanding nor for contemplation, but for simple assent, for a process of suspension in which the reader ceases to be himself and gives himself wholly, not to the poem, but to the poet. To abandon one's self-possession temporarily, as to suspend disbelief, is to participate in a ritual that calls upon our instincts of generosity in the interests of a pleasure and enlightenment that are ideally to repay our gesture. The work of art requests, as it were implicitly, that we be generous in the interests of our senses. At his worst, and even to some extent when he is not writing badly at all, Jeffers insists that we agree to heed what he says though there be nothing in it for us, not even the extension or stimulation of our imagination. Utterly without art, and without sympathy either for us or for the materials he manipulates, Jeffers coldly mocks our foibles, our dreams, our delusions. The ideological content of Jeffers' fine poetry here hardens into a mannered response to experience, so that no valid experience is lived through in the poem. What we have is a system of response, but nothing valid or poetically real to respond *to*. Confronted by such poems as "Unnatural Powers," we can have no alternative but to speak of arrogance and pretension.

How much less we are disposed to object to Jeffers' poetry when he reminds us of his mortality. We remain wary of prophecy in general, and of false prophets in particular, but we consent nonetheless to attend to Jeffers' prophetic rigors on occasion, perhaps even to be a little moved by the spectacle of a man obviously concerned for a purity of spirit, an integrity so hard for any man to come by. We are moved, for example, by "Shine, Perishing Republic," a poem too familiar to quote. It is not one of Jeffers' best things, but there is a fine tolerance for humankind in this poem that is attractive and that we respond to repeatedly. The theme of the poem is, after all, not so very new or terrible, having to do with the corruption of institutionalized life in the modern world, the tendency of mass culture to absorb protest and distinction and to heighten vulgarity in its citizens. Yeats had no less to say of such matters than Jeffers, and one need only think of those unbelievably awful poems of Lawrence's on the beastly bourgeoisie to realize how conventional among recent poets these concerns of Jeffers' have been. In fact, what is most responsible for the effectiveness Jeffers' poem has is the relatively understated quality it shares with some of the leaner lyrics that are not so well known. It is as though Jeffers were here dealing with realities too long pondered and accepted to fight over, and the assimilation of these contemporary realities to the perspective of eternal recurrence, ripeness, and decay allows Jeffers to speak of them with a calmness we admire. The poet's accents are firm, rather than petulantly defiant, as he counsels his children on the course he would have them follow: "Corruption / Never has been compulsory, when the cities lie at the monster's feet there are left the mountains." There is something almost plaintive in those words, "there are left the mountains," the procession of weak accents falling toward the final unaccented syllable, suggesting the encouragement of an option that is to be embraced only after others have been definitively abandoned, as they had been perhaps too casually by Jeffers himself.

What "Shine, Perishing Republic" lacks is a richness of sound and of metaphor. The language of the poem is not very interesting at all, dealing rather broadly in abstractions which yet do not confound, but which evoke, really, only other abstractions. If America is settling, as the poet claims, "in the mould of its vulgarity, heavily thickening to empire, / and protest, only a bubble in the molten mass, pops and sighs out, and the mass hardens," we can be expected to feel nothing more than modest dismay, for our sympathies have not been engaged by anything more than an issue, nicely stated, but hardly made manifest. And nowhere does the poem improve upon this initial evocation, the poet settling for modest effects, again largely concerned with assent rather than with intensifying our experience of a reality we are presumed to recognize as pertinent to our own.

I have no doubt whatever that Jeffers was more than aware of his inclination toward prophetic abstraction, toward the hollow exclamation patently ringing with WISDOM, as he was aware of a solemnity in his own demeanor that could degenerate into sententiousness in the poetry. But a brief sonnet like Jeffers' "Return" is so perfect in its way that to read it, again and again, is to forget Jeffers' faults and to wonder how a hard-boiled materialist often abused for the purple pride of his verse could manage to sound so much like Whitman, and yet like the Jeffers who was always so different from Whitman.

> A little too abstract, a little too wise,
> It is time for us to kiss the earth again,
> It is time to let the leaves rain from the skies,
> Let the rich life run to the roots again.
> I will go down to the lovely Sur Rivers
> And dip my arms in them up to the shoulders.
> I will find my accounting where the alder leaf quivers
> In the ocean wind over the river boulders.
> I will touch things and things and no more thoughts,
> That breed like mouthless May-flies darkening the sky,

The insect clouds that blind our passionate hawks
So that they cannot strike, hardly can fly.
Things are the hawk's food and noble is the mountain, Oh noble
Pico Blanco, steep sea-wave of marble.

Here at last is a poetry of sensation, of touch, in which form is
meaning and substance, in which a restless and mobile imagery is
the very whole and perfect embodiment of emotion. Here the
poet feels not about his materials, but into and through them—
things are his message, and as the poet thinks things he makes a
poem. He has seen that to the degree that he thinks primarily
thoughts he will cease to be a poet and become a philosopher, a
spokesman, a critic, anything but a poet. Does it matter that there
is a minimum of paraphrasable content in such a poem, as Winters argued against Jeffers' output generally? I think not, for
then, what would we do with a Herrick, or with a lyricist like
Hardy, were we forced to consider the content of a poem as the
quantity of ideas to be gathered therefrom? And indeed, what
more is Jeffers saying but "no more thoughts," not absolutely and
forever, but now, when we embody a poem, allow an image to
course through and work upon our sensibilities, when we would
be reverently humble, and grateful to life for what it is, which is
more than we usually deserve. How marvelous Jeffers' image of
thought as a swarm of "mouthless May-flies," and we need hardly
remind ourselves how often our poets have railed against the
intellect that darkens the possibilities of human feeling, that dis-
tracts and weakens both passion and pleasure. Are such com-
monplaces banal? Not as Jeffers has them in "Return" and in his
better poems, for Jeffers here proceeds through an intuition that
is more than an assertion of will. He is a poet, not of the world, but
of a world *he* knew well, a world partial at best, but firmly gripped
and eagerly loved, and his ability to make it known and real for
others is a measure of his success as a poet.

Who among us that has read Jeffers with devotion, though
critically, will not confess to an admiration for a man who could so
charge a created universe with a network of images so consistently
developed, so densely woven into the very fabric of the verse?
Who more earnestly than Jeffers has confronted the frailty of our
lives and engaged more desperately the attempt to reorient our
customary perspectives, to take us beyond pain into praise and
wonder? Jeffers knew all too well how men could suffer, and did;
and he knew why they suffered, and his awareness rarely failed to
leave him either angry or amused, or both, for he felt that most

human suffering was the result of unwarranted expectations, foolish illusions. His entire career was dedicated to the chastisement of a pity he felt and knew others felt, for he did not believe that pity was an essentially human quality, though for the most part peculiar to our kind. He felt that pity, and the suffering it often implied, was a product not of human emotion, but of human civilization, and with this he had no sympathy at all. Against this civilization, the pride of Western man with its "little empty bundles of enjoyment," Jeffers set the figure of the hawk, the eagle, the falcon, the vulture, predators all, and cast them winging alternately amidst towering rocks and seething waters, landscapes of permanence and of violent energy. The ambience of Jeffers' poems is characteristically stark, though rarely barren, and one has in them a sense of granitic harshness, as of objects tempered in a flame so blazing as to burn away all that is ephemeral and soft and pitying—everything, in a word, that is simply and merely human. But Jeffers' poetry is neither anti-human nor inhuman. It plainly works itself out within a system of values that includes much that is human, in terms of what we are capable of responding to at our most intense. As one would expect in a created universe of considerable density, though not of great complexity, there is a recurrence of specific symbols within the pervasive imagery of the poems and a consequent cross-fertilization of meanings, so that we are presented a vision of experience that is everywhere interfused, a frame of reference that cuts across entire groups of poems. Everywhere meanings seem to beckon away beyond themselves, so that in Jeffers' achieved works there is rarely an impression of a static quality, despite the weight of particular images.

Here is an irregular sonnet entitled "The Cruel Falcon," which ought to help us with some of the things we have been saying:

> Contemplation would make a good life, keep it strict, only
> The eyes of a desert skull drinking the sun,
> Too intense for flesh, lonely
> Exultations of white bone;
> Pure action would make a good life, let it be sharp-
> Set between the throat and the knife.
> A man who knows death by heart
> Is the man for that life.
> In pleasant peace and security
> How suddenly the soul in a man begins to die.
> He shall look up above the stalled oxen
> Envying the cruel falcon,

And dig under the straw for a stone
To bruise himself on.

With this extraordinary performance we move more securely into
that created universe which we know with every accent as Jeffers'.
The setting is harsh, the features of the landscape characteristic in
the marmoreal coldness of their surfaces, the poetic energies
intensely abiding in the carefully chiseled phrases. What we have
here is the movement and vitality, not of life, but of an art that
enhances life by appropriating its features in the interests of a
vision at once more passionate and more lovely than any vision of
life itself. Here is not that looseness of texture even discerning
readers like Brother Antoninus have sought to legitimize in their
defenses of Jeffers, for Jeffers knew that as a poet and as a man he
could achieve liberation only through scrupulous concern for
style, for form. There are no paradoxes in this mature vision, so
finely wrought, no telling nuances to qualify the poet's commitment; but everything is precisely placed, distributed its proper
weight, and there are elements of style so subtly woven into the
poem's basic structure that they largely escape observation. Notice
the delicacy with which Jeffers effects shifts of tense and mood in
this poem, moving from the conditional into the hortatory, to the
present indicative, to the future tense where he rests his case. It is
a little triumph of the prophetic voice, urging without sinister
overtones, stealthily proclaiming its insights without violence, for
it has earned the privilege of prophecy by the substantiveness and
accuracy of its representations in the course of the poem.

The language of "The Cruel Falcon" is, as we have intimated,
perfectly accurate, and if this language is without that exotic
strangeness we so admire in a Stevens, its dismissal of abstraction
and of the commonplace routines of experience is impressive
enough. And what precisely does Jeffers mean when he admon-
ishes us to "keep it strict," to speculate on the contours of a "pure
action," to abandon the "pleasant peace and security" that are the
extinction of the soul? I do not know why critical observers have
found it so difficult to explain these admonitions, why they have
resorted to the interpretation of inhumanism to explain the work
of a man all too frail, too human, and in his way enamored of a
beauty our best men have long sought to capture and identify.
Jeffers' concern in his poems is with the liberation of spirit from
what is gross. Human flesh is gross: the conventions by which men
cultivate the pleasures of flesh utterly ingenious and thoroughly
destructive of alternative values. Jeffers' concern is with a resur-

rection of spirit out of the ashes of human display, a religious
concern, and is frequently expressed in terms that have their
source in religious archetypes. The chastisement of flesh has, after
all, been a staple feature of religious practice for any number of
millenniums, though Jeffers' extension of this tradition has its
unique attributes. For Jeffers the god who creates and observes his
universe cares not what we do, so long as we do it well, so long as
life is clean and vibrant with energy and possibilities of renewal, so
long as it is whole, sufficient unto itself like the rocks Jeffers loved
to contemplate, like the white bone of the desert skull in his poem,
freed of gross desire, liberated to "lonely exultations."

If Jeffers is truly a religious poet, he can be said to worship
largely at the altar of art, for his resolution of the problems of
spirit is really an aesthetic resolution, just as his politics, if he did
indeed have a politics, is fundamentally determined by an aesthetic response to the world. Jeffers disparaged not human life,
but the ways in which human beings could destroy their world
and each other. There is nothing barbaric or fascistic about these
lines from "November Surf," generated by the poet's disgusted
observation of the summer refuse that litters the clean surfaces of
his beloved shoreline, with its smoldering waves and granite pro-
montories:

> The earth, in her childlike prophetic sleep,
> Keeps dreaming of the bath of a storm that prepares up the long
>   coast
> Of the future to scour more than her sea-lines:
> The cities gone down, the people fewer and the hawks more
>   numerous,
> The rivers mouth to source pure; when the two-footed
> Mammal, being someways one of the nobler animals, regains
> The dignity of room, the value of rareness.

It is distressing that at this late date one should feel it necessary to
defend such writing, when its intentions are so clear and so
fundamentally decent. Perhaps the crucial words in the passage
are "childlike," "dignity," "rareness." Yeats would have understood
Jeffers' meanings without any difficulty whatever, and though the
Irish poet could speak in certain poems of "all hatred driven
hence" and of the blight that is arrogance, he knew the value of
passions bordering on violence and of sudden purgation. And just
as Yeats could speak of ceremonies of innocence, so Jeffers sancti-
fies the "childlike prophetic sleep" of the elemental, innocent in its
contentment with the wholeness, the unity, of all things. For

Jeffers, the cities of man, representing industrial civilization, are a violation, an index to the disharmony and spurious competitiveness that have always distinguished our species. In the perspective of Jeffers' poems, human life is a defilement of all that is dignified and whole, and we are to listen to him not because he says we should, but because the poetic manifestations of his vision are sufficient to his message. How easy it is to ridicule Jeffers, to parody his preference of a hawk to a man; but given the terms of his vision, there is nothing in this to mock. For poetry is not a program, not a series of proposals which are literally to be carried over into the domain of normal human activity. Brother Antoninus has written eloquently on these matters in his books: "We must not shut ourselves off from the archetypal sources in [an artist's] vision by virtue of [our] revulsion from their social consequences when attempted politically in our time." The poet "makes his vision permanent by virtue of its inherent aesthetic, which protects it from misapplication in the phenomenal world, because once it is translated into another idiom it vanishes."

Jeffers' exaltation of the hawk, then, is not an exaltation of a naked violence that will see the destruction of man by man, but an exaltation of nature, of need, of instinct. For Jeffers the instinct of the hawk is tolerable, even majestic, because it does not seek to aggrandize itself at the expense of creation—it strikes according to its need and within a framework that does not threaten the fundamental harmony of other things. Its rarity he saw as a quality intrinsic to its nature, associated also with its reasonable relationship to its surroundings. At the point where the environment could not support increasing numbers of the species, the species by a law intrinsic to its nature would cease to multiply: not a matter of will but of nature. How different is man, clamoring for a little space, killing for programs and ideologies. And anthropological investigations into the similarity of human and animal aggressions, explanations of territoriality as a fundamental impulse of all life, would have left Jeffers no less secure in his mounting of the distinction, for Jeffers' thesis was not developed as fact, but as intuition. In the development of an ideal of what is beautiful and can authentically be meaningful to men, Jeffers' vision resists the disparagements of scientific critiques.

Jeffers does not succumb, it must be said, to pure aestheticism. His indictments of mass man, which is to say of man in our time, are not without a measure of conventionally *human* sentiment, and a number of the poems evoke a tension in which the resort to aestheticism is viewed as an element of necessity rather than of will or choice. The conflict in Jeffers is powerfully dramatized in the poem "Rearmament"—a poem in whose broadly undulating rhythms and the sweep of its long line the very quality and substance of Jeffers' message is embodied and reflected:

> These grand and fatal movements toward death: the grandeur of the
>   mass
> Makes pity a fool, the tearing pity
> For the atoms of the mass, the persons, the victims makes it seem
>   monstrous
> To admire the tragic beauty they build.
> It is beautiful as a river flowing or a slowly gathering
> Glacier on a high mountain rock-face,
> Bound to plow down a forest, or as frost in November,
> The gold and flaming death-dance for leaves,
> Or a girl in the night of her spent maidenhood, bleeding and
>   kissing.
> I would burn my right hand in a slow fire
> To change the future . . . I should do foolishly. The beauty of
>   modern
> Man is not in the persons but in the
> Disastrous rhythm, the heavy and mobile masses, the dance of the
> Dream-led masses down the dark mountain.

The rhetorical aspects of this poem are not as subdued as they might be, but a poem dealing with the disastrous currents of an entire civilization heading toward ruin need not apologize for a vocabulary that includes such terms as "fatal," "tearing pity," "monstrous," and "disastrous." It is a poem that teaches us a good deal about the function of art, or at least of an art that would transcend our sufferings and the evils we promote. It is an example of an art that through identification with the impersonal roots of all human behavior, of all activity in this universe, permits us to contemplate the reality of our foolishness and mortality without much pain, but with praise forming at the lips. Here, perhaps more clearly than in any other poem, Jeffers makes clear what we ought to have known even in his lesser work. To attribute, as Jeffers does, foolishness to the instinct to "burn my right hand in a slow fire / To change the future" is not to consign oneself to the perdition of the heartless, but to seek to forge out of futility a perspective in which futility can be relieved of its manifest failures, purified, rhythmically interpolated into a pattern in which it has meaning as part of that process that is life on this planet. The detachment that makes most great art possible is not heartless, nor is the distancing that is the process of the historical perspective, and that consigns to men the relative insignificance they deserve in the scheme of things, without its virtue. Throughout his career Jeffers tried to resolve the ambiguities of his vision in a direction that would take him further and further from concern with his fellows. How successful he was we can see in "Rearmament," with its persisting ambiguities and unresolved tensions. What is unmistakable, though, is the poet's steadfast refusal to counsel violence among men and his ability to achieve a perspective wherein the violence men would and did commit could be made tolerable, in a way even absorbed into the universe as an element of necessity. It is nothing less than a tragic vision; and if Jeffers in his poetry could not sufficiently examine and evoke the larger potentialities of man within his limitations, as could a Shakespeare and a Yeats, he did at least project a vision worthy of our attention and capable of giving pleasure. The felicities of Jeffers' poetry ought no longer to be denied, but received with gratitude. If he was not among our supreme poets, they have been few who were his equals.

The Problematic Nature of *Tamar and Other Poems*

Tim Hunt

The work of Robinson Jeffers presents a curious mixture of conservative and radical elements. Stylistically Jeffers paid little attention to the experiments associated with modernism. Although he abandoned rhyme sometime in 1920, his work is often descriptive and, by modernist standards, discursive and didactic. Worse, he chose to write narrative poems (a genre most professional readers had already judged oxymoronic—in spite of the then still recent example of E. A. Robinson). But even his contemporaries recognized that Jeffers was not simply a Victorian without rhyme. The violence of the narratives, the startling descriptions of California's Big Sur coast, and the judgments of contemporary politics and events were too unorthodox for that— too nihilistic, as some would have it.

Not surprisingly commentators have tended to stress Jeffers' content more than his style and form and to treat his work in isolation from that of his modernist contemporaries. The relative importance of Nietzsche and Schopenhauer as antecedents for the "philosophy" of the major narratives has been one line of study.[1] The structural and thematic role of myth and ritual has been another,[2] and the relationship of Jeffers' own psychology to his religious and poetic vision yet another.[3] (Jeffers' ecological vision has also attracted some comment and will most likely attract more.) Technical studies have been written of such matters as Jeffers' metric and his use of alliteration, but these discussions have tended to be relatively brief and have seldom considered the conceptual and thematic implications of Jeffers' choices.[4] They have not, that is, defined how his poetic—his orientation toward language and the making of poems—directs the writing and, by extension, our reading, so much as they have described aspects of his practice.

In part I want to suggest that this tendency to ignore the stylistic

issues of Jeffers' practice parallels our tendency to isolate him
from his period and his contemporaries. More, though, I want to
sketch an aspect of his poetic and its implications. In particular I
want to consider how the emerging sense of the nature of "nature"
in the work of the early 1920s combined with Jeffers' emerging
sense of style to define what might be termed his voice, how the
dynamics of this voice help clarify his vision, and how the conflicts
within this voice suggest the specific terms of Jeffers' modernity
(and its implications for understanding his place in modern poetry).

Tamar and Other Poems (1924) is the key source for studying
these matters. After two unsuccessful, imitative volumes (*Flagons
and Apples*, 1912, and *Californians*, 1916), the singular *Tamar*
quickly established Jeffers' reputation. But although *Tamar* marks
the emergence of Jeffers' mature style and vision, it is not a
unified collection and reflects at least two distinctly different styles
of work. Perhaps one-third of the work (like the apprentice volumes and apparently dating from 1917–19) is cast in rhyme,
stanzas, and traditional meters. The remainder (likely written
1920–23) is unrhymed, organized as verse paragraphs of varying
length, and often cast in long, accentual lines. The traditional
work is generally tentative and self-conscious; the unrhymed
work generally forceful and assured; and this disparity has contributed to the impression that Jeffers' mature work emerged,
essentially fully developed, when he abandoned rhyme.[5]

Viewed this way, *Tamar* becomes two collections: the last apprentice work, mature work, and little or nothing in between.
Jeffers' later suggestion that his poetic transformation stemmed
from a kind of visionary moment or awakening has helped reinforce this impression.[6] Jeffers, though, dated this visionary moment approximately in 1914, not only well before abandoning
rhyme but before *Californians* as well. Important as the episode is,
it took Jeffers some years of meditation and experiment to realize
its implications in actual work.

Another factor has also contributed to the sense of *Tamar* as two
collections. When Jeffers assembled it, he arranged the work with
little regard for chronology, which highlights the dichotomy between rhymed and unrhymed work but also obscures the more
subtle formal and thematic gradations of the unfolding project.[7]
The probable chronology shows that Jeffers' work continued to
evolve in fundamental ways through at least 1923 as he explored
different definitions of nature and different equations between

nature and the human world. As such, Jeffers' decision to abandon rhyme marks the beginning of his poetic maturation, not its realization.

The earliest unrhymed poems in *Tamar*, "The Maid's Thought" and "Divinely Superfluous Beauty," likely date from the spring or summer of 1920, as does "The Excesses of God," collected in *Be Angry at the Sun* (1941). Listed as a triptych in several early tables of contents, the poems are stylistically and tonally related (and were likely written within days of each other).[8] Each evokes nature as a positive force. "The Maid's Thought," for example, opens,

> Why listen, even the water is sobbing for something.
> The west wind is dead, the waves
> Forget to hate the cliff, in the upland canyons
> Whole hillsides burst aglow
> With golden broom.[9]

And it concludes with the maid's assertion, "it is time . . . to entangle our maiden bodies / To make that burning flower." To the extent that nature here frees the maid's erotic energy and makes her (or allows her to imagine becoming) a part of nature, the poem anticipates Jeffers' later practice. The poem, though, personifies nature to validate human experience, not to evoke nature's own meaning or comprehensiveness. However attractive the portrait, it subordinates nature to human desire, human meaning, and treats it as a metaphor to express the human situation. Similarly the "storm-dances of gulls, the barking game of seals" in "Divinely Superfluous Beauty" serve primarily to give meaning to human "joy," though this poem subordinates nature less clearly than "The Maid's Thought" (4).

Of the three, "The Excesses of God" comes closest to projecting nature as an independent reality, but even here nature is secondary and exists to mediate between the poem's primary figures, God and humans:

> Is it not by his high superfluousness we know
> Our God? For to equal a need
> Is natural, animal, mineral: but to fling
> Rainbows over the rain
>
> . . . .
> And make the necessary embrace of breeding
> Beautiful also as fire,

. . . .
There is the great humaneness at the heart of things.

(4)

Nature is God's expression to humans, God's language, but the language is secondary to the message, to who speaks, and to who listens.

The next poem, "To the Stone-Cutters" (fall 1920), appears to represent a major stylistic shift from the previous three. It begins in what becomes Jeffers' typical accentual measure and cadence, and it stresses, like later poems, man's insignificance and the relative impermanence of both humans and natural objects. But for all its stark imagery of stone and erosion, this poem, too, emphasizes the human world more than nature. It differs from "The Maid's Thought" in tone, but not conception. In spite of the way it contrasts human action and natural process and in spite of the way it argues that nature, though itself decaying, will endure longer than either individuals or the human race, the poem's concern is finally with stone-cutters, weathered monuments, and their significance for human imagination, and it emphasizes the way imagination largely sets the human world apart from nature and to that slight extent offers to redeem it. Although earth and man will both "die" and the imagination cannot change this, the imagination can create works that more nearly approximate nature's endurance, and these offer some relief from "pained thoughts" of mortality. The poem, then, centers on what imagination does or does not offer in the face of mortality, and nature is again a means to express what is specifically human rather than an end in itself. (Significantly, in "To the Stone-Cutters," the human realm colors the language that describes the natural: "For man will be blotted out, the blithe earth die, the brave sun / Die blind, his heart blackening."[10] Even as nature reveals the pathos of human imagination, the imagination projects this pathos back onto nature itself.)

"To the Stone-Cutters" gives nature less prominence as a source of value than does "The Maid's Thought" and its companion pieces. But if this makes it seem further from Jeffers' later work, its emphasis on human limits, decay, and endurance conversely seems to reach toward it. In spite of these differences, though, all four similarly weight the equation between man and nature toward the human world (even as they try out complementary aspects of the aesthetic to come) and in this sense mark a specific stage in Jeffers' emerging aesthetic in which nature becomes an end in itself, not a means, and where the human figures serve to express nature's structures and qualities, not the other way around.

In the second stage of unrhymed work, Jeffers began to subsume human life to nature, and not the reverse. And it is this shift in emphasis—even more than the abandonment of rhyme—that points to his mature aesthetic. The shift first appears in "Salmon Fishing" (probably written December 1920):

> The days shorten, the south blows wide for showers now,
> The south wind shouts to the rivers,
> The rivers open their mouths and the salt salmon
> Race up into the freshet.
> In Christmas month against the smoulder and menace
> Of a long angry sundown,
> Red ash of the dark solstice, you see the anglers. . . .

(6)

Here, the personifications highlight nature's own dynamic more than humanize it. This wind "shouts," but its message and the rivers' open mouths point to the landscape as natural action, not to its human-like qualities. Similarly, the human figures here become elements of landscape, of nature. They are no longer foreground, no longer a separate category. In "Salmon Fishing," nature itself is the subject; human meaning and action reflect and derive from it. The poem figures nature as an organism comprehending human life as one of its many elements (albeit a particularly problematic one).

In "Salmon Fishing" the human world can evoke and to some degree express nature but not control or explain it. As such, this use of the "pathetic fallacy" (if the term applies) enhances rather than lessens nature's otherness, and foreshadows contemporary ecological thought. "Natural Music" (likely written a few months later) further clarifies this new perspective:

> The old voice of the ocean, the bird-chatter of little rivers,
> (Winter has given them gold for silver
> To stain their water and bladed green for brown to line their banks)
> From different throats intone one language.
> So I believe if we were strong enough to listen without
> Divisions of desire and terror
> To the storm of the sick nations, the rage of the hunger-smitten
>   cities,

Those voices also would be found
Clean as a child's; or like some girl's breathing who dances alone
By the ocean-shore, dreaming of lovers.

(6)

As in "Salmon Fishing" the human figures and details of nature's
landscape are here a single category, and Jeffers' later comments
(from 1947) about composing the poem underscore this equation:

> I was by the mouth of the Carmel River in early spring, and noticed
> that the little flood-stream, on its rocks in the broken sand-bar, was
> making exactly the same song that the ocean was making on all the
> shores of the bay; the same pitch, the same accents. This was in 1920
> or '21, when fear and famine and civil war were abroad in the world as
> they are at present; and the two sides of nature, the human and the
> "elemental," both natural, came together in my mind and made the
> verses.[11]

The throats of birds, rivers, and ocean all express "nature," but
(the poem implies) viewing individual life and the life of societies
as separate, self-generating, and self-defining (rather than as each
limited facets of the more comprehensive organism nature) di-
vides experience into false categories. When this happens we fail
to "listen" and, by implication, we either lose voice altogether or
our voice loses validity. (Significantly, the human comes closest to
a voice in this poem when it sets aside voice in the usual sense and
dances its desire without thought.)

Jeffers seems to have realized that "Salmon Fishing" and "Natural Music" initiated a new direction in his work, but for several
months, perhaps a year, his writing only partly reflected it. "Consciousness" (an uncollected group of sonnets), for instance, explores the problem evoked by the figure of the woman dancing,
namely of a consciousness that alienates us from nature even as it
makes beauty available to contemplation; but its formality and
diction mark it as a regression, although thematically it anticipates
later work. "Age in Prospect," another poem omitted from *Tamar*,
tries "to listen without / Divisions of desire and terror" (9), but it
and "Wise Men in Their Bad Hours" deny rather than accept,
regressing to the attitudes of such early pieces as "Promise of
Peace" and "Suicide's Stone" even as they recover something of
"Natural Music's" line and cadence.

The clearest example of Jeffers' uncertainty in this period is "To
the Rock that Will Be a Cornerstone of the House." In it the
speaker pours "Wine and white milk and honey" on a rock, invit-

ing his "old comrade" to trade its "stone strength of the past" for his "wings of the future" (11). This improvised ritual, though, falls short of "Natural Music's" vision of a comprehensive, living nature, except for one image: the rock's "Wing-prints of ancient weathers."[12] Here, weather is implicitly a giant bird acting on the life of stone, a transaction that contrasts with the speaker's own posing elsewhere in the poem and which suggests that Jeffers was searching out his new direction by trial and error, not abandoning it.

By early 1922 Jeffers had sufficiently clarified his new poetics of nature to begin using it all but programmatically. "Not Our Good Luck," for instance, notes how "the ancienter simple and silent tribe of the stars / Filed" above the "filth of Babylon" and then claims that the same "God who walks lightning-naked on the Pacific [and] has never been hidden from any" can also be "Espied . . . in the eyes of a temple harlot" (12). Although the images stress the human realm more than those in "Natural Music," they express the human as a dimension of the natural; thus nature is again a single reality rather than a series of discrete realities. Similarly, "The Cycle" portrays human migrations and historical cycles as natural, rather than historical, actions, and "Shine, Perishing Republic" (also written at this time) applies the same perspective to America's growth and decay. Finally, "Continent's End," from late winter or early spring 1922, expands the rhythms of earthly nature—along with those of poem, birth, and human history—into figures for the more encompassing rhythms of stars and universe, the "tides of fire," "the older fountain" (17).[13]

The view of nature is "Salmon Fishing" and the poems that followed it shows how sharply Jeffers' assumptions had come to differ from those of his modernist contemporaries. Charles Altieri has traced "the assumptions and concerns" that "generate" modernism back to two distinct but related modes of romanticism: an immanentist mode typified by early Wordsworth and a symbolist mode typified by Coleridge.[14] He suggests that the modernists, faced with "Victorian attacks on attributing any moral or teleological functions to nature," almost inevitably rejected Wordsworth's faith in the poet's ability to discover value in the natural world and ordinary experience and elected instead the symbolist impulse with its allegiance to "the creative mind as the source of value."[15] In short, the modernists, rather than accept the flux and conflict of post-Darwinian nature as a source of value, based their practice on "the ideal of creative culture," not "the force of creative nature."[16] Jeffers, though, had come to take "the force of creative nature" as the basis of his work in spite of the position's inherent difficulty.

The logic of Jeffers' adaptation of the dormant Wordsworthian mode to the un-Wordsworthian view of nature he had inherited from modern science is particularly apparent in "Continent's End," the concluding poem of *Tamar's* second stage of unrhymed verses.[17] In it nature is both an immediate manifestation—the Pacific Ocean, the "mother" from which we came—and an ultimate dimension of process ("tides of fire") that comprehends the lesser rhythms of ocean and individual human life:

> . . . you have forgotten us, mother.
> You were much younger when we crawled out of the womb and lay
>   in the sun's eye on the tideline.
> . . . .
> The tides are in our veins, we still mirror the stars, life is your child,
>   but there is in me
> Older and harder than life and more impartial, the eye that watched
>   before there was an ocean.
> . . . .
> Mother, though my song's measure is like your surf-beat's ancient
>   rhythm I never learned it of you.
> Before there was any water there were tides of fire, both our tones
>   flow from the older fountain.

The poem assumes the nature of modern science: the human species is one phenomenon unfolding "naturally" among others. But simultaneously the poem gives this nature "moral or teleological" implications in two ways. First, it projects the "tides of fire" (though these are also literally descriptive) as an overarching analogy that unifies nature's more immediate, earthly aspects and its cosmic phenomena. Second, it simultaneously defines nature as "the eye that watched," thereby transforming nature into a kind of sentient being: a divine organism that is both the process of destruction and renewal and the awareness of that process. While the figure of process ("tides of fire") gives the poem its unmistakably modern quality, the second figure, the figure of nature's awareness ("the eye that watched"), recovers nature as a creative force that can reveal (when contemplated properly) meaningful ways, in Altieri's phrase, to "participat[e] in objective laws."[18]

In "Continent's End" the interplay between the perspectives of individual, species, earthly nature, and universe help make the poem's metaphors compelling, but the metaphors themselves point to the inherent duality in Jeffers' conception of nature and its ontological status as process and awareness of process. They also point to his sense that only nature, in its ultimate sense, is fully and simultaneously both. For Jeffers, this seems to be nature's divinity, which the speaker can share but not fulfill. To imitate nature, the human speaker must accept his destruction in that "older fountain" of fire, even as he struggles to transcend its flux sufficiently to contemplate it. Similarly his transcending glimpses of beauty and joy will have meaning only if they remain yoked to a process that ends in death, since these moments are at once the product of process and the escape from it. The human condition, then, contributes to nature's divinity but fails to realize it: as process, the human figure is only a limited moment in time and space; more significantly, human consciousness allows one only to be fully process or fully awareness of process—not both simultaneously. These modes of being alternate, or when simultaneous, exist partially and in conflict with each other. As such, humans are always at least partially alienated from themselves and from nature—neither fully process nor awareness—though their imagination can posit the simultaneity and wholeness of a nature that is fully both and create the illusion of that simultaneity in such products as poems.

The third stage of unrhymed work in *Tamar* is a single long narrative, the title poem, and its emphasis on a violent, introverted human world is in some ways a radical departure from the exploration of a poetics of nature begun in "Salmon Fishing." In part "Tamar" was a return to an earlier stage of Jeffers' work.[19] *Californians* included narratives, and from 1917 to 1919 Jeffers drafted several more, which he chose, with one exception, to leave unpublished.[20] The earlier narratives were relatively unsuccessful, in part because Jeffers was unable to find suitably flexible rhythmic, metrical, and stanzaic schemes, and his abrupt shift to unrhymed lyrics in 1920 was likely in part a reaction to (and recognition of) this problem. It is not surprising, then, that Jeffers was apparently ambivalent at first about setting the lyrics aside to return to narrative. The earliest notes for "Tamar" (on the same sheet as the manuscript for "Continent's End" and apparently contemporaneous with it) conclude with the exclamation, "My last story!"[21] But whether or not Jeffers initially recognized it, the logic of his recent lyric work made narrative a plausible direction.

Although the lyrics of 1921–22, especially "Continent's End," demonstrate that the flux of modern nature could serve as a source of value (and that a modern poetry could affirm what might be termed creative acts of perception without regressing nostalgically to an earlier view of nature), these poems only partly explore what they evoke. Their reliance on a single meditating speaker observing a single scene restricts Jeffers' portrayal of human action—human process—to what can be glimpsed from the outside. Correspondingly this restricts his treatment of the relationship between human process and awareness. Thus these poems of the second stage often have a static quality. Each presents a tableau or a meditation on a tableau. "Salmon Fishing" shows men fishing but not their awareness of it; "Continent's End" enacts the awareness but does so by abstracting the speaker from the process that produced the meditation, thereby obscuring or muting (and repressing) the implications of his own status as an object within nature.

Narrative offered a way beyond these limitations, though Jeffers' sense of this was likely more implicit than explicit when he veered off to begin "Tamar." Jeffers may also have sensed that his vision of nature in the recent lyrics offered an alternative explanation for the failures of the early narratives. He may, that is, have seen that they failed less from their formal problems than their confused treatment of nature as a context and value. The early narratives at times cast nature as a source of human norms but did so by regressing to a kind of pre-Darwinian view that was finally sentimental and unconvincing. The early narratives that attempted to portray the flux and violence of the nature of modern science were more "modern," but the characters in them violate society's patterns only to discover that nature has no interest in their affairs and that society (with its own seemingly arbitrary and unconnected logics) was unlikely to discover or punish their behavior. These poems escape sentimentality only to drift toward a nihilistic vision where the structures of nature are either unknowable or irrelevant to human meaning and being.

In "Tamar," though, Jeffers came to treat his characters and their actions (even their violence and introversion) as elements of nature.[22] As in the recent lyrics he viewed the human figures as expressions of the landscape's force and structure, but rather than treat these relationships as a tableau, he set them in motion. By assuming that his characters exemplified nature's physical immediacy and process—while yet partially reflecting or refracting its inherent being and consciousness—he could, that is, turn narrative into an extended exploration of the duality of "tides of fire" and "the eye that watched." As such, his narratives became a series of situations that forced human figures to act as natural force and process while simultaneously confronting—or struggling to avoid—their consciousness of nature and self. In this way narrative action became a means for exploring what might be termed the natural status of human action and the implications of this for human consciousness, especially consciousness of nature.

The final stage of lyric work collected in *Tamar* clarifies "Tamar's" importance (and perhaps its necessity) for Jeffers' attempt to shape an aesthetic that would express the nature of modern science as a source of value. Although he seems to have been primarily concerned with narrative in the months after "Tamar," Jeffers did draft a few shorter pieces during the spring and summer of 1923, and these differ significantly, if subtly, from the lyrics written before "Tamar."[23] They show that the work with narrative had actually made nature a more problematic image and had led as well to a more active and dramatic sense of the lyric speaker's role.

In the lyrics of 1921–22 the speaker, having discovered nature's drama, posits its unity and transcends his own transience by identifying with it. The speaker's interaction with the scene is largely implicit and precedes the poem's action. After "Tamar" the lyrics assume nature's drama as a starting point, but the speaker must then struggle to clarify his place in it. In these later poems, the speaker interacts with the scene as the poem unfolds, which shifts attention from nature's drama to the speaker's drama of meditation, which, among other things, transforms lyric and narrative into complementary modes of a single aesthetic of process. The difference between them becomes a matter of scale and emphasis. In one the speaker explores his own consciousness of his fictional inventions. In both, though, the speaker confronts the problematic status of human consciousness.

"Point Joe" illustrates these developments. Like the earlier lyrics, it begins with a specific scene, but this description emphasizes objects, not actions, which (oddly) makes landscape a less static image than in the earlier poems, where nature's processes suggest a kind of timeless recurrence. In "Point Joe" the objects indicate a world where things change as much as they recur and where, at least at the human level, recurrence and change are experienced as conflict. "Point Joe's" opening verbs underscore its difference from the earlier work. In the 1921–22 poems, active verbs and simple tenses typically intensify the landscape's presence as action; in "Point Joe" passive voice, perfect tenses, and participles empha-

size the objects' presence as objects. Additionally Jeffers places the
landscape's actions in the past. The point, strewn with "spars and
planks," has "torn ships"; its pines are "wind-bitten"; "the flat sea-
meadows . . . were plated / Golden with the low flower called
footsteps of the spring, millions of flowerets, // Whose light suf-
fused upward into the fog flooded its vault" (90).[24] These choices
(whatever we make of the light) stress the present as an unfolding
where some things recur (spring flowers) for a time while others
(trees and ships) are altered or destroyed, and it makes nature a
text, a history inscribed in the trees and debris, that the speaker
must read and interpret.

Significantly the only action in the present is human action. The
two verbs "saw" and "wandered," which control the first four
couplets, describe the speaker, not nature, and both suggest his
active (if initially undirected) role. The speaker's full stake in the
scene emerges in the fifth of the poem's nine couplets when he
notes an "old Chinaman gathering seaweed from the sea-rocks"
(90). The participle "gathering" leaves open whether this "glean-
ing" figure is part of the speaker's active (if wandering) human
present or part of nature's recurring, yet not merely recurrent
process. This ambiguity defines "Point Joe's" difference from the
lyrics of 1921–22. When human figures occur (other than the
speaker) in the earlier pieces, they demonstrate nature's inclusive-
ness. As details of landscape, their will or consciousness is not an
issue for the speaker or reader. In "Point Joe," however, our status in
nature and the status of consciousness are questions. Nature is a
problematic text, and the "old Chinaman," human yet seemingly
timeless in his act of "gathering," confronts the speaker with his
own ambiguous status, thereby raising the question of how consciousness affects our participation in nature:

> One other moved there, an old Chinaman gathering seaweed from
> the sea-rocks,
> He brought it in his basket and spread it flat to dry on the edge of
> the meadow.
>
> Permanent things are what is needful in a poem, things temporally
> Of great dimension, things continually renewed or always present.
>
> Grass that is made each year equals the mountains in her past and
> future;
> Fashionable and momentary things we need not see nor speak of.
>
> Man gleaning food between the solemn presences of land and ocean,

On shores where better men have shipwrecked, under fog and
    among flowers,

Equals the mountains in his past and future; that glow from the
    earth was only
A trick of nature's, one must forgive nature a thousand graceful
    subtleties.

                                  (90–91)

In the poem gleaner and poet are complementary, and their
interplay again demonstrates Jeffers' sense that one cannot both
contemplate and fully be nature. As object, the "gleaner" is process but not awareness. Conversely, the speaker, the poet, enacts
consciousness but thereby separates himself from the permanence he celebrates. He can imitate "the eye that watched," but the
power that makes him aware of nature's issues isolates him in his
own watching and mortality. Nature, thus, leaves us neither fully
acting object nor knowing subject. Only nature can fully know and
be the beauty at the same time. Only nature is fully knowing and
doing. Its unity of expression and consciousness, of object and
subject, is beyond comprehension (in both the usual and root
sense of the word). For us, its temporary and contingent manifestations, nature's fullness of being—its unfolding completion,
its un-unified unity—is as inscrutable as any deity.[25]
    In a sense the 1921–22 lyrics look at the answers nature offers;
"Point Joe," in contrast, looks at the questions it poses and finds
nature's beauty a paradoxical "trick": a temptation to fall into an
individual consciousness that chains us to mortality, yet is our
grace-full link to nature's recurrence. This shift in what can be
known undercuts the speaker's authority. In an earlier piece like
"Continent's End" the speaker can assert what is and address
nature as "you"; in "Point Joe" the speaker can only speculate
about what "is." (If "Point Joe" has a "you," it is the speaker's silent
companion, invoked at one point by "we," or the reader, cast at
another point as "one.") But this shift in what can be known also
enhances the speaker's presence as a dramatic character by stress-
ing his attempt to know, affirm, and cope. It alters the emphasis
from nature in and of itself to the problematic emphasis found in
the narratives from "Tamar" forward—the problematic of consciousness within nature.
    "Point Joe," then, stands as a kind of Janus poem. It gathers the
aesthetic strands that had been emerging in conjunction with
Jeffers' sense of nature through the stages of unrhymed work in
Tamar and it anticipates their future exploration. It also suggests

reasons for such staples of Jeffers' mature practice as his emphasis on "permanent things," his willingness to resort to explicit, even didactic, statement, and his penchant for a dramatized speaking voice when others of his generation were seeking to discourage the reader from identifying the poem's "voice" with the poet's.[26] First, "Fashionable and momentary things" offer no insight into nature's organism and moreover are likely to distract us from the way nature's larger mystery grounds our individual consciousness. Second, "Point Joe's" explicit claims and statements have to be read as part of its overall dramatic development. They (though Jeffers means them as "true") play against each other to evoke anomalies that outstrip language but that we must try to intuit—just as the poem's speaker tries to read the truths of nature's text to intuit what he cannot hope to grasp fully. And this in turn suggests why Jeffers would retain the illusion of a speaking voice (even in the narratives where the first-person interpolations call attention to the narrator's stake in his tale). If consciousness is the individual's curse and blessing and its paradox something necessarily experienced as an individual, then one must explore and testify individually. This voice, though, suggests neither confession nor dramatic monologue, since it must be stripped as much as possible of the "temporary things" that mark personality and must be generated as much as possible from the dimensions of self that are permanent and of nature. The version of self, then, in the mature lyrics is not a personality, a Jeffers egocentric enough to believe he has answers to preach, but a self that struggles to assume the role of a voice in nature that would, by virtue of becoming part of nature, speak with an authority prior to and beyond ego—would be, that is, one "voice" among the many and able for that reason to "intone [the] one language" ("Natural Music").

In some ways the four stages of unrhymed work in *Tamar* confirm (even as they complicate) a common model for Jeffers' career, in which he discovers a way beyond the conflicts of the politics and history (and the confusions of his own political poems from the First World War and shortly after) by assuming nature as his subject and authority (at the point he abandons rhyme). The impetus of this new vision and style then carries him well into the 1930s, when the drift toward a second world war draws him back to explicitly political and historical themes (and a body of less successful work). This scenario suggests that Jeffers' best and most typical work rests on an antithesis between nature and history (or nature and politics), and nature (at least when understood as the simultaneity of "tides of fire" and the "eye that watched") becomes the measure of other categories of experience. Nature, that is, is either beyond history and free of it, or (probably more accurate to the work) nature subsumes and redeems history ("Natural Music" and "Shine, Perishing Republic" could be cited here). Although partly right, this view underestimates the importance of history and politics for Jeffers—even when he seemed most concerned with a poetry of nature in the early 1920s—and posits nature, history, and politics as overly discrete and stable categories. Here, too, the specific evolution of *Tamar* complicates the picture, and it is at this point that the dialectical interplay between Jeffers' project and various modernist projects can be glimpsed.

In the years after *Californians* Jeffers apparently considered a number of groupings for publication (and submitted at least one) before settling on the form of *Tamar and Other Poems*.[27] The surviving tables of contents for these intermediate collections suggest that each built from a cluster of poems from 1916–20 (some in *Tamar* as published) and that Jeffers progressively added the lyrics of 1920–22.[28] The first contents page to include "Tamar," though, breaks this pattern. Instead of simply adding the most recent work (and paring some of the least recent), it shows that Jeffers deleted recent work (including pieces eventually in *Tamar*) while adding several explicitly political and historical poems he had long discarded and would never actually publish.[29] Moreover, he used these specific poems (written during and about the First World War) to frame "Tamar," not his more recent nature lyrics. In other words, Jeffers at first contextualized "Tamar" as a political poem, even though Tamar's incest and destruction of herself and those around her is in no way explicitly political.

Jeffers' choice of context may reflect his sense that the violence of war would make "Tamar's" violence seem less excessive. Or he may have considered "story" (at least at this point) as inextricably bound to the world of politics and history he had seemingly set aside when he began "The Maid's Thought" and the unrhymed lyrics that followed it. (It may be worth noting that "The Coast-Range Christ," the last and only rhymed narrative from 1917–19 included in *Tamar*, is—like "Tamar"—set during the First World War and that its plot hinges specifically on whether or not to fight in the conflict.) But either explanation calls attention to the vision/dream that several characters experience independently and that imagistically equates the imploding violence of the Cauldwells to

what "Tamar" represents as the simultaneously imploding violence of Europe.[30] These scenes do not preclude reading the
poem (as many have done) as an exploration of the mythological
or philosophical or psychological implications of our human place
in nature (or lack thereof), but they do suggest that for Jeffers the
Cauldwells' tragedy at some level expresses (and is at another
caused by) the political and that readings of the poem need to
account for this dimension and the equation it implies between
"nature" (including the psychology of the individual and the dynamics of the family as a kind of organism) on the one side and
"history" and "politics" on the other. It should be noted that
similar scenes and explanations occur in the other narratives of
the 1920s, most importantly in *The Women at Point Sur* (1927).[31]

Jeffers' treatment of the lyric "Shine, Perishing Republic" also
suggests the importance of this equation. It assumes (like other
1921–22 lyrics) a nature of conflict and process. It is also, though,
explicitly political and portrays historical process as a kind of
natural process in which the human task becomes finding the
proper way (the proper consciousness with which) to regard both
history and nature as figures of the more comprehensive process
of growth and decay. Written about the same time as "Continent's
End," it was added to the collection along with that poem,
"Tamar," and "The Murmansk Landing" and "The Dance of the
Banner" (the early war poems that initially framed "Tamar"). Not
surprisingly, Jeffers omitted both these early poems from *Tamar,*
but he also omitted "Shine, Perishing Republic" along with them,
even though a year later he would add this to his newest work as
part of the "Roan Stallion" grouping in *Roan Stallion, Tamar and
Other Poems* (1925).

"Shine, Perishing Republic" itself points to the importance for
Jeffers of a kind of equation between nature, history, and politics,
but his uncertainty about whether to print it (along with his
shifting sense of how to contextualize "Tamar") suggests that late
in his work on *Tamar* his sense of these categories was not yet
firmly fixed. Here again Jeffers' post-Darwinian sense of nature
may be a factor. A nature that is unfolding and becoming is itself a
kind of history; and if nature is a kind of history, then conversely
history becomes a kind of nature. Both become (to some degree
equatable) examples of the material process of "tides of fire." But
here again the duality of nature for Jeffers required complicating
the matter further. For poetry was not only a record of flux (of
change in both nature and history) but also an assertion of
beauty—a claim that this flux offered to the right sort of con-

templation an experience of a beauty somehow in and of time yet transcendent ("the eye that watched"). In other words, the problem was not simply to visualize a nature that assumed the materialism of modern science in a way that would comprehend historical, social, and political process. It was how to do this while affirming (yet redefining) that most traditional of aesthetic values—beauty. And it is precisely at this point that Jeffers' problematic relationship to the projects of his modernist contemporaries begins to be visible.

Although in the 1920s Jeffers tended to express "beauty" and "history" in terms of "nature," the general unfolding of his work (and the details of specific poems) suggests that these were for him categories that constituted and required each other. They were interdependent facets of his attempt to articulate a modern aesthetic that would credit the material basis of experience while yet demonstrating the "reality" of transcendence. Jeffers, that is, like his modernist contemporaries, was crucially concerned with visualizing a modern beauty and deriving a rationale for it. But where a poet like Stevens might stress the imagination's power to make a beauty unique to it, Jeffers stressed the imagination's power to apprehend and celebrate a beauty already inherent in the world. Although this underscores Jeffers' difference from the high modernists, the concern he shared for finding a modern (yet traditional) ground for beauty raises the question why the New Critics, speaking for their modernist clients (whether or not they wanted speaking for), would find Jeffers so worthy of attack and be so eager to cast him as some kind of nihilistic demon in the poetic garden when they might more simply have complained that his sense of line was clunky (if it was) or questioned his choice of the narrative mode. The interdependence and instability of "nature," "history," and "beauty" in Jeffers provides part of the answer.

In *The Beauty of Inflections* Jerome McGann examines how most of the English romantics rejected the work of George Crabbe as defective and anachronistic. McGann questions these conclusions and suggests that one way to "begin to define precisely what the Romantics took their stand upon" is to consider what it meant for them to reject Crabbe, whom McGann takes seriously in spite of the judgments of Coleridge and Wordsworth. McGann reads these judgments as "part of a polemic on behalf of certain poetical criteria" to demonstrate that romanticism was not the exclusively relevant poetic ideology in this period, even if the "relative truth," the "partisan view" of the romantics and their successors successfully marginalized Crabbe's contrary project.[32] (McGann here and elsewhere notes the ironic place this conventionalized narrative of the romantic episode creates for Jane Austen's work.) For McGann, Crabbe was by no means irrelevant to the romantics. He suggests that the romantics were forced to ignore Crabbe, in spite of his strength, because confronting his work seriously would require confronting what was problematic in their own ideological and aesthetic assumptions. As such, Crabbe figures dialectically as a kind of shadow romantic, the invisible term that reveals the visible.

Jeffers bears a similar relationship to his modernist contemporaries, and his example raises the same questions about what it means for one group or position to define the terms used to read another. In other words, Jeffers' still somewhat marginalized status may point less to his actual marginality than to his centrality, his dialectical relevance to the positions and figures who established the rationale for excluding his work. But why, more specifically, might the modernists and New Critics reject Jeffers? I suggest that it is because in the several varieties of modernism the dichotomies between culture and nature, history and nature, and how they defined beauty were—as for Jeffers—similarly dialectical and problematic and that to interrogate Jeffers or be interrogated by his work would require confronting the instability of the categories and terms, the ideology, that made various modernist projects possible. Jeffers, that is, differs from Stevens, Eliot, or Pound, but not enough to be neutral or safe.

What does this mean about reading Jeffers? First we need to treat his categories as inherently complex, not simple, and to see how over time the play of the work, the career, articulates a serious and modern project. It also means that we should interrogate Jeffers' practice with that of his modernist contemporaries—and vice versa. And it may mean that we will have to reconsider the implications of his decision in the later 1930s and 1940s to return to poems that again foregrounded the political and view these not as a radical veer from the work of the 1920s, but as a moment where (in the midst of crisis) the collision (and potential slippage) of categories becomes more apparent and where what is both radical *and* traditional about Jeffers becomes particularly explicit.

If so, we will be closer to realizing that part of what makes Jeffers relevant (and threatening enough to some to be worth ostracizing) was not that he ignored history and culture as shapers of the human imagination, but that—seeing them—he shaped a response just different enough to be troubling, because if Jeffers' struggle with nature was a way to envision history, society, and humanness (not simply reject them), then it was implicitly and legitimately an interrogation of the tendency in some modernist practice and modern culture (at least as imagined by the academy) to visualize a history, a humanness, that so domesticated nature as to erase it altogether.

NOTES

1. See, for example, Arthur B. Coffin, *Robinson Jeffers: Poet of Inhumanism* (Madison: University of Wisconsin Press, 1971); William H. Nolte, *Rock and Hawk: Robinson Jeffers and the Romantic Agony* (Athens: University of Georgia Press, 1978); and Radcliffe Squires, *The Loyalties of Robinson Jeffers* (Ann Arbor: University of Michigan Press, 1956).

2. See, for example, Robert J. Brophy, *Robinson Jeffers: Myth, Ritual, and Symbol in His Narrative Poems* (Cleveland: Case Western Reserve University Press, 1973), and Frederic I. Carpenter, *Robinson Jeffers* (New York: Twayne Books, 1962).

3. See, for example, [William Everson] Brother Antoninus, *Robinson Jeffers: Fragments of an Older Fury* (Berkeley, Calif.: Oyez, 1968), and Robert Zaller, *The Cliffs of Solitude: A Reading of Robinson Jeffers* (New York: Cambridge University Press, 1983).

4. See, for example, Lawrence Clark Powell, *Robinson Jeffers: The Man and His Work* (1934; reprint, New York: Haskell House, 1970), 115–43.

5. *The Selected Poetry of Robinson Jeffers* (New York: Random House, 1938) seems to confirm these divisions: Jeffers omitted altogether poems from *Californians* (1916) as "only preparatory exercises," included only four of the early *Tamar* pieces as "sample[s] of the metrical experiments that occupied my mind for awhile," and kept nearly all of the unrhymed work.

6. Introduction to *Roan Stallion, Tamar and Other Poems* (New York: Modern Library, 1935), vii–x.

7. William Everson has commented extensively on the chronology of the early poems in his three Jeffers compilations: *Californians* (1971), *The Alpine Christ* (1974), and *Brides of the South Wind* (1974) (all Cayucos, Calif.: Cayucos Books). The chronology, though, for the somewhat later poems discussed in this essay is based in part on a packet of three hundred manuscript pages at Occidental College first made available to researchers in 1987. A full discussion of that evidence will appear in the fourth and final volume of *The Collected Poetry of Robinson Jeffers*, ed. Tim Hunt (Stanford: Stanford University Press).

8. Two were written the same day, and the third either shortly before or after. Two early contents pages for what developed into *Tamar* are at the Beinecke Library, Yale University, and are reproduced in Sidney S. Alberts, *A Bibliography of the Works of Robinson Jeffers* (1933; reprint, New York: Burt Franklin, 1968), 17–18. A third, held by the Harry Ransom Humanities Research Center, University of Texas, is reproduced in Everson's *Brides of the South Wind*, 135. A partial revision of one of the Beinecke contents pages has not been published. These contents provide additional evidence for the chronology for the *Tamar* period.

Note that the early manuscripts and first two appearances of "The Excesses of God"—*University Review* (1939), 238, and in Edith Greenan, *Of Una Jeffers* (Los Angeles: Ward Ritchie, 1939), 45—show that Jeffers substituted "can understand" for the original reading of "understands" when he prepared it for *Be Angry at the Sun*. The original reading ends the poem on a more optimistic note about our ability to perceive nature and act in accord with it, which is perhaps the reason he omitted it from *Tamar*.

9. *The Collective Poetry of Robinson Jeffers: Volume One, 1920–28*, 3. All other quotations of Jeffers' poems follow this text, except where noted, and page numbers are noted parenthetically in the body of the essay.

10. *Tamar and Other Poems* (New York: Boyle, 1924), 125. The quotation is from the poem's original appearance. "To the Stone-Cutters" is one of the few poems Jeffers revised after collecting it. In *The Selected Poetry of Robinson Jeffers* line 8 reads, "Die blind and blacken to the heart." The change in emphasis is slight, but removing the possessive pronoun "his" somewhat blunts the personification, and to that degree makes the 1938 form more consistent with the change in Jeffers' work I am claiming begins to occur the following year with pieces such as "Natural Music."

11. *California Poetry Series* (San Francisco: Book Club of California, 1947).

12. The reissue of the poem in *Roan Stallion, Tamar and Other Poems* (New York: Boni & Liveright, 1925) reads "Wind-prints" rather than "Wing-prints." The corrected galley proofs for *Roan Stallion* at the Beinecke Library confirm that this was the typesetter's change.

13. It might be noted here, as well, that the likely chronology of Jeffers' short poems from 1920–22 shows that as his sense of nature and its æsthetic implications evolved, his verse line grew progressively longer.

14. "From Symbolist Thought to Immanence: The Ground of Postmodern American Poetics," *Boundary 2* (1973): 606, and *Enlarging the Temple: New Directions in American Poetry during the 1960s* (Lewisburg, Penn.: Bucknell University Press, 1979), 29.

15. Altieri, *Enlarging the Temple*, 29, 37.

16. Ibid., 37–38.

17. For a brief summary of Jeffers' scientific training and its possible impact on his early work, see the introduction to *The Collected Poetry of Robinson Jeffers: Volume One, 1920–28*, xvi–xx.

18. Altieri, *Enlarging the Temple*, 37.

19. In this essay the poem "Tamar" is indicated by quotation marks, the title of the collection by italics.

20. "The Coast-Range Christ," included in *Tamar*, is from this period. An unused preface for the *Tamar* collection dated August 1923 shows that Jeffers did consider using several more of these narratives. See Melba Berry Bennett, *The Stone Mason of Tor House: The Life and Works of Robinson Jeffers* (Los Angeles: Ward Ritchie Press, 1966), 108.

21. The sheet, the verso of a bank statement dated 17 February 1922, is held by the Beinecke Library.

22. Although the limited scope of lyric, at least as he had conceived it and for his purposes, seems to have been a major factor in Jeffers' return to narrative, his response to the depth psychology of Freud and others and the then still new anthropology popularized by Frazer's *The Golden Bough* is another factor that should be noted. Like others of his generation, Jeffers was intrigued by this work, though here too his greater familiarity and ease with the perspective of

modern science seems to have led him to a different response. For someone like Eliot, Freud's work seems to have revealed the psyche as the source of an imagination requiring the aesthetic act to order and redeem it; for Jeffers, Freud seems to have demonstrated the psyche as "natural" force and the essential unity of nature and imagination as analogous forces or energies. Similarly for Eliot, Frazer's work on primitive myth seems to have suggested that the structures for imaginative experience might be implicit in cultural groups, while for Jeffers Frazer's emphasis on primitive ritual seems to have demonstrated these same groups participating in, and acting as, natural force. Together Frazer and Darwin may have helped shape or confirm Jeffers' sense of the human species as a social organism responding to natural force as natural force, suggesting that social units such as the family could themselves be treated as forms of nature. John B. Vickery discusses Jeffers and Frazer in *The Literary Impact of The Golden Bough* (Princeton: Princeton University Press, 1973), 157–61. Brophy develops Jeffers' use of mythic and ritual elements more fully in *Robinson Jeffers: Myth, Ritual, and Symbol in His Narrative Poems* but without claiming a specific influence. Jeffers' letter of 24 April 1926 to his editor Donald Friede is also relevant. Referring to *Point Alma Venus*, the precursor to *The Women at Point Sur*, Jeffers wrote, "The story, like Tamburlaine or Zarathustra, is the story of human attempts to get beyond humanity. But the superman ideal rather stands on top of humanity— intensifies—ends in 'all too human'—here the attempt is to get clear of it. More like the ceremonial dances of primitive people; the dancer becomes a rain-cloud, or a leopard, or a God. . . . The episodes of the poem are a sort of essential ritual, from which the real action develops on another plane." See *The Selected Letters of Robinson Jeffers*, ed. Ann N. Ridgeway (Baltimore: Johns Hopkins University Press, 1968), 68. (These comments are expanded from Tim Hunt, "Robinson Jeffers: The Modern Poet as Anti-Modernist," *Critical Essays on Robinson Jeffers*, ed. James Karman [G. K. Hall], 1990, 245–52).

23. The image of golden flowers recalls "The Maid's Thought" but without that poem's humanizing metaphors of dancing, games, and love, and the landscape might almost be Gothic (is there a faint echo of the upward beating light in Poe's "The City in the Sea"?) if the flat, deliberate tone did not so clearly accentuate the literal.

24. In a sense, nature in the earlier poems is a realized text waiting to be read; in "Point Joe," a text constantly writing itself and fully knowable only by the infinitude of "the eye that watched." Nature is still an image of value, the fundamental reality to be realized, but the speaker's limited ability to know shifts the emphasis from celebrating nature to questioning how to stand in relation to it. Even if nature somehow unifies change and recurrence in its own sight, the difference remains real in human experience, since our consciousness requires recognizing the contrast between nature's duration and our own.

25. For an analysis of the modernists' sense of voice and the particular form and dynamics of their transformation of Victorian models, see Carol T. Christ, *Victorian and Modern Poetics* (Chicago: University of Chicago Press, 1984). For a somewhat fuller discussion of this point, see my "Robinson Jeffers: The Modern Poet as Anti-Modernist," op. cit.

26. Everson prints a rejection letter from Macmillan dated 2 April 1920 in *Brides of the South Wind*, 134. The original is held by the Harry Ransom Humanities Research Center, University of Texas.

27. See n. 8.

28. The manuscripts of these two poems, "The Murmansk Landing" and

"The Dance of the Banner," are part of the newly available material at Occidental College. See n. 7.

29. Brophy is one of the few critics to discuss these passages. See *Robinson Jeffers: Myth, Ritual, and Symbol in His Narrative Poems*, 48–49.

30. Jeffers' uncertainty following "Tamar" shows in other ways as well. After hesitating some months before submitting the poem at all, he chose to print the book at his own expense, and then, even after the printer he had selected enthusiastically offered to serve as publisher, Jeffers delayed months more before proceeding, perhaps hoping to finish a new narrative to complement "Tamar." In the same letter of 24 April 1926 to Friede cited in n. 22 Jeffers writes, "I began [Point Alma Venus] quite cheerfully, soon after Tamar was written I put it aside because it was too exciting, and ever since has been a struggle to keep it out of my mind by writing something else" (*Selected Letters*, 68). Long sections of various drafts of "Point Alma Venus" are held by the Harry Ransom Humanities Research Center, and these show that the poem was a precursor to *The Women at Point Sur* (1927). When that project stalled, he considered adding the group of narratives he had written after *Californians* and drafted the unused August 1923 preface that encourages the reader to view the narratives as a single, evolving project. *Tamar and Other Poems* would have been ample with "Tamar" as its only narrative. But Jeffers may have wanted the narratives, not lyrics, to dominate the collection, or he have wanted other "stories" to reinforce the patterns that grounded "Tamar's" lurid sensationalism, or have simply felt a volume containing several long poems would be taken more seriously. Whatever the case, his uncertainty about how to present "Tamar" suggests he did not initially realize how his new sense of nature unified his work independently of politics or landscape, narrative, or lyric.

31. *The Beauty of Inflections: Literary Investigations in Historical Method and Theory* (New York: Oxford University Press, 1985), 295.

32. "Invasion," published originally in *The Double Axe and Other Poems* (1948) is a useful example of the interplay of "beauty," "nature," and "history" as categories in Jeffers' later work.

Reading Robinson Jeffers: Formalism, Poststructuralism, and the Inhumanist Turn

David Copland Morris

In 1977, fifteen years after Robinson Jeffers' death, his self-acknowledged disciple, William Everson, assessed Jeffers' legacy of environmental wisdom: "The ecological crisis has driven home with great force the pertinence of Jeffers' insistence that man divorced from nature is a monstrosity. By wrenching attention from man to cosmos he has served as a powerful counterbalance to perennial human egocentricity, and his witness in this regard is only beginning. No matter what civilizations survive this one, the pertinence of his vision will go on, because it is not possible to state the case more emphatically."[1] Even ambivalent readers such as James Dickey recognized the importance of Jeffers' environmental prophecy and the power of the poetry in which it was embodied:

> One thinks, uneasily, that the prophetic tone may be more than just a tone, remembering that Jeffers was telling us long before Hiroshima that the ultimate end of science, of knowledge, and of tool-using, is not comfort and convenience, but unrelieved tragedy. It is extraordinarily strange how the more awful and ludicrous aspects of the atomic age have come to resemble Jeffers' poems. In a film like *Mondo Cane*, for example, one sees the dying sea turtles, disoriented by the Bikini blasts, until they cannot even find the Pacific Ocean, crawling inland to die in the desert, and one thinks compulsively of Jeffers.[2]

Jeffers chose the provocative term *inhumanism* for the compelling vision that swept Dickey up against his will. This inhumanist vision, I believe, projects a state of mind necessary (though not sufficient) to resolve twentieth-century civilization's environmental crisis and the nihilism that accompanies it. Leo Marx, a cultural historian who has thought hard about the causes of the destructive behavior that has led to the environmental crisis, concludes that something quite opposite to inhumanism is at fault: "The philosophic root of this dangerous behavior is an arrogant conception of man, and above all, of human consciousness, as wholly unique—as an entity distinct from, and potentially independent of, the rest of nature."[3]

It is precisely this arrogant conception of humanity as separate and superior from nature that Jeffers' inhumanism resisted. In the poem "The Answer," Jeffers writes, ". . . the greatest beauty is / Organic wholeness, the wholeness of life and things, the divine beauty of the universe. Love that, not man / Apart from that, or else you will share man's pitiful confusions, or drown in despair when his days darken." In his letters as well there are numerous expressions of thought directly opposite to the environmentally destructive philosophy criticized by Marx. For Jeffers clearly human consciousness is not the sole source of value, nor is it something he considers separate from or superior to the rest of creation: "I don't feel consciousness alien to the rest. The animals are aware of external things and inner sensation; no doubt all life is, in some degree; and as life shades down into chemical and physical process, so it seems to me that consciousness shades down into something not alien to it."[4] How strikingly different this type of thinking is from the harsh dichotomies between the human and the natural handed down by the major tradition of Western thought from Plato to Descartes to Sartre. And how gracefully Jeffers can give both consciousness and the nonhuman world their due: "The feeling of deep earnestness and nobility in natural objects and in the universe—these are human qualities, not mineral or vegetable, but it seems to me I would not impute them into natural objects unless there were something in not-man that corresponds to these qualities in man. This may be called delusion, or it may be called mystical certainty, there is no external proof either way."[5]

In taking this position Jeffers opposes the major thrust of Western thinking—the detestation of the fallen material world and the exclusive glorification of the human spirit. Jeffers saw clearly that a subjectivity feeding only on itself feeds on nothing and starves, while at the same time it casually and tragically destroys its only true source of nourishment, the external world. He was not the first to achieve this insight; anomalous passages such as the voice from the whirlwind in the Book of Job, or Thoreau's meditations on top of Katahdin in *The Maine Woods*, contain expressions of the inhumanist view, and it may be said to permeate

much of romanticism generally. However, it may be fairly claimed
that Jeffers' work provides the most thorough and profound
development of inhumanist thinking.

At the present time investigations of cultural perspectives similar to inhumanism are taking place in several fields; among those
engaged in such inquiry are the philosopher Mary Midgley and
the theologian Frederick Elder. In his interesting book *Crisis in
Eden*,[6] Elder sees Western thinking as divided into two camps:
close-up "inclusionists," whose thinking corresponds to inhumanism, emphasize humanity's connection to the physical world,
while "exclusionists" stress humanity's alienation and distance.
Without question, the exclusionist strain has been dominant historically in the West. When Elder contemplates the environmental
crisis brought on by societal action derived from exclusionist
thought, he sees the following solution: "I contend that what is
needed is the substitution of minor Western traditions for what
are currently the major ones."[7] As the earlier quotations from
Everson and Dickey suggest, Jeffers offers a powerful expression
of the minor tradition that must now become primary if environmental catastrophe is to be avoided, and if the nihilism disguised
by blind technological expansion is to overcome.

If Everson's and Dickey's assessments of Jeffers' value are valid,
why, it may be asked, has the revival of his reputation been so
slow? If Jeffers' work is so important, why has it been given such
limited space (sometimes none at all) in the major contemporary
anthologies of American literature? Why so little attention in the
dominant critical journals? The reasons are complex, but without
doubt the legacy of censure handed down by the hyperformalist
New Critics has affected the climate of debate. Jeffers' poems did
not evidence the particular brand of irony and tightness that the
narrow New Critical ideology called for. But now, of course, the
influence and prestige of New Criticism have greatly declined;
might we expect a corresponding rise in Jeffers' stock? There is
one major reason to be pessimistic: the rise of a new dominant
hyperformalist paradigm, poststructuralism, which is also inap-
propriate as a perspective from which to read Jeffers. Poststructuralism is founded on the same principles of cultural arrogance
and alienation that Jeffers spent his poetic life resisting.

The deconstructive approach emerging from the poststructuralist philosophy of language can serve a valuable purpose: it
can help assure that discussion of content (or of the relation of the
poem to the world) does not näively ignore complex issues of
mediation. Indeed, the earlier New Critical emphasis on the au-

tonomy of the art object was salutary in breaking up simple-minded equations of the poem with either its effects on readers or with the intentions of its author. No one would deny that some benefits accrue from a formalist approach, be it New Critical or poststructuralist; but issues of mediation are not the sole, nor often the most fruitful subjects for criticism. To privilege such issues absolutely is to fetishize them, and thus to pervert critical inquiry; it is to cut us off from a source of wisdom about how to live.

A typical example of such fetishizing may be found in the work of J. Hillis Miller, a leading poststructuralist critic, who writes: "for all writers generally in the Western tradition literature is distinguished from other uses of language by the explicitness of the orientation toward language rather than thematic concerns for Nature or for selfhood. This orientation, however, can only be expressed in language that invites its thematic misreading."8 Viewed from Miller's perspective, Everson's or Dickey's assessment of Jeffers is clearly a misreading. If we accept Miller's critical principles, then one of the strong claims for Jeffers' importance is ruled out of order since Jeffers himself firmly believed that his poetic vision was indeed oriented toward "thematic concerns for Nature" and selfhood. Specifically he claimed that his work "offers a reasonable detachment as a rule of conduct, instead of love, hate and envy. It neutralizes fanaticism and wild hopes; but it provides magnificence for the religious instinct, and satisfies our need to admire greatness and rejoice in beauty."9 These are large and important claims, especially so in the context of the ironic shoulder shrugs and sad little sighs of much contemporary poetry. I argue here that instead of abandoning our appreciation of Jeffers on his own terms, we should recognize the limitations of poststructuralist methods of criticism. We must escape the narrow hyperformalist or textualist assumptions within which poststructuralism would confine us if we are to receive the generous gift Jeffers has bequeathed.

Because poststructuralists see themselves as opponents of humanism they would seem at first glance to be important potential allies for a doctrine such as Jeffers' inhumanism. To be sure, the poststructuralist attack on the notion of absolute metaphysical truth and on privileged conceptual schemes should in theory help open the way for new perspectives such as that of Jeffers'. The emphasis of a writer like Richard Rorty on keeping the conversation of culture going is particularly pertinent because the inhumanist view, at least as represented by Jeffers, has been resisted in some quarters in a manner that suggests a simple refusal to listen.

However, certain key poststructuralist tendencies are counter to inhumanist thinking. In fact, it is grimly ironic that poststructuralism can be seen as repeating in many ways the environmentally destructive attitudes of human separation and superiority noted by Leo Marx. For example, when Jacques Derrida stresses how much of the way we see the world is bound up in the structure and history of language, there is no denying the strength of his insights, but when he says, "Now I don't know what perception is and I don't believe that anything like perception exists. . . . I don't believe there is any perception,"[10] his thought is perverse and leads toward an ideology of extreme anthropocentrism. One result of downplaying perception and emphasizing the determination of consciousness by the structure of language is that consciousness comes to be seen only as a by-product of language. Geoffrey Hartman put it this way: "Even the self, that is, has its boundaries fixed and unsettled by language."[11] An important result is that this extreme, language-centered view of consciousness naturally emphasizes the separation of animals and humans since humans are the only species with access to language, or at least to writing. Derrida sees no fountain of perception that we share with animals that might refresh the stream of language. Jeffers intended that his own work achieve "a shifting of emphasis and significance from man to not-man; the rejection of human solipsism and recognition of the transhuman magnificence,"[12] but there is no possibility of transcending human solipsism or of representing linguistically a transhuman magnificence if we see language only as a prison-house, or as an endless hall of mirrors, as it appears to poststructuralism. It is crucial to remember, however, that seeing language in this way is an ideological choice: it is not an alternative dictated by the character of language itself. The prison-house is a metaphor that is sometimes useful, sometimes not, in describing how language operates in different situations.

If a critical ideology such as poststructuralism collapses nature into language, or asserts that there is an unbridgeable gulf between the two, then literature will necessarily be seen as always self-reflexive or "about language," and the most highly prized texts will be those whose texuality is most prominent. Works of referential character that emphasize themes of nature and selfhood will not be highly regarded. But again, we must see such evaluations for what they are—the products of ideology. To cite

Geoffrey Hartman again: "Derrida tells literary people only what they have already known and repressed. Repressed too much, perhaps. The fullness of equivocation in literary structures should now be thought about to the point where Joyce's wordplay seems normal and Empson's *Seven Types [of Ambiguity]* archaic."[13] *Finnegans Wake* is the prime text for poststructuralism, but it is evidently not enough to find it a great work in some ways—it must now be seen as "normal," that is, normative. The judgment is incorrect on simple empirical grounds; Joyce's wordplay is not the statistical norm, nor is it normative outside of certain limited critical circles. One can say that the subject of *Finnegans Wake* is language, but that does not mean that the subject of all other significant literary works is also language.

What, then, is the motive behind the skewed view of literature that wishes to see *Finnegans Wake* as normal? The result of its adoption, says Hartman, is that "A thousand and one nights of literary analysis lie before, a Scheherazade to keep the emperor awake beyond his intentions."[14] This statement is depressing in its frivolous sentiment, its rather ponderous punning, and its would-be "playfulness." In opposition to Hartman, I believe that once the consideration of texts is severed from concern for intentions, criticism becomes arbitrary. Poststructuralism reveals itself here to be a kind of English professor's employment act—an infinite field of meaning (or nonmeaning) requiring an infinite number of interpreters. Hartman's view represents, in the most uncharitable light, the exercise of privilege by an elite, for under his schema the only ground an interpretation can have is the professional reputation of the critic writing it.

As a way into a perspective on literature different from poststructuralism, let us look at D. H. Lawrence's evaluation of Joyce, Hartman's touchstone. Lawrence says of Joyce's writing in *Ulysses:* "My God, what a clumsy olla putrida James Joyce is! Nothing but old fags and cabbage-stumps of quotations from the Bible and the rest. . . . what old and hard-worked staleness, masquerading as the all new!"[15] And elsewhere: "But James Joyce bores me stiff—too terribly would-be and done-on-purpose, utterly without spontaneity or real life." I do not endorse this view of Joyce, but it stakes out a formidable position directly counter to that of Hartman. Undoubtedly, a deconstructionist would look at Lawrence's comments and say that "spontaneity" and "real life" were mere constructions of the reader and that Lawrence was hopelessly naïve in believing that these terms represented some "presence" in the text. Jeffers too would be vulnerable to similar poststructuralist objections, for he, in criticizing the tradition of

Mallarmé, makes similarly "naïve" realist claims: "The modern French poetry of that time, and the most 'modern' of the English poetry, seemed to me thoroughly defeatist. . . . It was becoming slight and fantastic, abstract, unreal, eccentric. . . . It must reclaim substance and sense, and physical and psychological reality."[16] There is some validity to the post-structuralist charges that could be brought against the views of Lawrence and Jeffers, at least in the uncompromising form expressed by these quotations, but they in turn would probably see such objections as decadent and trivial, and so it would go with no resolution. The point to be made is that both sides possess a notion that can have merit, and neither may be completely dismissed.

One way to put the poststructuralist view in perspective is to remember that while some literary critics spend a thousand and one nights analyzing the wordplay in such texts as *Ulysses*, there are also pub tours in Dublin tracing the adventures of Stephen and Bloom. Self-reflexiveness and reference exist in the same universe, and to eliminate either one is to be false to experience. What is disturbing is that Hartman conveys the impression that it is obvious and beyond debate that Joycean wordplay is the norm, and that his own brand of indeterminism is the only viable critical stance.

Another way of putting poststructuralist criticism in perspective is to distinguish its strength from its weakness. It is clear that poststructuralist approaches can be fruitful when applied to poetry like that of Mallarmé, one of the ideology's heroes. Jeffers, however, specifically rejected Mallarmé's work as a model for his own:

> It seems to me that Mallarmé and his followers, renouncing intelligibility in order to concentrate on the music of poetry, had turned off the road into a narrowing lane. Their successors could only make further renunciations; ideas had gone, now meter had gone, imagery would have to go; then recognizable emotions would have to go, perhaps at last even words might have to go or give up their meaning, nothing be left but musical syllables. Every advance required the elimination of some aspect of reality, and what could it profit me to know the direction of modern poetry if I did not like the direction? It was too much like putting out your eyes to cultivate the sense of hearing, or cutting off the right hand to develop the left.[17]

In discussing Jeffers it is necessary to keep the mind open. No one can see him properly while believing Mallarmé's poetry or *Finnegans Wake* to be the only models for significant literature.

My argument, then, is essentially against reductive and dog-

matic limitations on methods of criticism. Hartman says of Derrida: "He shows how much metaphor remains and must remain
(in philosophy), how much equivocation and palimpsest-residue.
But he doubts that philosophy can get beyond being a form of
language."[18] And certainly if philosophy does not escape language, according to this view, neither does literature. What I want
to suggest here is that it is also significant to show how much in
literature is *not* equivocation and palimpsest-residue, but instead
new knowledge about this world and new wisdom about how to
live in it.

Let us look at some of Jeffers' verse directly in order to evaluate
the different critical approaches that might be applied to it. In a
short poem, "Return," he writes:

> I will touch things and things and no more thoughts,
> That breed like mouthless May-flies darkening the sky,
> The insect clouds that blind our passionate hawks
> So that they cannot strike, hardly can fly.
> Things are the hawk's food and noble is the mountain,
>   Oh noble
> Pico Blanco, steep sea-wave of marble.[19]

Surely these lines lend themselves to deconstruction. There is in
them an expressed preference for action and matter over consciousness and language, yet the preference is expressed in a
poem, a product of both; there is a valorizing of the immediate,
but it is expressed in a deliberate act; there is a valorizing of the
world, but it is expressed in the medium of language. Is Jeffers
praising nature or self-consciousness? J. Hillis Miller says that in
most Western literary works, "Nature is no more than a major
resource of figurative language";[20] could the same be true in
Jeffers? There is indeed a perspective from which we could see
the subtext for Jeffers' poem as an imperative to write, to make
use of nature as a source of figurative language. At least, may one
not say that language perpetrated an ironic reversal on Jeffers?
He has not touched "things," a present source of energy and
renewal; he has merely been caught in the process of language
unfolding itself in a stream of signs. The effect of the poem, then,
from a deconstructionist view, is to stress our difference and
distance from nature, an effect quite different from the apparent
"intended" one.

Jeffers' avowed intentions are indeed the opposite: "But my

subject is what it used to be: my love, my loved subject: / Mountain and ocean, rock, water and beasts and trees / Are the protagonists, the human people are only symbolic interpreters."[21] And elsewhere he says: "To feel / Greatly, and understand greatly, and express greatly, the natural / Beauty, is the sole business of poetry."[22] But even these notions could be deconstructed to show that they reveal, despite their surface meaning, a preoccupation with interpretation and expression as much as with nature.

In his foreword to the *Selected Poetry* Jeffers provides evidence for both modes of interpretation. He says that his move to the Carmel coast was a decisive factor in writing the kind of poetry he did—poetry that, in his words, was "at least in my own voice." In other words, the subject matter determined the style and gave the poems "substance" and "reality." But he also says that even had he not come to Carmel, "some kind of verse I should have written, of course, [but] not this kind,"[23] which seems to support the idea that the writer's theme, as always, is simply writing. The contradiction is deepened when, in another poem, Jeffers says, "The poet . . . wishes not to play games with words, / His affair being to awake dangerous images / And call the hawks. . . ."[24] A poststructuralist would ask pertinently, "But isn't the image of calling the hawks just a verbal construction, the result of a game with words? A game, moreover, that is played, as much by language as by the writer? Isn't language, in fact, always in the foreground?"

The answer, I believe, is that there are no external standards for deciding what should be placed in the foreground and what in the background; it is a matter of mood. Hartman says that Derrida's great accomplishment has been the "foregrounding of language," and this is true. But it must be kept in mind that to foreground language as a critical maneuver is not to prove the primacy of language as a metaphysical fact. The foregrounding of language can be subjected to criticism as readily as other more content-oriented critical approaches. Ironically, the deconstructionists, in their single-minded concentration on the issue of language, often appear to be as limited as the most unsophisticated and literal-minded of earlier critics. To see *Walden*, for example, as solely about language shows a narrow-mindedness similar to that found in readers who dismiss Thoreau's thoughts on nature because of his sometimes inaccurate labeling of bird species. It is valuable to stress issues of linguistic mediation in Thoreau, but it would be a distortion to completely collapse his concern for nature into a concern for language.

If we go back once more to the lines from "Return," we can

grant the deconstructionist that there is pathos in them to the degree that the poet admits being trapped in the prison-house of language, trapped in his difference and distance from nature. Jeffers is, after all, denigrating mediation by means of an ordered verbal construct. Yet there is also exhilaration in the degree to which the poet *is* able to overcome alienation and imprisonment by turning language outward. If, in his reading, a critic like Paul de Man chooses always to foreground pathos rather than exhilaration, such is his prerogative; but his choice is not binding. His stance may help to prevent overly simplistic readings, but it also may be regarded as somewhat forced or even hypocritical in its skepticism. De Man represents a questionable contemporary orientation that I would call sentimental nihilism. Mary Midgley suggests that "the hypocrisy of past ages was usually classical and dogmatic; the hypocrisy of this age is romantic and skeptical. We pretend *not* to know. Instead of trying to see, we shut the curtains and revel in the tragic darkness. . . ."[25] If, as readers, we orient ourselves differently than a deconstructionist would, then Jeffers' poem can be seen as an act of praise turned outward, and the primary motivation of the writer can be perceived as the desire to give homage, to thank. Stanley Cavell has pointed out there is an etymological link between thinking and thanking, and he sees this notion as central to Emerson, one of Jeffers' early heroes.[26]

The will to write, then, can be linked to the desire to thank, and "Return" may be seen as an expression of thanks. In considering such an expression, we do not regard it primarily as a linguistic structure whose verbal complexities call attention to its own problematic status as language. Or rather, we can think of it this way but conclude that it would be clearly perverse to do so. The purpose of an expression of thanks is to thank, and we can judge it on how well it does that job. The poem can appropriately be said to be about language in the sense that it is an exploration of how we can use language to express thankfulness. But this view of language would be far from the introversion of the poststructuralist paradigm. In other words, as critics we can focus on how language carries out the intention of the writer to praise and how well he convinces us that an object worthy of praise exists, or we can become fixated on how language reflects only itself and its inability to register an external world. As Jeffers himself said when pondering whether beauty exists in the outer world or only in our minds, there is no external proof either way. But there are practical consequences, both psychological and environmental, in choosing one view over the other. From the standpoint of complete subjectivity, everything, as Nietzsche remarks, is permitted. But from an environmental standpoint, clearly everything is not permitted. The external world presents possibilities and constraints that we ignore at our peril.

To interpret the poem as a successful act of praise or expression of thanks requires a recognition of the limitation of the poststructuralist conventions for reading. To say that most literary texts are self-reflexive in some degree does not require us to say that they are *only* self-reflexive, just as to say that humans are in some ways alienated from nature is not to say that alienation is their only mode of relation. The allure of such dogmatism may be strong, but it can be resisted.

A close look at the text of "Return" will suggest some of the ways in which the writing turns outward. In the last two lines of the poem Jeffers has done something unusual and important, I think. A return to an archaic mood of relationship with the natural world, almost a kind of animism, is enacted within a modern geological perspective. Jeffers' archaic diction in ". . . noble is the mountain, oh noble / Pico Blanco . . ." invites an ironic reading. It is truly nostalgic (in the pejorative sense of Derrida) because it attempts to re-enact an animistic viewpoint at a moment in history when such a viewpoint is hard to take seriously. But Jeffers reverses the irony by linking the animist stance with a geologic view of the mountain that "reanimates" our wonder at its nobility. The coastal mountain Pico Blanco is seen as a "sea wave of marble." It is a sea wave, first visually, and then conceptually, in the sense that it was formed into its wavelike shape when the rock that composes it was plastic like the ocean. The beauty of a metaphor that thus partakes of a modern scientific view of natural process inspires a renewed feeling of wonder about the world, but based on a sense of unity rather than the fragmentation that science often engenders. Jeffers is able to connect the pagan spirit of place worship to the objective spirit of science—they are both avenues to value—and in this sense the poem is in no way nostalgic. The "return" of the title is a return to the satisfactions of a unified or organic vision, but it is a new vision, and as such a recovery of the old emotion on new terms. The poem is a dramatic enactment of the satisfaction of the desire for worship. Jeffers has not expressed his frustration but rather his fulfillment.

If we can see a Jeffers text as an act of mind achieving satisfaction amidst great obstacles, then his value becomes clearer. Consider, for example, these two lines from a late poem: "It is only a little planet / But how beautiful it is."[27] Here Jeffers absorbs the

Copernican revolution, the phenomenon that began the displacement of humans from the center of the universe, and finds that it
can be a source of value. The lines move us from the humanist to
the inhumanist vision. The first clause places the earth and humans in a new perspective, and the attitude it dramatizes toward
what is seen is strikingly novel. Jeffers sees the diminution of the
earth relative to the rest of the universe as a reason for valuing it
in a new way; it is no longer just the old antagonist, the howling
wilderness that must be colonized and dominated. We can now use
language in reference to the world that would normally be used to
refer to a vulnerable child; the implication is that the attitude of
care we adopt toward a child is now appropriate, almost required,
toward the earth. Certainly the earth seems small and vulnerable
when we see it floating isolated in space and when we have the
capacity to destroy it. The injunction to subdue the earth, characteristic of traditional Western culture, is turned inside out. The
scientific view has, ironically enough, converted the earth into an
object of tenderness. The diminution of the earth has only highlighted its abiding value—its beauty. In the context of the lifeless
agglomerations of gas and stone that are its closest neighbors, its
beauty becomes more precious.

Again, in these lines, thinking is tranformed into thanking. The
great blow to the human-centered conception of the universe
becomes an occasion for praise. The lines quietly and serenely
turn outward. In them is dramatized the turn toward inhumanism.

This inhumanist turn is eloquently expressed in poem after
poem by Jeffers. I conclude by offering a reading of one of the
representative lyrics; I hope that I can demonstrate through it an
approach that will make visible the rich values available in his
work.

OH, LOVELY ROCK

We stayed the night in the pathless gorge of Ventana Creek, up the
    east fork.
The rock walls and the mountain ridges hung forest on forest above
    our heads, maple and redwood,
Laurel, oak, madrone, up to the high and slender Santa Lucian firs
    that stare up the cataracts
Of slide-rock to the star-color precipices.
                                  We lay on gravel and
    kept a little camp-fire for warmth.
Past midnight only two or three coals glowed red in the cooling
    darkness; I laid a clutch of dead bay-leaves

On the ember ends and felted dry sticks across them and lay down
    again. The revived flame
Lighted my sleeping son's face and his companion's, and the vertical
    face of the great gorge-wall
Across the stream. Light leaves overhead danced in the fire's breath,
    tree-trunks were seen: it was the rock wall
That fascinated my eyes and mind. Nothing strange: light-gray
    diorite with two or three slanting seams in it,
Smooth-polished by the endless attrition of slides and floods; no fern
    nor lichen, pure naked rock . . . as if I were
Seeing rock for the first time. As if I were seeing through the flame-
    lit surface into the real and bodily
And living rock. Nothing strange . . . I cannot
Tell you how strange: the silent passion, the deep nobility and
    childlike loveliness: this fate going on
Outside our fates. It is here in the mountain like a grave smiling
    child. I shall die, and my boys
Will live and die, our world will go on through its rapid agonies of
    change and discovery; this age will die,
And wolves have howled in the snow around a new Bethlehem:
    this rock will be here, grave, earnest, not passive: the energies
That are its atoms will still be bearing the whole mountain above:
    and I, many packed centuries ago,
Felt its intense reality with love and wonder, this lonely rock.[28]

This poem is an example of how Jeffers can dramatize the
emergence of value from a contemplative stance toward nature. It
is an enactment of the inhumanist vision, a model for the mind
finding value and satisfaction outside itself.

The movement from the flatly declarative first sentence
through the rapidly accelerating rhythm of the second creates a
sense of significance. One is drawn out of oneself as one's eyes are
drawn up the valley walls to the precipices and as the line itself
rushes onward to its conclusion with no resting place for the voice.
The language here is both ordinary and mythic; the firs "stare" in
the only figure Jeffers employs, yet we are in the realm of the
numinous. The first sentence is matter-of-fact; only a hint of
something beyond the ordinary is suggested by "pathless." The
word literally indicates that the poet is entering a wilderness, but
"pathless" also comes to refer to an opportunity to explore a new
realm of experience.

The next five lines describe a static scene but manage to infuse it
with a sense of motion or tension. The rock walls are actively
hanging the forests one on top of another as if the scene were a
display in a gigantic gallery, and as if it took energy to hold them
there. The trees "stare" upward, as do the poet and the reader;

the whole scene seems to be reaching. It is one scene, one immense but unified manifold of sensation: the different kinds of trees seem with the rock to compose one transcending entity for which there is no name. This entity, while possessing a powerful unity, is also richly diversified. We are disoriented—one forest on top of another—and the whole scene is superhuman in scale. But despite the scale there is an inherent order, expectant, and yet in a sense already fulfilled, and astonishing too in the economy of means with which this has been accomplished.

The second stanza is abruptly calmer and returns us to the human scale—a father camping with his son. The first nine lines of the second stanza are perfect; Jeffers' own particular economy of language is well illustrated here. It is easy to take language like this for granted in Jeffers. His description of his actions around the campfire unerringly builds up the picture of consciousness composing itself, making itself still and transparent. The language is completely uninflected and yet the little motions Jeffers makes come to seem like the gestures of a religious ceremony. More accurately, perhaps, they seem like the original gestures that will come to comprise a ritual in some future religion. These are the lucky, spontaneous motions that only later will be seen to have invoked the epiphany. It is possible for anyone; it requires no priest, only the attentive mind. There is a feeling for the man and the two boys *in* the setting; the human tenderness that is implied in the situation is not opposed to the setting but enhanced by it. An atmosphere of human love is already evoked as Jeffers fulfills his responsibilities as a father. But, while the human attachments are important, Jeffers moves quickly beyond them. In the next lines the boys and rock wall are both seen as valuable; indeed, the rock is characterized as having a childlike innocence or earnestness.

The key point that Jeffers builds to is the notion of a fate going on outside our own. He sees the rock as having certain virtues, like constancy or endurance, that we can understand, but he avoids mere sentimentality because his affirmation is so restrained and muted. It is a small moment, perhaps, but an intense one, and it is on such moments that the inhumanist vision rests. By making himself very quiet and attentive, Jeffers is able to appreciate a state of being different from his own, a state of being entirely other, and yet not alien, even a stimulus to love. The rock is seen as both "light-gray diorite with two or three slanting seams in it," and as an entity exhibiting passion, nobility, and loveliness. The language of geology and the language of feeling can both apply, but each alone is too limited. The poem does not assert the absolute truth of its own description, but represents an act of mind. The act of mind serves as a model for how to apply alternate descriptions in order to reflect value that eludes a single mode or expression.

In "Oh, Lovely Rock," Jeffers dramatizes the experience of feeling the reality and value of an objective world. He exercises an "impassioned empiricism," to borrow a phrase Santayana used in describing the thought of William James. Our glimpse of the world revealed by this impassioned empiricism should not be blocked by restrictions on the modes of critical inquiry that stem from the fashionable skepticism of our day. Another lonely twentieth-century realist, Alfred North Whitehead, suggests the motivation for constantly trying to revitalize the notion of an objective world and the value inherent in it: "It appears . . . that we are *within* a world of colors, sounds, and other sense-objects, related in space and time to enduring objects such as stones, trees, and human bodies. We seem ourselves elements of this world in the same sense as are the other things which we perceive. . . . My point is, that in our sense experience we know away from and beyond our own personality."[29] This is the fundamental intuition from which Jeffers also starts. I submit that knowing away from and beyond ourselves is the necessary precondition for any sane environmental policy, as well as the very state of sanity itself.

Jeffers believed that "man is a part of nature, but a nearly infinitesimal part; the human race will cease after a while and leave no trace, but the great splendors of nature will go on. Meanwhile most of our time and energy are necessarily spent on human affairs; that can't be prevented, though I think it should be minimized; but for philosophy which is an endless research of truth, and for contemplation, which can be a sort of worship, I would suggest that the immense beauty of the earth and the outer universe, the divine nature of things, is a more rewarding object. Certainly it is more ennobling. It is a source of strength: the other of distraction."[30] Jeffers' poetry too can be a source of strength, but only if we are strong enough to read it with what he called the "whole mind."

NOTES

1. William Everson, foreword to *The Double Axe and Other Poems*, by Robinson Jeffers (New York: Liveright, 1977), xiv.

2. James Dickey, *Babel to Byzantium: Poets and Poetry Now* (New York: Ecco Press, 1981), 188.

3. Leo Marx, "American Institutions and Ecological Ideals," *Science* 170 (1970): 946.

4. *The Selected Letters of Robinson Jeffers*, ed. Ann N. Ridgeway (Baltimore: Johns Hopkins University Press, 1968), 286n.

5. Ibid., 262.

6. *Crisis in Eden: A Religious Study of Man and Environment* (Nashville, Tenn.: Abingdon, 1970).

7. Ibid., 140.

8. J. Hillis Miller, "Nature and Linguistic Moment," in *Nature and the Victorian Imagination*, ed. V. C. Knoepflmacher (Berkeley and Los Angeles: University of California Press, 1977), 440.

9. Robinson Jeffers, *The Double Axe and Other Poems*, xxi.

10. Jacques Derrida, "Structure, Sign, and Play in the Discourse of the Human Sciences," in *The Languages of Criticism and the Sciences of Man: The Structuralist Controversy*, ed. Richard Macksey and Eugenio Donato (Baltimore: Johns Hopkins University Press, 1970), p. 272.

11. Geoffrey Hartman, *Saving the Text: Language/Derrida/Philosophy* (Baltimore: Johns Hopkins University Press, 1981), v.

12. Jeffers, *The Double Axe and Other Poems*, xxi.

13. Hartman, *Saving the Text*, 20.

14. Ibid., 23.

15. D. H. Lawrence, *Selected Literary Criticism*, ed. Anthony Beal (New York: Viking Press, 1966), 148.

16. *The Selected Poetry of Robinson Jeffers* (New York: Random House, 1959), xiv.

17. Quoted in Melba Berry Bennett, *The Stone Mason of Tor House: The Life and Works of Robinson Jeffers* (Los Angeles: Ward Ritchie Press, 1966), 76.

18. Hartman, *Saving the Text*, 23.

19. *Selected Poetry*, 576.

20. Miller, "Nature and Linguistic Moment," 445.

21. Jeffers, *The Beginning and the End and Other Poems* (New York: Random House, 1963), 50.

22. Jeffers, *Selected Poems* (New York: Random House, 1965), 94.

23. *Selected Poetry*, xv.

24. Ibid., 459.

25. Mary Midgley, *Beast and Man: The Roots of Human Nature* (New York: New American Library, 1980), 261.

26. Stanley Cavell, "Thinking of Emerson," *New Literary History* 1 (1979): 172.

27. *The Beginning and the End and Other Poems*, 29.

28. Tim Hunt, ed., *The Collected Poetry of Robinson Jeffers: Volume Two, 1928–1938* (Stanford: Stanford University Press, 1989), 546–47.

29. Alfred North Whitehead, *Science and the Modern World* (New York: Macmillan Co., 1967), 89.

30. *Selected Letters*, 342.

Robinson Jeffers' Ordeal of Emergence

William Everson

I: *CALIFORNIANS*

The justification for reissuing any immature work by a major artist lies chiefly in one thing: what it can tell us of the greater achievement to come. And this is so because there is no more mysterious and fascinating moment in human creativity than the transformation of a tentative and groping artist into a powerful and accomplished one. This fascination overrides all the objections, legitimate though they be, which can be brought against the policy, even though that policy, on the face of it, seems to patronize mediocrity.

The protest that the recent reissue of Jeffers' first book, *Flagons and Apples,* does his career a disservice at the present time is tenable. But so poignant is our need to share whatever light can be thrown upon the crystallization of the man's major achievement that it overrules our reservations. We brush aside the obvious objection in our need for background material pertinent to the greater work itself. For instance, I have heard it maintained that the qualitative gulf between Jeffers' early and late work is one of the most emphatic in all literature. This is untrue, but until now the reader has had no way of estimating such a break. *Flagons and Apples* has simply not been available.

When I was approached, therefore, to write the introduction to the present volume, Jeffers' second, I found myself more confident than I might otherwise have been. My satisfaction with the reissue of *Flagons and Apples* had dispelled whatever lurking apprehensions the rumored reissue of *Californians* gave rise to. And in this new confidence I found myself wanting to look at the book not from the perspective of Jeffers' mature work, where I know its

Reprinted from *On Writing the Waterbirds and Other Presentations: Collected Forewords and Afterwords, 1935–1981,* ed. Lee Bartlett (Metuchen, N. J.: Scarecrow Press, 1983), 182–225, 232–58.

value lay, but to see it as he wrote it, see it from the point of view
within which he poured it out. For an artist rarely sees his future
course when he writes; he sees the immediate vision. Composing
at white heat, he creates out of the awesome impetus of a masterpiece being born. In his view it *is* a masterpiece, and it is terminal,
final. He subsumes his whole past as he produces, which is what
gives it its absolute character. Unfortunately that sense of psychological absoluteness accounts as much for its faults as it does for
any virtues which may survive in it. Before a man's sensibility
matures nothing is more total than his conviction of the ul-
timateness of what he does. The adolescent poet pours out his first
poem to his first girl and is convinced by the totality of his feeling
that both the girl and the moment are immortal. And he is right;
for his moment is archetypal, and hence is indeed immortal. It is
only *what he makes of it* that crumbles with time and fades.

So I began *Californians* seeking to reexperience Jeffers' impetus
as he wrote it. This volume I had avoided all the years of my study
of Jeffers because I never had the need to approach it from so
basic a point of view. Granted, it stood in the open stacks at the
Fresno Public Library when I foraged downtown from Fresno
State to expand my knowledge of this prophet who hit me so hard
that he changed the direction of my life. But even then I knew
Californians could not serve my need, and I did not care to dilute
the purity of revelation by lacing it with conventional predecessors. Lawrence Clark Powell's synopsis of it in his basic book on
Jeffers contented me. I think I was right. When the present publisher sent it to me, I unwrapped the rare package with curious
respect and began to read it in the light of the newly tasted *Flagons
and Apples.* I felt immediately, of course, that I was witnessing a great
step forward in the evolution of a poet. But that of itself meant little.

However, it was not surprising that despite my good intentions
I was unable to read *Californians* at the hoped-for level of involvement. Only a little of that came through: an increase of craftsman-
ship brought about by a focusing of intellectual energy, and hence
a more elaborate diction than is evident in *Flagons and Apples;* the
marmoreal presence of conventional meters, and out of it a kind
of formal authority, tending inevitably toward the creation of
"memorable lines," a value that our current "projective verse"
movement has pretty much discarded.

And in fact when Jeffers published *Californians* in the midteens
the modernist revolution that would lead to our current proj-
ectivist emphasis in poetry was already launched. Imagism was in
the air, denoting the need for a more explicit diction to replace
the idiom of the period that was even then proving exhausted in

the hands of the Georgians. But in *Californians,* Jeffers, using that idiom, seems quite unaware of the threat. He has no sense of a man writing in a beleaguered mode, a mode on the verge of exhaustion, one that has to be insisted upon against the rising star of innovators. Obviously, he feels his medium is adequate to his message, and obviously the best work of the book rests in that feeling. What we have is the effort of a worthy poet striving, as every committed poet does, to bend a fit instrument into transcendent use, and in the better passages he succeeds:

> *Odi et amo!* "Loving thee I hate!"
> The tenderest fieriest mouth of Roman song
> Cried to his strumpet-goddess from the long
> Passion, the wild desire, the vain regret,
> Cried to his strumpet-goddess—greater wrong
> Urges who cries to men: For love of you
> Hatred of all exceeds my love of few!
>
> (Maldrove, IX)

Taken in stride, even the jarring final rhyme seems lifted out of constriction, as we see such rhymes often lifted in, say, Shakespeare, by the sense of plenitude invested in a marriage with the idiom, giving the supremely confident poet his stretch of freedom. In *Californians* Jeffers is no Shakespeare; but it is apparent that he often feels the exultation of one.

As I say, then, well-intentioned as was my original resolve to read the work as Jeffers wrote it, I soon began to encounter elements that swept me forward into the greater work ahead: prefigurements, parallels, a recurrence of evocative devices that here exist principally *in potentia*. Looking back on them from the plateau of the higher achievement, there indeed seemed a lack of finality in these initial manifestations. And I began to recognize that even after making allowance for the idiom of the period this lack of finality, increasing as one progresses, emerges as the chief limitation of the volume.

For instance, the hermit in "Stephen Brown" is clearly the prototype of the later "A Redeemer" and "An Artist," but Jeffers does not yet know what to do with him. Emilia, of the poem by that name, dances alone as Tamar will later dance, but Emilia's decorous sarabande has no issue. In this poem, too, her sister invokes the rain-glutted road to welcome respite from a persistent lover. Jeffers would use it later, chiefly in the prologue to "The Women at Point Sur," where Myrtle Cartwright seeks out her profane love because her husband cannot return across the bridge-spewing coastal creeks, and likewise young Howren's mother's false vision in *Such Counsels You Gave to Me* touches Jeffers' sense of isolation from the world which rain on the road seems to evoke in him. Then there is the astonishing prefigurement, to one familiar with the later work, in "The Vardens," where the death cry of the father dissociates itself from the flesh and soars, harkening ahead to Jeffers' unprecedented depictions of souls-at-death in *Cawdor* and "At the Birth of an Age." But in "The Vardens" the poet has not yet got the cosmic sense to clinch the issue in a true catharsis. All is as yet earthbound, swaddled in sentience. The amorphousness of earth and the earth-mood maintains an unquestioned authority over his poet's soul, and he cannot really spread his wings. As I read on I wondered, why? The religious spirit is here, the pantheism and, yes, the mysticism. All are here, indeed. But the spirit remains unliberated.

But it was "The Three Avilas" that made the underlying implication of these prefigurements really jolt my mind. For in this poem Jeffers touched the ancient theme of incest, always so powerful a symbolic subject for him, touched it for the first time, the theme that gave his breakthrough-to-come such a smashing impact on his period, and the one which stimulated much speculation as to the meaning of his preoccupation with it. Some have accused him of morbidity, which is not surprising, but in a recent essay Robert Brophy touches on its correspondence to Shelley's use in "The Cenci" and, in relating it to the great tradition, gives each poet a clean bill of health.

> In the case of both Shelley and Jeffers, incest as a dramatic device comes not from a prurient mind as much as from an artist's precise need for a structure-shattering symbol.[1]

No one reading "Tamar" today can doubt the justness of this conclusion. But in reading "The Three Avilas" something very different emerges. In this first use of incest Jeffers has no such objectivity as "Tamar's" theme to discipline his direction. The same earthbound mood that invests the whole volume shows the incestuous motif as something more deeply subjective, more intimately involved in the dynamics of the poet's own psyche. On the basis of it one is compelled to question Brophy's conclusion and ask: Is it possible that with Jeffers the motif comes not from the need for a structure-shattering symbol, but from an incestuous mind?

I believe that it is. But in conceding it, one wishes to precisely limit the implications, otherwise we find ourselves back at the discredited attribution of a prurient mind, not to speak of a sick one. Clearly such an attribution oversimplifies the profound psychology of the artist. For the deeper psychological analysis probes the poet's soul, the more it finds that its workaday categories of normalcy and aberration are subsumed in a far deeper dimension.

First of all, "The Three Avilas" is a confessional poem in the way that "Tamar" is not, and therefore stands upon another footing. The crucial part of the poem is addressed directly to the poet's wife, Una, and it is startling, from our wary, post-Freudian point of view, to observe Jeffers—in a poem about incest, mind you—addressing Una as his sister!

Now it is obvious, of course, that Jeffers, in "The Three Avilas," uses incest strictly as the analogy of his sense of personal misconduct. In the narrative he describes how a brother and sister, reared separately in Mexico, learn of their blood relationship only after they have already fallen deeply in love. Rather than renounce each other they flee to the California coast, but ere long are pursued by a vengeful brother and dispatched forthwith in an execution-murder. As outlined, the plot is unalloyed melodrama.

But Jeffers then recalls how he and Una themselves fell in love before they could be said to be aware of the consequences, giving rise to the conjecture that when Jeffers first beheld Una in class at the University of Southern California he might well have been smitten before realizing she was a married woman. At any rate they too, he tells us, in the full recognition of their adultery, decided to opt for consummation rather than the prescribed moral code, and themselves came to this same "spot of incest," the dank, weed-grown defile near Carmel. Here, the poem narrates, every day Jeffers and Una paused to rest while carrying driftwood back from the beach, and here, he further tells us in his note to the poem, the foreboding place so touched his spirits that the poem "grew up like a plant from the ravine described in it." In other words, daily pausing here to rest, surrounded in that dank nook that he populates, in the best Gothic tradition, with bloated toads, bats, tank weeds, slimy fungus, and blood-swollen sunsets, the trouble in him, his problem of conscience, stirs awake. He conceives this tale of incest in order to set down something about Una and himself that he could touch in no other way.

Limited to this bare outline, what the poem states is no more than that the forbidden love of Avila and Marina (incest) finds a correspondence in the equally forbidden love of himself and Una (adultery). But what the diction, the urgency, the creative involvement reveals is something far deeper—namely that in the rifts of his unconscious, his own love for Una is recognized as itself something incestuous. To Una he says, revising the place where in his imagination the inces' of Avila and Marina occurred:

> Lie still and stir not! while I quietly
> Tell my deep heart's own sister, my desire
> And dear delight, your living misery.
> O sister of my heart, . . .

(Verse 21)

Then, after narrating the course of the incestuous lovers, he exclaims:

> O, do you see in hardly alien fate
> Our imaged own? We also are come from burning
> The world behind us . . .
>
> My deep heart's dear one sister and lone mate,
> Yes we would weep—but would we long go mourning—
> Were it not also joy—if us like them
> One tree had borne, twin-blossoms of one stem?

(Verse 28)

In declaring that even if he and Una had learned too late that they were brother and sister they would likewise not have forgone physical passion, Jeffers is saying psychologically that Una is his sibling. In his crisis of conscience he is all but declaring that their adulterous love is the incestuous love of brother and sister.

Nor does the matter end there. For psychology tells us as well that the physical love of brother with sister is actually the Oedipus complex operating at an imponderably deep level. Sexual union of brother and sister is symbolically the sexual union of son with mother. Not only so, but psychology also tells that the passion of an unmarried youth for a married woman, and in this case a woman his senior, is itself oedipal. No matter what construction he puts upon it, she is in fact a maternal symbol. No prudent psychologist, of course, would declare such an oedipal ingredient to be necessarily the ruling motive in such a liaison. But he would nevertheless insist on its presence, and if any objective evidence emerged in the course of analysis to back up his hunch, he would not hesitate to elevate an underlying ingredient to the position of a ruling motive. Reading "Tamar," this hypothetical psychologist would be tempted to see such evidence in the poem's incestuous theme. Reading "The Three Avilas" he would have no doubt.

What I am seeking to trace is the genesis of a major artist who could create an objectively universalized statement like "Tamar" out of a subjective confessional theme like "The Three Avilas." And I do not use the word "confessional" in a pejorative sense. In that poem Jeffers without doubt was disburdening his soul of the guilt of an objective sin, adultery. By hindsight we can see that he was doing so because his creative destiny demanded that the incestuous ingredient in his adultery be resolved at the personal level before he could later approach the archetypal implications of the theme in "Tamar." What I am suggesting is that below his relationship to Una the current of that universal volition (incest) ran through his relation to his mother, but beyond her to the even deeper dimension, the secret clue to the inner life of any artist. Erich Neumann in his "Leonardo da Vinci and the Mother Archetype"[2] has dealt at length with the artist's closeness to the archetypal feminine as ruler of the creative unconscious, and of the rewards and perils of him who by destiny is launched upon the artistic vocation. What "The Three Avilas" affords us is a perspective from which the convergence of two strains, the personal and the archetypal, can be glimpsed.

Does art, then, defer to the hypothesis of psychoanalysis? It does not. "Tamar" exists. "The Three Avilas" exists. We estimate each on the basis of its relative aesthetic achievement, asserting that "Tamar" is primary whereas "The Three Avilas" is not. But we have already seen that the principal reason for studying the preliminary work of a master is not so much for what it is in itself, but for what it presages about the greater achievement to come. What, then, can "The Three Avilas" tell us about "Tamar," save that each concerns incest? It is the answer to this question that throws us back on the motivating psychology of the poet, and therefore upon his biography. For clearly, the two poems are not saying the same thing.

In my essay "Archetype West"[3] I spoke of Jeffers as the prophet par excellence of the Western movement, and I placed its apotheosis in "Tamar." I wrote of that poem's long societal preparation, stating that Jeffers' historic moment could not have been better. I further affirmed that neither could the moment in his own soul have been better:

When the mother of Robinson Jeffers died in 1921, liberating, as the death of the mother so often does, the creative energy fixated in the soul of her son, the breakthrough poem which Jeffers poured out gave the Western archetype its fiercest clench and its prospective apotheosis.

And I went on to conjecture that:

The long life of the mother forced him to bank his interior fires, enduring her omnipresence till death could grant him release from the unconscious maternal authority over his soul.

The point has been questioned, if not challenged.[4] What I meant was that when an artist espouses a formerly married woman older than himself, clearly his moment of psychic leave-taking of the maternal archetype has not yet arrived. His body is mature—it needs physical confirmation on the being of a woman—but his soul is still nascent, still hovering under the long maternal nurturing, still being fed on the evocative and sentient maternal instigation, so that to take, in a woman, a mother in the bride, is to instinctively prolong the maternal nurturing, even as he enters manhood in the taking of his mate. Not having yet read *Californians* I went on to say:

Thus two inferior books enabled him to jettison the purely cultural overlay of received poetic forms and be free for a new technique when his breakthrough moment arrived.

This is true, but in the light of "The Three Avilas" it is distinctly secondary.

Actually, what the death of the mother does for such an artist is to open the way for his long-deferred entry into the patriarchy. Speaking symbolically, this means a transition from the childhood primacy of mood (the maternal) to the adult primacy of ideas (the paternal). Without doubt, not the least interest of *Californians* is that it shows Jeffers' intellect struggling to be born. Which of the symbolic patriarchal images available emerged to displace the primacy of the maternal, effect the transfer from mood to ideas that is traditionally the role of adolescence,[5] and which in the artist is generally deferred well into manhood, is difficult to say. Certain it is that his assimilation of the intellectual giants of his time—Nietzsche, Freud, Spengler—had been long augmenting.

Una herself, however, attributed the transformation to his contact with stone, one of the archetypal symbols of his verse. In a letter to Powell she wrote:

The conflict of motives on the subject of going to war or not was probably one of several factors that, about this time, made the world and his own mind much more real and intense to him. Another factor was the building of Tor House. As he helped the masons shift and place the wind- and wave-worn granite I think he realized some kinship with it, and became aware of strengths in himself unknown before. Thus at the age of thirty-one there came to him a kind of awakening such as adolescents and religious converts are said to experience.[6]

Because of its coldness and permanence stone is a patriarchal symbol, and constructive preoccupation with it undoubtedly was instrumental in preparing Jeffers for the crossover. But the year 1918 bore no poetry that we can point to as marking the crystallizing psychic event that "Tamar" manifestly is. For until the mother passes, actually or symbolically, these particular images are retained in the soul of the artist in a state of suspension. It is only when the mother herself releases the son that the complex is dispelled, and until that happens, there can be no accounting for the convolutions and thrashing of the poet's psyche in its struggle for liberation.

Some of these convolutions are dramatic in the extreme. Jeffers, facing prospect of death symbolized by America's entry into the First World War, threw himself into an extramarital love affair. He spells it out in "Mal Paso Bridge," one of the works in *Tamar and Other Poems* that obviously predates the title piece. No more telling revolt at Una's maternal grip on his life is possible. *But it was still the mother!* For his new love was herself a mother:

Under Mal Paso bridge the long-maned sea-waves
Beat up into the stream, on the other bank
A woman with a little child was standing,
Her daughter three years old, the woman's face
Though it seemed white against the storm was brown,
Her body and face I thought were beautiful
Her eyes and hair were stormier than the cloud,
I trembled when she turned her eyes upon me.

This act of violational liberation was at least partially efficacious in terms of the creative emergence I am tracing, for he attributes to it a major stylistic innovation in his work:

Therefore I swore to drink wine while I could,[7]
Love where I pleased, and feed my eyes

With Santa Lucian sea-beauty, and moreover
To shear the rhyme-tassels from verse.

Be it noted in this regard that in the collective unconscious the maternal image presides over the world of convention, whereas the image of the father presides over the world of principle. To shear the rhyme-tassels from verse is to cancel convention in a bid to live by creative principle. It was a salutary resolve, but as the work itself shows, it could not be truly liberating. The real moment had not yet arrived.

And indeed with the Armistice and the passing of the death-threat of war, the poet could truly begin his work of transformation, ready himself for the crossover. It would, however, take another three years. For truly, more than rhyme-tassels must be sheared; the umbilical cord itself must be cut. In the death of the mother the artist's own demeaning death is assimilated, and finally, and at terrible lengths—lengths of shame, lengths of doubt, lengths of debilitation and impotence—he can stand forth in the actuality of liberation and write his release. In charting the graph of the creative evolution of Robinson Jeffers, that release we know as "Tamar."[8]

But if the death of the mother can be credited with the release of a new dynamism in the poet, it cannot explain the radical change in tone, the mood that so markedly sets *Tamar and Other Poems* off from *Californians*. To explain it, the disillusionment following the war is most often adduced, but it seems like something far more personal must have occurred, some trauma, precipitating the soul into aspects of itself previously unsuspected.

In support of this there is an incident that Jeffers relates in "Come, Little Birds" from the *Be Angry at the Sun* volume of 1941. He describes a séance in which, through the help of a seeress, he is able to penetrate to the world of the dead, to Endor, as he calls it, after the biblical First Book of Samuel. In that account the seeress slaughters a calf to revive King Saul, stunned by the prediction of his death on the morrow. Jeffers, however, moves the calf-killing up to furnish the blood through which the spirits are summoned, as in the sheep-slaying to evoke the dead in the eleventh book of the *Odyssey*. Among those summoned appears his father. The prodigal asks forgiveness of the sire whose code he has offended, and indeed receives his absolution. But in the very same moment he meets the quintessential feminine spirit whose story, when he tells it, will launch him upon the course of his creative destiny. "I am Tamar Cauldwell from Lobos," she commands him. "Write my story. Tell them I have my desire."

The use of the calf in both accounts seems to indicate a merely literary situation employed by the poet, but he positively identifies the séance as having occurred in 1920, and there is indeed something about "Come, Little Birds" that carries the stamp of direct reporting. It might well be that at an actual séance the killing of a calf led Jeffers to make the association with the biblical Endor. In any case the incident is prefigured in *Californians* by the poem "The Year of Mourning."

Dedicated to his father and modeled on the classical elegiac form of Milton's *Lycidas*, the poem was written across the year 1915 following his father's demise the previous December. It is also dedicated to his daughter, Maeve, who had been stillborn the previous May. These two deaths he places together, almost as one. It is unquestionably the best poem in the book, and it tells us more about Jeffers' relation to his father than any other thing so far published. In the ninth part he asks:

> Shall I seek darker counsel, shall I take
> Resort to such as murmur in the gloom
> With tortured Pythian lips familiar names
> And tongues of mortal slumber? Must I fee
> That lost king's Endor-witch to answer me?

Then he writes as if he had indeed sought help of a medium, and indeed heard his father's loved voice, rejecting it as a mere projection of his own need. The whole incident is obviously rhetorical. But it is possible that such a medium actually lived near Carmel, that Una and Jeffers had heard of her. If so, she comes to mind when he writes the poem, but he rejects recourse to her.

But five years later, in the psychological impasse that a prolonged sojourn under the maternal hegemony imposes, with the long-deferred paternal blessing unavailable, guilty under the weight of his new adultery, with all of its incestuous overtones, and hungering deliverance into the positive intellectual crystallization that will transmute his impasse into relevance—it could well be that he sought out such a seeress. As I say, what he writes of this event has all the stamp of direct reporting, quite different from the dismissal set down in "The Year of Mourning." Now he does hear his father' voice, but he no longer discounts it as the projection of his own need. In "Come, Little Birds" he gives every evidence of accepting his father's presence as authentic.

And the actuality of such an event seems confirmed by an obscure passage that Jeffers excised from the manuscript of the poem "Theory of Truth." I looked at it in the Lockwood Memorial Library of the University of Buffalo, where together with a letter of presentation from Jeffers dated "Tor House, May, 1941," it is kept with the drafts of the other three unpublished poems that close the *Selected Poetry* volume of 1938. In the poem referred to, the struck-out passage follows the tenth line, the one beginning, "And godless Buddha . . ." The excised passage reads:

> By the Big Sur narrows I meet my father and mother—a dear friend
> "whom I will not name"
> And Cawdor perhaps and certain others. Cawdor is disillusioned
> and might tell Macbeth.

Above this is written, "I betrayed him to death, but not viciously. He laps the blood." But it is not clear to whom the reference is intended.[9] And finally there is a marginal note in parentheses that reads: "(In the same volume print "The Pit in the Pinewood," written in 1919)."

The introduction of this Big Sur Narrows incident into the poem is fortuitous and had to be excised. But that argues for rather than against a specific event.[10] Often the actual does obtrude into the creative vision simply because it *is* actual, but, as here, does not have sufficient relevance to survive in the speculative or aesthetic dimension of the completed poem. But doubtless this pertinence of actuality led Jeffers to directly recall the incident in "Come, Little Birds," as well as to employ the motif in the masque "The Bowl of Blood," all written about the same time. Clearly the approach of World War II was taking him back into something fearful and ominous in his past that he had long left quiet.

If the incident is indeed an actual event, and if Jeffers is correct in recalling (as he does in "Come, Little Birds") that the séance occurred in 1920, his mother was still alive. If he meant to write "I meet my father and daughter," as would seem most likely from "The Year of Mourning," the slip of the pen is most revealing. In that case he means "daughter," writes, "mother," and in "Come, Little Birds," introduces "Tamar"! Such is the awesome power of the eternal feminine in the soul of the poet.

But if Jeffers is wrong in his date—if indeed it was his mother's death early in 1921 rather than something in 1920 that induced him to actually seek out the seeress, as he declined to do in 1915 following his father's death, then his recall of almost twenty years later is equally revealing. And indeed from this point of view it matters little whether the incident actually occurred or not: it is the symbolism that is so telling about the disposition of the soul that evolves it. For he writes: *"By the Big Sur narrows I meet my father and mother. . . ."* But in the gestation of his art what emerges is not his mother in the flesh but his mother in the spirit, daughter of incest and spirit of holy violation, who burns pure because she burned beyond equivocation—Tamar Cauldwell of Lobos—who had only one thing to say to the world from beyond the grave: "Tell them I *have* my desire!"

To sum up, then, what emerges as the principal impression of a first reading of *Californians* by one long familiar with Jeffers' work is an emptying, or depotentiation, of the agonized Jeffersian landscape, a kind of insular unrealization that leaves it merely pastoral and inert. There is as much emphasis on actual place-names as would later occur, but they are approached from a different segment of the psychic hemisphere. The torment is quite lacking, and we hardly seem to be in the same world. One is left with the impression that if the mother's death did liberate the soul of her son into intellectual realization, something equally powerful, something twisted and misanthropic, awesome and terrible, had simultaneously occurred.

What the event was that changed the pastoral landscape of *Californians* into the tortured landscape of "Tamar" doubtless will never be certainly known. But unquestionably between the two works something radical and conclusive did occur. With the later work a new world has been entered, and it is truly "real" in a way that the natural landscape of *Californians* never is. I believe that this super-real unreality is the result of a direct penetration into the parapsychological dimension, the awesome reality of the world beyond.

For with Jeffers, as with Yeats, the depiction of the occult and preternatural has about it the authenticity of personal experience—not something derived from literary sources, but something experienced and accredited, something rendered as true and hence believable. Until other evidence emerges (and it may well be that the unpublished poem "The Pit in the Pinewood" holds the key) I myself will continue to place the transformation from the relativity of the real to the absoluteness of the unreal in a very definite "descent to the dead"—the poet's memorable encounter with the world beyond, the son's finding of the long-sought father, and the fiery liberation of the spirit of his mother, who loved him not only like a mother but like a lover, and, as true lover, became Tamar. If this conjecture is accurate it denotes a most significant change in names (Mother-Tamar), the lisp of the lover infusing in the name of his beloved both her sacred and her profane essences. Such a transposition would not at all be far-fetched. We have Jeffers' own statement that it was performed under the tutelage of that supremely accomplished mythical mother, the Witch of Endor.

Notes

1. "Tamar, The Cenci, and Incest," *American Literature* (May 1970): 241.
2. *Art and the Creative Unconscious* (New York: 1959), 3.
3. Reprinted in *Regional Perspectives: An Examination of America's Literary Heritage,* ed. by John Gordon Burke (Chicago: American Library Association, 1973).
4. I might as well acknowledge at the outset that my intuition regarding the liberation of Jeffers' creative spirit following the death of his mother is basically introspective, founded on my own experience. The increase in universality after my mother died in December of 1940 is evident in the turn taken by my writing shortly thereafter. Quite unaware of any connection between that death and my literary activity, the course of later psychological investigation brought home to me how marked a turning point in my creative life it was. I cannot apologize for the introduction of subjective criteria here, because in the absence of something more concrete, introspection must suffice.
5. As in the immortal refutation of the Christ-child, when at puberty, missed from the caravan returning to Galilee, he was found by his parents in the temple back in Jerusalem conversing with the elders:

> And when they saw him they were amazed: and his mother said unto him, Son, why hast thou thus dealt with us? behold, thy father and I have sought thee sorrowing.
> And he said unto them, How is it that ye sought me? wist ye not that I must be about my Father's business?
> And they understood not saying which he spoke to them.
>
> (Luke 2:48–50)

Christ was a man who had no time to spare, but it is not infrequent that the poet is unable to pronounce these words until he is in his twenties.
6. Lawrence Clark Powell, *Robinson Jeffers: The Man and His Work* (1940; reprint, New York: Haskell House, 1970), 17. The relevance of this statement gains immeasurably when one realizes that the words are Jeffers' own. A draft in the poet's hand survives at the University of Texas in Austin. He not infrequently had Una answer inquiries he felt too self-conscious responding to personally. Seen in this light, the episode emerges as a salient ingredient toward the solution we are pursuing.
7. In that "while I could" we see a tacit acknowledgment of the impetus of the death-threat behind his bid for liberation. I am not speaking of personal coward-ice, but of the youthful artist's need to hoard and preserve his vision until it is

written out. For truly the prophet who is threatened with death before he has divested himself of his message is an entirely different figure from the serene sage who steadfastly accepts death after he is well assured that his message is out of his guts and on its way in the world. When the citizens of his own city of Nazareth sought to hurl Christ from a cliff in the first year of his ministry, he extricated himself from their hands and vanished. But after his work was completed he permitted himself to be crucified despite Pilate's efforts to free him.

8. Unfortunately the actual date of composition is not known. In *The Colophon; No. 10,* his account of breaking into print, "First Books," Jeffers places the poem as "1920 or 1921." When queried by S. S. Alberts, his bibliographer, who doubted it would be that early, Una replied, "He says 1921 or 1922 for Tamar is the nearest he can recollect." Alberts then goes on to record the discovery of a fragment of preface dated June 1922, written by Jeffers for a collection of poems in which "Tamar" is not included. He concludes from this that it was not yet written. However, the dating of a preface is often adjusted to the anticipated date of publication rather than applying to the date of its actual composition. At any rate, in the prefatory fragment itself Jeffers speaks of developing a "rhymeless narrative measure of my own; but the poems are not finished and not included in this series." Since he uses the plural it is evident that the narrative work following "Tamar" was already begun, putting that poem already in the wrap-up state when the passage was written.

9. George Sterling seems most likely. In *The Overland Monthly* for November 1927, Jeffers gives his account of Sterling's death: "One night a year ago I dreamed about the interior of an ancient church, a solid place of damp stone about which the earth had crept up, beautiful in its ruin, somewhat like the Carmel Mission before they restored it. Sterling and I were there in the stone twilight, among many worshipers, and I said though it was pleasant we mustn't stay, it was time to return outdoors. But he preferred to stay, and I returned alone, and awoke. The afternoon after that night a newspaper reporter came to tell me that Sterling had died. We had not seen him for several months but were expecting a visit from him that week or the next."

10. Some will say that the poet's provisional interjection of such literary figures as his own Cawdor and Shakespeare's Macbeth demonstrated that the episode is completely fictional. I disagree. Rather I would say that the episode was real enough, as demonstrated by its forced intrusion into the scenario of "Theory of Truth," whereas the accommodation of such figures as Cawdor and Macbeth merely shows the poet's frantic attempts, caught unprepared by the precipitate intrusion of this archetypal event into his poem, to accommodate it into the thesis.

II: *THE ALPINE CHRIST*

In tracing the evolution of Robinson Jeffers the most important interval is the murkiest—the interval that changed him from an accomplished but stilted poet in *Californians* (1916) to a decisive and transcendent one in *Tamar and Other Poems* (1924). That interval has never come into focus. Jeffers had only slight interest in chronology—for him the message was all—and at least one poem written in 1918 appeared as much as twenty years later, when it came once more to his attention, and he saw a use for it.[7] Conversely, many truly significant poems relating to his creative development were never published at all. Until this potent but obscure interval is clarified, the emergence of the Jeffers we know will remain a mystery.

This book is a first attempt at the shaping process. It is one of two that will endeavor to bridge the transitional years by presenting available materials, published and unpublished poems alike, in viable sequence, structured so that the creative evolution is emphasized. This sequential approximation I have attempted to resolve partly by the dates assigned to certain pieces; partly by specific internal evidence in the work. But in the end it has been more my own sense of the evolving sensibility as evidenced from intangibles in the poems themselves that has guided me. In other words I have tended to trust what the poem is, its intrinsic spirit and mood and its level of precision of technique, more than I have trusted the specific dates assigned by later researchers, even when assisted by Jeffers himself. As I say, he cared little for chronology and would concede too much to the importunities of others hot on their particular theories. My own decisions cannot plague him now.

These decisions I have attempted to explain, if not justify, in my introduction and in my notes. But in the end it is my intuition of the whole picture that is most responsible for my placements. To do this I have had to enter deeply into the spirit of the verse. The fact that none of it is Jeffers' best has presented problems. Immersed in so much provisional verse, with sheer subjectivity playing so large a part in the overall estimate, it would be remarkable if I made no mistakes. For those guesses that future scholarship proves to be wildly wrong I apologize in advance. But for those that prove me only a little bit wrong, I say nothing at all. It is at best a risky business, and a near miss is as good as a hit.

Since writing the introduction to *Californians* a year ago a much clearer picture of Jeffers' evolution as an artist has come home to me. The better part of that year has been taken up with searching out, and weighing in depth, the unpublished material pertinent to the whole plan. But though I have a clearer picture, it does not make the writing of it any easier. With knowledge comes increased responsibility, a deepening irritation of detail, and a heckling indecisiveness. These clearly militate against strong and interesting writing; and in presenting work that Jeffers himself rejected the presentation is almost as important as the text.

Nevertheless, because the process has been fascinating to me, I hope something of that has crept into my writing. I truly believe the evolution of a major artist is of utmost importance, both for our understanding of his work, and for knowledge of humanity as a whole. Somehow we learn most about human nature from the lives of the most singular, idiosyncratic people; and of the singular people of our time few give greater pause than Robinson Jeffers. More than any other poet his awesome contradictions and his passionate transcendence of them are naked in his message. This, of course, is as it should be. The trouble is that the message stops you in your tracks.

Not here, however. What we have here is the work of a single year, 1916. In it we can see the forging of a soul, the soul of a man sensitive in the extreme, undergoing the purgation of a great loss and bracing himself for a terrible affront to his spirit: a war that fascinates even as it revolts him. Something in him is festering. Bearing an abscess that has yet to be lanced, he hungers blindly for the blade. We watch him suffer, but we cannot hand him deliverance. Only destiny can do that—and it will.

I am writing from a remote cabin on Long Ridge, the extended hump of mountain that separates Rocky and Bixby creeks on the coast south of Carmel. It is basic Jeffers Country. At the mouth of Bixby is the sheer headland that took the somber close of *Thurso's Landing*. Rocky Creek itself is Cawdor's canyon, and up the hill, on the far side of the slope above me, is the site of the great rock that Jeffers put there, transplanted in his imagination from the Sierra Nevada, to effect and memorialize the death of Cawdor's son, the fate-driven Hood. To the south are the abandoned Mill Creek lime kilns where Onorio Vasquez lived; and, late in the thickening loci of Jeffers narratives, the site of "Mara" lies hereabout. Nor are the literary associations exhausted by these specifically Jeffersian references. Down on Bixby is Ferlinghetti's cabin, where Jack Kerouac wrestled his midsummer demon and made it the source of his novel *Big Sur*.

It is early morning. The sun, peering over Mescal Ridge, leaves its near flank in shadow. The giant redwoods that line Bear Trap Canyon, huddled together without distinction, are deep in shade. I know that by noon each one will stand out like a green cone under the straight descending light. By nightfall the sun at my back, shining flatly through, will reveal the skeletal structure of trunk and paired limbs. That, however, is ten hours away. What I hope for today is to synthesize in writing my strongly diverse impressions of the most important Jeffers "find" that has come to light since the poet's death. I mean the lost lyrical drama, "The Alpine Christ." Reflection in depth can come later but what I need now is the uninterrupted flow of consciousness to pull together my clustering intuitions. For this I have given myself all day.

And it will take all day. My wife and child have driven into Monterey, there to see the sights and pick up a few supplies. When they return I have promised to broil a steak over open coals, and if this day has gone well, will yield myself at last to the ambience of evening. Now, feeling the stretch of solitude about me, the wide contemplative silence under the redwoods and out over the canyon, I have every hope of converting into clear energy-flow my fixity of absorption in this work, my race against time pulling the critical instinct into point-focus. Seated on the porch in a comfortable chair, a stack of books beside me on the plank floor and, on my knee, a pad of writing paper clamped to a board, I flip through the long sheets of "The Alpine Christ" a final time before I take up my pen.

Last night I read it in typescript—a xerox print of Jeffers' own copy—late into the night; and when I snuffed out the candle I felt that I had in my hands one of the purest documents we shall ever possess as to the shaping of the man's eventual attitude. This morning that impression holds. I believe future scholars will go to the final speech of Manuel with almost as keen an interest as they now go to Orestes' words closing "The Tower Beyond Tragedy." Orestes' declaration is far more important, no denying that, for it defines the place where Jeffers eventually arrived. But Manuel's speech, just as undeniably, defines the place from whence he got there. The difference between them holds the mystery of his evolution as an artist.

I have come to Long Ridge on vacation, impatiently bringing the typescript with me. I say impatiently for I have been working all year trying to assemble the lost Jeffers manuscript *Brides of the South Wind,*[2] the unpublished interim volume between *Californians* and *Tamar,* and on this vacation I hoped to get away from that. I needed to erase the poetry of Jeffers out of my head, so to speak, and recharge my energies on primal Jeffers landscape instead. But a series of delays has kept this particular manuscript out of my hands for a fortnight; nothing will do, therefore, but that the poem comes along as well. And that means also the published books of Jeffers, and the commentaries on Jeffers, and even the basic reference works, the tools a writer uses to forge the blade of his speech. All have gone into the Toyota with the skillet and axe.

I first encountered "The Alpine Christ" last winter. Peter Bartlett, publisher of Cayucos Books, commissioned me a year ago to do the introduction to *Californians,* which he was then preparing to reissue. Work on this led me to formulate a proposal for a Jeffers "Collected Poems" in the *Robinson Jeffers Newsletter,*[3] and this in turn put me on the track of the lost *Brides.* Peter and I set out to reconstitute it, insofar as that was possible, from surviving manuscripts in private holdings. In Alberts' *Bibliography of the Works of Robinson Jeffers* we noted references to *"An* [*sic*] *Alpine Christ"*[4] among the collection of John Hay Whitney, surviving on the versos of the holographs of two major narratives. Since Alberts' succinct description of the work cannot be bettered, I quote his summary in its entirety:

> Of *An Alpine Christ,* written in 1918, destroyed by R.J. in MS., Una Jeffers writes: *It was a long lyrical drama somewhat modeled after Shelley's "Prometheus." It was written during the war, and R.J. found it rather naive after consideration.* The poem was written as the first part of a projected poem to be called *Witnesses.*
>
> It is unfortunate that *An Alpine Christ* was destroyed, because it stands in a transitional position—in point of time at least,—between the poems of the early period and *Tamar.* The typescript of the poem consisted originally of 227 numbered sheets of white laid paper watermarked *Berkshire Parchment Linen U.S.A.,* 8¹⁵⁄₃₂ × 13¹⁄₁₆ inches, typewritten on one side only, double spaced. Thirty-two of these sheets, numbers 54, 84–85, 87–93, 99–101, 113, 118–122, 194, 216–227, on the versos of which portions of *Roan Stallion* and *The Tower Beyond Tragedy* were written, are extant, in the collection of John Hay Whitney. It is R.J.'s wish that these fragments remain unpublished.[5]

As far as anyone could expect, that was all we were ever likely to know about the specific configuration of "The Alpine Christ."

Though it does not occur in the table of contents of *Brides of the South Wind,* it seemed important to present "The Alpine Christ" in lieu of poems that are missing. We therefore sent for the pages, John Hay Whitney's gift to Yale, which were readily provided in reproduction by Donald Gallup, curator of the Beinecke Library there. The thirty-two pages seemed enough with certain other poems, to piece together a Part 1 for an interval volume of the *Brides* period, even though the *Brides* itself was clearly beyond recall.[6] With the sheets from Yale in hand (which I related to the

Californians period) I set the drama aside to get into the integral section of work we were tracing: the crucial years after America's entry into World War I, the breakover point in Jeffers' evolution as an artist.

But the deeper we got into the material surviving between *Californians* and *Tamar,* the more evident it became that an abundance of text, greater than the selective synthesis that Jeffers made for the *Brides* manuscript, in fact exists. This material actually falls into three parts. There is the post-*Californians* period, of which "The Alpine Christ" is most significant. There is the crisis of America's entry into the war, which centered around "Mal Paso Bridge" and a lost narrative "Peacock Ranch," and, finally, there is the postwar period leading up to *Tamar.* These three periods are clearly defined, so much so that they yearn to be clarified in distinct formats.

But "Peacock Ranch" refused to be found—by early summer only four pages of the typescript emerged on versos of other Jeffers poems. Besides the holdings at Yale, which include the surviving narratives up through *Give Your Heart to the Hawks,* the most important by far is the rich Tor House collection which went to the University of Texas at Austin. Cataloguing there not being complete, if the matter of "Peacock Ranch" were going to be resolved, I must see for myself. Late in July I boarded a plane for Austin.

At the Humanities Research Center at the University of Texas I found an old friend, Bill Holman, formerly chief at San Francisco Public Library, newly installed as librarian. There followed a halcyon three days, surrounded by congenial spirits and choice manuscripts. Hour by hour pouring over the drafts, papers, notes, sketches, bits and snippets that Jeffers left behind in Tor House when he died, I lived in a kind of intellectual transport. Those days stand out in my mind as a benchmark of biblio-poetic largesse.

Even so, after the first two days, it began to look as if, so far as anything major goes, my trip would prove inconclusive. There was everything I knew but little that I needed. Then, on the last day, working up through the final cards of the catalogue, I discovered, hidden on the versos of an early version of *The Women at Point Sur,* more of the self-same typescript that Jeffers used in writing *Roan Stallion* and "The Tower Beyond Tragedy." These versos are, of course, those of the typescript that carry the fragments of "The Alpine Christ" we received earlier from the Beinecke Library. I almost got down on my knees in gratitude to that angel who guides all seekers to the term of their desire. For it seemed to me that surely among such an abundance the illusive "Peacock" must survive.

I was cruelly mistaken. The more I pressed on, leafing the long legal-size sheets, the more hope dwindled. It was almost an anguish to turn up page after page of such quotidian stuff as "Coast Range Christ" and "Fauna," lengthy poems we already have in print—and, to be sure, "The Alpine Christ," but this I brushed aside at first in my impatience, for I knew from the Yale sheets that it looked back to the Jeffers of the past, whereas "Peacock Ranch" promised a gateway to the future, first of the powerful narratives of violence that were to become the singular Jeffers *forte*. Finally, to appease me, one page emerged, the opening page, and I thanked my angel for crumbs—but in fact I was deeply disappointed. Then, with a sigh, I began to go back over the bundle to see what it all amounted to. It was only at this point that I realized that I had before me over a hundred new pages of "The Alpine Christ."

This, of course, was staggering. And to tell the truth I was not too happy about finding it. Such a mass of material would simply overburden the opening part of the book I was fervently trying to reconstruct. I had no time to read it there, but ordered reproductions, and came back home. When "The Alpine Christ" pages finally arrived on the eve of my departure for Long Ridge, and I laced them together with the thirty-two pages from Yale, I found that of the entire drama we now have almost two-thirds. I then realized we had to issue our prospective Part I separately, as a distinct volume in its own right. Sheer bulk demanded it. *The Alpine Christ & Other Poems* rose naturally to mind for title.

It is, I see by the sun, midmorning, and I pause a moment to relax. I get up to go inside for a cup of lukewarm coffee left over from breakfast, but a stirring deep in my entrails tells me it is time for the morning ablutions. I start along the trail to the outhouse. It lies a hundred feet or so downslope from the cabin, and is built without a wall to the front, so that you can sit there and gaze out into tranquil space, the sunlight falling about you, and ease yourself as people have done for thousands of years before the invention of plumbing. It is, as always a relief to have the weight of so much dross taken from one, and, musing there in the aftermath of purgation, I let my gaze rove over the vast panorama before me. A lizard races around my toe and fixes me with unflinching eyes. I stare back at him unblinkingly and he moves on, impelled by a curiosity for marginal areas I deeply share. When I have finished the small ritual of cleansing, I stand up and fasten my clothes, then walk slowly back the trail to the cabin. Up in the yard I go under the redwoods where the spring is piped and wash my hands in the tin basin with a piece of soap. I toss the water into the ferns, and, not finding a towel, I wave my hands gently in the air to dry them. Going back to the cabin I get the lukewarm coffee I started for earlier. It is too savorless now to sip, so I gulp it down, then light a cigar. I could easily kill an hour or so like this, but soon put the cigar aside and get back into my chair. Crossing my legs with a sigh I take up my pen and pull together my thoughts.

Una Jeffers' letter to S. S. Alberts had noted, it will be remembered, that "The Alpine Christ" was based on Shelley's lyrical drama *Prometheus Unbound*. It is a work I have never read. Consequently I have taken along a copy from an 1861 set of English verse, for it gives the notes of Mrs. Shelley, and these prove useful in coming to terms with the poem. I spent the first day at Long Ridge reading it. As I sum it up in my mind preparatory to tackling the Jeffers, it seems evident that the real hero of Shelley's poem is not Prometheus but the Demogorgon, the being who represents primal power, and who effects the overthrow of the tyrant Jupiter. Prometheus's role is simply to hold firm under duress, endure until the moment of Demogorgon, the "moment of truth," arrives. And this is what Shelley conceived of as his own role. He was a social radical who scorned compromise, disdaining Aeschylus's reconciliation of Jupiter and Prometheus as a sellout. "I was averse," he tells us in his preface, "from a catastrophe so feeble as that of reconciling the Champion with the Oppressor of mankind." These are the sentiments today of all good protestors. Since Jeffers cited Shelley as his model I naturally looked to him to pick up on those implications.

But as it turned out in "The Alpine Christ" Jeffers has no interest in extending Shelley's revolutionary implications. True, he approximates the overthrow of Jupiter by Demogorgon to the overthrow of God by Fate, but it is no matter for celebration. Too much is being lost, too little is being gained. His mood is mournful, not celebrative. And it leaves his Promethean figure, Manuel, not liberated, but saddled with the immense responsibility of sustaining universal value alone. The archetype here is not the "freedom from God" of the eighteenth-century persuasion, which

Shelley was recapitulating, but rather the mournful "death of God" of the latter nineteenth, the disenchanted looking back from under the pall of industrialism and reductive scientism to the lost ambience of religion.[7]

Nor is the background of "The Alpine Christ" Greek. It derives from the Old Testament Book of Job, the familiar confrontation between God and Satan, and issues in a new lease accorded Satan to test mankind. Satan stirs up trouble in the Balkans, then extends it from a mere local conflict to a universal conflagration, World War I. Christ once again descends to save mankind, this time to be reincarnated in a half-witted deaf-mute named Manuel Rüegg. The encounter between Christ and Satan is enacted out in the Alps, situated above the military conflict, and Satan is defeated. But the testing of humanity rebounds on the testers, for the extremity of the conflict results in the jeopardy of all value, and occasions the emergence of that naked Fate which renders the concept of a beneficent God superficial and unreal. In the disappearance of God, Christ as Manuel is left alone, the Promethean figure remaining to assert Christian ethic as a kind of residual substantive value despite the disappearance of the Being from whom it derived. Jeffers clearly had a deeper outworking in mind, for "The Alpine Christ," as Alberts noted, is only the first part of a larger drama, to be called *The Witnesses*. But this was as far as he was able to develop it.

So it is apparent that Jeffers had no interest whatsoever in extending Shelley's revolutionary opportunities. In his drama the emergence of naked Fate to replace God was not an evolution, as Shelley saw it, but a devolution, the reduction of ideal value through a stripping away of illusion in anguish. Jeffers had no intrinsic interest in social reform. An idealist he certainly was, with a healthy interest in contemporary affairs, but he lacked social *passion,* the essential ingredient that gives Shelley's drama its creative force. Rather, Shelley's model gave him the opportunity for three things: the overthrow of God; the figure of Promethean endurance in spite of hopelessness; and a fresh (for Jeffers) literary vehicle in which to work out the implications, the lyrical drama, or as we call it today, the dramatic narrative.

Thus "The Alpine Christ" is significant in that it is the first instance we have of what would later become a powerful Jeffersian genre. Many times, later on, he would use it to body forth his ideas: "The Tower beyond Tragedy," "Dear Judas," "At the Fall of an Age," "At the Birth of an Age," "The Bowl of Blood." These stand apart from his true dramatic works such as *Medea* in that they were not intended to be staged. But whereas under the traditional ordering of Jeffers' poems the genre seemed a subdominant one that developed after the full flowering of his narrative skill ("The Tower Beyond Tragedy" follows, and is inferior to, "Tamar"), here it is evident that he mastered the idiom well before a comparable fluency with narrative skills was effected. "The Alpine Christ" simply dwarfs the tentative narratives in *Californians* which preceded it.

It is apparent, then, that Jeffers perfected his powers of dialogue before those of description. He would soon develop his descriptive powers in his lyrics, but the fusion of the two in narrative form would come last, though of course it stands as his chief achievement. But the power of dialogue is here so evident that it forces us to reevaluate its weight in his narratives. The fact that he created his mood through his descriptive power has tended to overshadow his skills of dialogue. "The Alpine Christ" demonstrates that those skills are primary, and the aptitude surfacing here for the first time probably accounts for the great success of his plays on stage.

Here in his first employment of dramatic narrative we can see its use for him. The form enabled him to touch on a number of diverse concerns that the limitations of straight narrative do not permit. Here, among purely fictional or mythological characters, Jeffers introduces historical events and contemporary figures at will. One encounters Francis Ferdinand, archduke of Austria; King Albert of Belgium; Roger Casement; Lord Kitchener; Oyama, the Japanese field marshal; Rupert Brooke; Queen Elizabeth of Rumania. Behind them we see the invasion of Belgium and the battle of Jutland. These concurrences indicate his intense interest in contemporary affairs. Truly basic, it was not something of an aftereffect emerging with the shift in focus occasioned by World War II, and sometimes associated with an alleged depletion of his creative power.[8] This also indicates how markedly the drift of contemporary affairs was responsible for his mood. Jeffers created his best work in a period of political stasis between the Treaty of Versailles and the Reichstag Fire. Both before and after, however, when war threatened the world, he was dragged down to the calendar of events, episode by episode, battle by battle. Critics have been distressed by this penchant, but Jeffers' acuity of reaction at least gives us a timing device, what we might think of as his personal Carbon 14 Dating Factor, enabling us to place with some accuracy the moments of his various wartime compositions.

This is especially helpful during the World War I period, emerging as our chief aid in enabling us to chart the matter of his creative evolution.

As a matter of fact, in "The Alpine Christ" that kind of specificity never becomes the ponderous limiting factor. What a fantastic vision Jeffers projects after the closed world of *Californians!* We are forced to advance his long-debated "intellectual awakening" by several years. For the first time we glimpse the vast cosmic sweep, Jeffers' eagle-vision, the blazing prophetic gaze. From the lofty vantage point of the Alps his eye sweeps across Europe. He sees the souls of the slain mounting up to heaven between the forces of preternatural evil and preternatural good. He sees God and Christ and Satan, and does not scruple to put words in their mouths, set deeds to their hands. He knows the passion boiling beneath the archetypes, and with powerful strokes he fleshes it in, bodies it forth. Wholly swept up in a new genre he makes it all live.

And it does live. Though Jeffers is as yet nowhere near his mature style, here for the first time he is cracking the mold of traditional verse in order to make it register the flow of his imagination. In this he is not yet following modernist precept, but is forging out a new instrument by dint of necessity. And it is exciting to see him at work. Certainly the poem has enormous flaws; it is forever lapsing through untried, haphazard forays, provisional solutions that have no issue. But it keeps rising again: it both limps and soars. A steadily recovering intuition is constantly lifting it back into the bid for consequence. The overall effect is impressive, even awesome. Last night, with its pages in my hand, I thought: if this poem had been published when it was written, before our modernist tenets completely unseated traditional verse practice, it would have been hailed as the most splendid attempt of the wartime interval. For sheer scale of ambition, no American poem of the period that comes to mind approaches it.

Looking up from my page I see by the sun that it is nearly noon (or, by daylight saving time, one o'clock) and time for lunch. I get up and go into the cabin and take out a loaf of bread and some cheese. Outside in the cooler over the spring are butter and milk, and in a bag under the eaves some apples and grapes. I make a sandwich and eat it slowly, gazing reflectively out in the void, thinking as I chew. A slight haze has thickened against Mescal Ridge, but the cool of the morning is not all dispelled. The distant redwoods, as I anticipated, stand out like phallic flames, each green core thrust at the sun. Bear Trap Canyon kinks its wrinkle up the groin of Bixby Mountain. Time seems to hang over the world, suspended. After my sandwich and milk I slowly peel an apple and munch it. I would like some raisins and nuts but I have none, and instead eat the grapes, crushing them refreshingly in my mouth, spitting out seeds. I remember how, as boys, we used to wander the vineyards of the San Joaquin, finding the bunches of grapes the pickers had missed, gulping them down, spitting seeds before us as we roved. When I finish my meal I walk a bit through the cool redwoods back where the road curves in. I freshen my eyes on another view, west toward the mouth of Bixby Canyon, and the level sea. Then I return and sit down to my work again. In my mind I gather together the threads of the poem, and pick up my pen.

In our estimate of Jeffers' creative development, the significance of "The Alpine Christ" lies in the deep identification between the passing of his father in death and the passing away of civilized values under the barbarism of war. The erosion of a belief in a personal God had long been accomplished, but its consequence was struck home only with the concurrence of the death of his father and the impact of war. Institutional Christianity had been living on momentum through the Victorian era, a complacency of belief in a situation of metaphysical vacuum.[9] The war exploded that vacuum resoundingly. Jeffers, well aware of the vacuum, but existing within it in a kind of unconscious ambience of post-Christian idealism, was equally unprepared. The conjoined death of his father and the breakup of civilization in war virtually overwhelmed him. "The Alpine Christ" makes this fact unmistakable.

The final words of Manuel, in Jeffers' mind, clearly constitute the quintessential Christian affirmation, the only kind of Christian he deems capable of surviving at all. But more than that, the deep commitment in Manuel's expression lets us know that this value is Jeffers' own in a way the speeches of Christ in "Dear Judas" never are. For the Gospel of Love has persisted in civilized values beyond the Death of God. Now this gospel as well was being rendered bankrupt on the battlefields of Europe. Both were being exposed as illusions—the religious ideal and the civilized ideal alike. The death of his father, the patrician, corresponded with the death of civilization, that is, the death of patrician values. In the poem "The Cloud," here presented, the depression Jeffers complains of is the cloud of culture shock that hit to the bone. The unconscious assumption of the received values of Christian civilization are, of course, everywhere evident in *Californians*, but the closing speech of Manuel in "The Alpine Christ" is important because the threat posed by war caused Jeffers to sum those values up with a nostalgic eloquence transcending his previous unconscious assumption of them, and that here makes them memorable.

In a letter dated 12 March 1927 to Donald Friede, who inquired about the drama he noticed on the versos of the *Roan Stallion* holograph just sent him, Jeffers reacted emphatically. "The Alpine Christ," he said, "was useless and absurd; written just ten years ago. It had some passages of poetry that I can easily understand may have caught your eye when you saw only fragments, but it was vitiated by essential absurdities—exaggerated importance attached to the war that was contemporary then—naïf use of Christian mythology—general childishness."[10] His repudiation of the poem, and all it stands for, is complete.

But that phrase "exaggerated importance attached to the war," while well enough said in the midtwenties when dismissal was his purpose in a world bent on forgetting its war, reveals the real depth of his involvement. For Jeffers was a scrupulous and close-mouthed man. When at last he exaggerates it is only because his reserve is overborne by his feelings. And in just such a way the phrase "naïf use of Christian mythology" is indicative. It denotes Jeffers' deep psychological adhesion to the values of Christianity, which were his father's values, even though the doctrine was manifestly abandoned. Thus when he sought to make a summing up of what the carnage of war was calling into jeopardy for him, he instinctively had recourse to the Christian *mythos* rather than the Greek one. This reveals how deeply held those values were, and how closely they were identified with the parental image. One of the most pathetic figures in the drama of the Alps is The Young Man Mourning For His Father, clearly Jeffers himself. When he dismisses all this as "childish" we can see how the childhood part of his soul was overwhelmed by the collapse of both image and ideal occasioned by the war. The pain was clearly incepted in "The Year of Mourning" in *Californians;*[11] it took another year for it to overflow in "The Alpine Christ." And on its heels came the dawn of the hard, bitter misanthropic will: Jeffers toughening himself against his own vulnerability.

Thus there is a basic interlock, a direct continuity between the final poems in *Californians* and the collection of verse here presented. It is an interlock of mood occasioned by the war that the early poems in *Californians* do not share. It is this continuity that makes the separate publication of what is a single entity so wrenching, requiring an act of creative synthesis on the part of the reader himself, the imaginative grasp to see the inner unity in the bibliothetic cleavage. But though the continuity between the two works is direct it is not thereby simple.

Four main strands can be detected. First there is the theme of the lost father and the collapse of ethical value, running from "The Year of Mourning" to its apotheosis in "The Alpine Christ." Next there are the tentative attempts to come up with alternative values, such as the "Ode on Human Destinies" in *Californians* and "Moral Beauty," its sequel, here. There is also the prolongation of the traditional narrative form initiated in *Californians* and completed here in "A Woman Down the Coast." And last, running like a counter movement beneath them, is the fascination with the new science of flight, offering a hope for another world, a new life on a different planet. This is the underlying yearn for transcendence for which Jeffers will find a less superficial solution in his later thought. The interlock between the two volumes, this direct continuity, ought to yield to a tentative reconstruction of the events of Jeffers' life from 1914 to 1917, and I turn to his biography.

Pausing in my writing I look out over the vast expanse of Bixby Canyon. It is midafternoon. The sun is beginning to slant down toward the western rim, but the solar intensity is still at crescendo. Down below me a redtail hawk circles and dips, his remorseless gaze searching for prey on the slopes beneath. After a time he gives up and cries angrily, disturbed by something intruding below him that I can't see. In the redwoods over my head a jay answers the hawk feebly, only a scrawny imitation of the master he cannot rival. I get up and go over to a patch of sunlight splashing the cabin yard. On the slope to the east a group of wild pigs, almost rust color in the strong afternoon light, scampers out of the brush. Slipping inside the cabin I get my binoculars and in a moment I have them in focus. They pause tentatively to snuff the air, their weak eyes blinking, and move along again. I have seen their sign everywhere hereabout. The cascara berries are ripe, and the pigs, gorging themselves, discover in the painful way that it is a powerful emetic. Across the slope they disappear into the brush, and I put the glasses down, exhilarated by this sudden manifestation from the wild. I go over to the spring, and from the dipper I gulp down a long draught of cold water, and am refreshed. Deceived by strong light I have the illusion that time is still young, and experience a momentary feeling of lassitude, but the urge to get on with it is nevertheless relentless. Going back to my chair I pick up the story of Jeffers' life. In order to piece the wartime years together and relate the poetry we have to the events we know, I scan its pages.

In September of 1914 Jeffers and Una came to Carmel. They had planned a European trip, but the outbreak of war in August had diverted them; hence Jeffers' very finding of his place, his creative center, depended on the war. Here under the impact of the region, he wrote "The Three Avilas," the poem that, in *Californians,* separates the Carmel verse from the southern California narratives.

In December of that same year, 1914, the couple was called back to Pasadena by the death of his father.[12] There he wrote the poem "Return to Paradise"—a Carmel paradise of only three months' founding, but already recognized as archetypal. Returned, he composed across the year 1915 the coast pastorals that complete the narratives in *Californians.* That the cloud following his father's death and the deepening war in Europe was already on him is attested by their basic unreality of theme and mood. Then in December of 1915 something jelled and he wrote "The Year of Mourning," the stilted but splendid ode of his grief, followed by "Ode on Human Destinies," which completes the volume; for his biographer tells us that the book was assembled early in the new year.[13] Finally, he probably wrote "Invocation," which, though it opens *Californians,* is, I think, its epilogue.

In the winter of 1916, then, would come at least some of the poems whose titles we know from existing tables of contents, but which have not themselves survived—save for "Moral Beauty" and "The Stars," both here in first appearance. At this time, too, he must have written that second most impressive poem offered in this volume, the remarkable "A Woman Down the Coast." It must certainly precede "The Alpine Christ," for it is clearly the last of the old-style *Californians* type of narrative, and it is hard to see him going back to that after the breakthrough of the lyrical drama.

The discovery of "A Woman Down the Coast" is a joy, for it is so much greater than its predecessors that it lets us know Jeffers was able to perfect the form he had expended so much energy on and which the *Californians* attempt never quite realized. "A Woman Down the Coast" is the summation of those tentative narratives. One encounters something of Frost's laconic verse-story recourse, giving rise to an interesting speculation as to the course of Jeffers' verse had he kept to traditional meters, heretofore a question idle in the extreme. But though clearly a more resolved aesthetic achievement than "The Alpine Christ," it cannot rival it. The ideological impress of the latter, its scale of conception and its cosmic sweep, leave its supremacy here unchallenged, fragment though it be.

On the typescript at Austin of "A Woman Down the Coast" the narrative's original title is crossed out and in its place, struck across in Jeffers' hand, is written: "Storm As Deliverer." I have retained the early name because it long stood so in Jeffers' mind, even serving for a title to one of the provisional collections he assembled before *Tamar*.[14] I feel that the apocalyptic tenor of "Storm As Deliverer" is as yet too extreme, still too far away up the line of Jeffers' psychic evolution, to truly reflect his mood at the time he wrote the poem. The germ is there. He would use its theme and its characters again. And indeed when they reoccur in the Prelude to "The Women at Point Sur" we recognize a work for which the title "Storm As Deliverer" is truly apposite.

But a reading of this poem in no way confirms that its storm delivers in nearly so positive a sense as will be true of the Prelude's archetypal hurricane. Jeffers could hardly have conceived such a title until the upheaval told in "Mal Paso Bridge" sheared him from the loyalties sustaining him, confirming the unconscious tendency that spoke through this poem before it manifested in his life. After that the title "A Woman Down the Coast" must have seemed simply too inert. But for us, approaching it from the other way, up from *Californians*, we are in the same situation as was Jeffers when he first titled it. So, even as with him, it serves us better to find it as he found it.

One happy result of the discovery of "A Woman Down the Coast" is the light it throws on the problem of violence in Jeffers' work. This is usually attributed to a later date, associated with his reaction to the war; but the attribution, though plausible, has never really seemed positive—something more fundamental is clearly responsible. As Radcliffe Squires puts it, "The influence of the war is complicating. No violence appears in Jeffers' verse until after 1918."[15] This poem corrects that without entirely controverting it. Jeffers locates the action in August 1914:

> He seemed no nearer to her nor more a part
> Of her existence than the people were

That over land and ocean eastward far
Were opening to the old agonies of new war

The naked organs of human suffering
That hour, that August day . . .

This indicates some association in his mind between the sensual
violence he depicts and the overthrow of the rule of reason in
Europe by the war.

Actually, the first infusion of violence in Jeffers' verse was "The
Three Avilas" in *Californians*, by my account written in 1914, and
can be attributed to the impact of the weird Carmel landscape on
his psyche. He was so taken aback by the region's extravagance
that, as he says in the poem, he slept at night with a pistol by his
bed. But he did not yet know how to interpret it; for explanation
he could only have recourse to the occult. But "The Three Avilas"
is clearly the inception of the strain of thought that will find its
most complete rationale in "Apology for Bad Dreams," namely:
"This place crying out for tragedy. . . ."

When, then, was "The Alpine Christ" composed? Alberts, working with Una, placed it in 1918. We have seen that in his letter to
Donald Friede Jeffers himself placed it roughly in 1917. I have no
doubt it was completed then, but to me it has all the earmarks of a
1916 production.[16] Clearly it was written before America's entry
into the war. Jeffers says as much when, fairly early in the work,
he has The Young Man's Spirit state:

My land has peace,
A happy, fat, and cancerous peace. . . .

Nevertheless, the work's special quality sets it emphatically apart
from the poetry preceding it. Thus something must have intervened to break the *Californians* mood and start him on a new
.course, for "The Alpine Christ" has no precedent whatsoever in
his poems. Something sets it apart in time as well as in concept.

My hunch is that when Jeffers took Una back to Pasadena in
June of 1916 for the birth of the twins[18]—which, however, did
not occur until November 10—this move not so much broke the
cloud that had shrouded Jeffers' imagination as it enabled him to
focus what had been distractingly amorphous. Separated from
the obsessive Carmel landscape, in the family home presided over
by the presence of his mother, with the mementoes and the
memories of his lost father everywhere about him, and with his

own paternity approaching, the long-nurtured psychological inertness broke, and he wrote "The Alpine Christ" at intense heat.

Shelley had situated his *Prometheus Unbound* in the Caucasus, where the Greek tradition placed it. Jeffers set his drama in the Alps. It was Switzerland, after all, which typified for the world the ideal of a lofty transcendence above the bloodbath. For Jeffers, too, the convergence of the dearest memories of his father with Switzerland was unmistakable, and surely gave him the motive to place "The Alpine Christ" there. The germ exists in "The Mountain Village," which opens this volume. That it had been powerfully gestating is shown in "The Year of Mourning" in *Californians*. This convergence indicates how densely interwoven the ingredients of Jeffers' psychological depression, his "cloud," had been. Now the form of the dramatic narrative, with its fast-changing shifts of scene and situation, enables him to gather the strand together, touch them rapidly and put them by, in the creative orchestration through which an artist bodies forth the incredibly complex intermesh of forces that motivate him.

But in our search for the emergence of the "new" Jeffers, the man who was so soon to become a truly major artist, there is still not the crystallizing factor we are seeking. A new facility, yes, quite astonishing, considering the work that preceded it; and certain a positive brilliance that denotes a new focus of intellectual powers. But the attitude is really the summation of the old, not the imminent emergence of the new. There would have to be an interlude, an event effecting a change in consciousness before any such revaluation could occur.

That, however, is another story, and must wait for the sequel to this work, the central interim volume to follow. But from the place where we have arrived, it can be seen that in the two years' interval between the close of 1914 and the close of 1916 one of the major psychological ordeals of Jeffers' life was met. It was, however, not his alone. What he endured was something the whole world was suffering.

At the end of 1914 the world at large still thought of the war as just another European power-struggle, an extension of familiar Balkan cockpit rivalries. But by the end of 1915 it realized that it was in the grip of a totally new kind of nightmare, and it was terribly afraid. By the end of 1916 fear had impacted into something more desperate. At last the world, its post-Victorian opulence shattered in the horror of its own brutality, was truly shaken and appalled. The carnage stunned the soul of Europe to the root.

The balance of violence hung on month after month, year after year, without resolution, without purpose, without cessation. Europe, bled white, still could not reluct. Armaments continued to pour from the factories, conscription bit deeper and deeper into the manhood of Europe, and still no one could foresee the end. From this point of view the plunge of America into the war was no mere adventitious political intervention, as we tend to look back on it today. It was the desperate impulsion of humanity as a whole to bring the awful nightmare to a close, to stop the slaughter. And when it came Robinson Jeffers, believing neither in the cause nor the purpose of that war—but impelled by the force of his shattered ideals—was ready to lay down his life to end it.

Now, at last, my ear picks up the sound of the Toyota toiling up the long three-mile grade from the old coast road at Division Knoll. Behind me, over Long Ridge, the sun is sinking. The flat light, striking the side of Mescal Ridge, plunges its rays deep in the crooked canyon, the zigzag bear-trap jaws clamped on the thigh of Bixby Mountain. Like a luminous flood the light pours in and drenches each redwood on the slope, staining the tall trunks and the graceful, paired branches, which noon had hidden in dense shade, with living gold. It is the moment for which I have been waiting, the last leveling of the day. Now is the time to put down the pen, the time for the lighting of fires and the pouring of wine. But I have been stirred by a singularly compelling poem, a work of unformed genius, inchoate and bizarre, a work that will take years, and stricter minds than mine, to bring into focus.

My gaze, lingering on for a moment, perceives that the skeletal redwoods, pressed flatly together by the enveloping light, are like fossils of fish, matted on the sea floor silt many aeons ago. Trunk and branches are now spine and ribs, and the soft pointedness of each conifer is the fish-shape of long-gone forms palpably impressed in the retentative element, retrieved out of time.

And I marvel at the subsuming power of life. As living forms we carry the fossils of our future within us, the unconscious element, ignored in our passion for objectivity, inexplicably to survive. "The Alpine Christ," cast aside by its author, endures in fragments on the versos of truly permanent poetry, only a fossil in the evolution of Robinson Jeffers. But from the bones of no more than a single vertebrate what may not the peering paleontologist, seeking the telltale links between lives, astutely surmise? From the petrified bones he senses the living nerves, and supporting the nerves the palpable flesh, and in the form of the flesh the manifest spirit of the life. Like a fish sunken in silt "The Alpine Christ" retains all the gathering intensity of a soul tormented by the collapse of its world. But it also contains the germ of new forms, new life, new courage.

For many weeks following my return from Long Ridge I experienced a certain uneasiness, a vague sense of disquiet regarding some of the implications offered in my introduction. This unrest had to do with Jeffers' attribution of "The Alpine Christ" to Shelley's *Prometheus Unbound.* Side by side the two poems do not seem to have enough in common to support the claim. True, the overthrow of God and a certain Promethean stature about Jeffers' hero, Manuel, are evident; but beyond that the *form* of Jeffers' drama is too radically different from Shelley's to convince of any meaningful derivation. Yet if not *Prometheus Unbound,* then what? If not Shelley, who precipitated Jeffers into so sudden an eruption of creative consciousness as "The Alpine Christ" signifies?

Then one night a reference chanced on in Frederic Carpenter concerning a later dramatic narrative gave me pause. "The Bowl of Blood," he observed, "is narrated in the manner of Hardy's *Dynasts,* but its murky symbolism suggests Wagnerian opera."[19] Of course! Hardy's somber and disregarded masterpiece! Among poetry readers it has a kind of mythical renown, but since it is perhaps the most unread major poetic work in twentieth-century English literature, it simply did not come to mind as constituting the influence of anything. Brought into focus, however, as epic drama it is the manifest fountainhead of Jeffers' prodigious effort. What *The Oxford Companion to English Literature* has to say of it goes a long way toward understanding the underlying impetus of his own attempt:

> This great work is written mainly in blank verse, partly in a variety of other metres, partly in prose. The stirring events of history with which it deals are recounted in the descriptive passages and stage directions. The whole centres around the tragic figure of Napoleon. . . . By the side of the major scenes are little "patches of life" seen at close quarters, episodes showing how these great events affected English rustics in Sussex, private soldiers, camp-followers, and other humble folks. And above them all, "supernatural spectators of the terrestrial action," are certain impersonated abstractions or Intelligences, called Spirits, the Ancient Spirit of the Years, the Spirit of the Pities, the Spirits Sinister and Ironic, the Spirit of Rumour, with their respective choruses; also the Shade of the Earth, and the Recording Angels. At the head of them is the immanent Will, the force, unconscious and heedless, that moves the world.[20]

The slightest glance at this synopsis persuades that in "The Alpine Christ" Jeffers is attempting to produce nothing less than *The Dynasts* of World War I.

On Long Ridge, with this knowledge in hand, I would have directed my introduction along a somewhat different course. But on reflection it seems for the best that things have gone as they have. After all, what I wrote was based on Jeffers' own attestation as to the primacy of *Prometheus Unbound* in the genesis of his poem; and in any case, where all is speculation, two points of view are perhaps better than one. I have, therefore, decided to present my conclusions in the form of an afterword. Not only is this the order in which my impressions evolved, but, sans any indication from the author, these reflections fittingly stand somewhat apart.

In reviewing my course of study, then, I will first take up my hypothesis concerning the poem's inception. Upon Jeffers' return to Los Angeles in mid-1916, it will be recalled, I conjectured that his sequestration in the family home provided the change of atmosphere needed to dispel his prolonged depression. If so, it could well be that at this time he chanced across *The Dynasts*, either in his father's library or elsewhere. For, ranging downtown in the invariable wont of the provincial writer visiting the city, he would seek out the bookshops. Browsing the stalls, impelled by pure intellectual hunger no less than by the need to know what was current, he might easily have encountered Hardy's poem. After all, a new edition appeared only the year before, and would still be active on the shelves. Carried home and devoured, the relevance of the tragic epic to the savage European conflict then in progress would provide the impact, the torch needed to ignite the combustible emotional complex he was hugging within. And with the impact of theme came the solution of form. Given the stimulus and the model, all his throttled passion, his anguish of loss, the rising threat of war, and underlying them that primordial dogged resoluteness trenchant in his nature—everything exploded into the poem we have.

All this is pure conjecture. It is, however, conjecture aimed at meeting the crucial question: how does one explain the sudden eruption of the drama in his life at this time? For what can hardly be dismissed as conjecture is the immense influence of *The Dynasts* on "The Alpine Christ." To immerse oneself in Hardy's poem is to be convinced of Jeffers' source. Its form, its content, its very methodology, are too obvious to doubt.

Why, then, did not Jeffers point to it rather than to *Prometheus Unbound*? This, at first, is puzzling. But when queried in the twenties about "The Alpine Christ" he had very good reasons for not putting the public on the track of any Hardyesque influence. Shelley was comfortably remote from all he was trying to say; but Hardy, still alive, was much too close. Any attribution from that quarter could not but confuse people regarding Jeffers' own, by then more evolved, intentions.

For Hardy's popular novels had made his name a household world in both England and America; what that name stood for was Pessimism. Moreover, *The Dynasts* is Hardy's masterpiece, and is the summation of Victorian poetry; whereas Jeffers, dismissing "The Alpine Christ" in 1926, was just then being hailed as something wholly new and unprecedented. Though the power of *The Dynasts* is enormous—in my view it is the most convincing realization of epic in English since *Paradise Lost*—in attitude it looks back rather than forward. The monumental scale of the action, the supremely impassive detachment and the illuminating perceptions of the Spirits, all taken together constitute one of the great achievements of the English tongue. But it is an achievement that impels through sheer visionary grandeur and the massive organization of historical events, rather than through lyric intensity, which it almost completely lacks. This must be accorded the chief reason why it is so seldom read.

But "The Alpine Christ" lets us know just how much the shape of Jeffers' intransigent negativism stems from that grim womb— an attribution one can safely make because no more than the tendency exists in Jeffers' verse prior to this poem. As a potentiality, that negativism was certainly there from the beginning, but it is now clear that it was the grandeur and conviction of *The Dynasts* that gave it an epic feasibility in Jeffers' mind. In this regard it is a pity we do not have it entire. The speeches of Jeffers' two main mouthpieces—Manuel, the voice of his passing values, and The Aquiline Person, the voice of his emergent ones—have not survived in their fullness. The most significant gap in the drama is the forty-nine-page hiatus in Book Four, a hiatus relieved by only one page of text, a single leaf. That leaf, however, is given to The Aquiline Person, and it is not unlikely that the missing pages carry the burden of his thought, speaking for the author in a way no other character in the drama is permitted to do. From what we can gather about him he appears to be the personification of creative skepticism. Thus Jeffers' emergent negativism seems directly traceable to the skeptical Spirits in *The Dynasts*. Their acute, transterrestrial overview of reality is something he would never forego. Yet here all such presences fade. The surviving value expressed in "The Alpine Christ" is the affirmation of Manuel, who proclaims through the desuetude of his world the truths that shaped him.

Yet this affirmation, poignant as it is, cannot match the exalted religious celebration of Jeffers' mature work, its passionate attestation to the omnipresence of God. He had not arrived at that. As it turned out, he would in time prove to be perhaps the most consummate transcendentalist in the whole spectrum of modern thought. When his time came he would secure the dwarfing of man not through the crude enginery of Fate, as did Hardy, but through the stupendous beauty of the living God. It is no wonder, then, that he steered clear of any identification with Hardy, however slight, being unwilling to further confuse an already perplexed public. After *The Women at Point Sur* he was severely enough misunderstood as it was.

It can be no surprise, then, that when measured against the monolithic achievement of *The Dynasts*, "The Alpine Christ," for all its intensity, is seen to be thin. Looked at through the frame of its progenitor it is manifestly something of a brainstorm, precipitating its author into areas and events he is too close to in time to resolve. Lacking Hardy's dispassionate distance from his chosen field, the Napoleonic wars, Jeffers' poem gives off a feverish heat of precipitate concern. This, however, in no way diminishes its value for us as the key to his attitude on the eve of America's entry into World War I; in fact it clarifies it. And it makes plain something previously unsuspected; we perceive that underlying Jeffers' eventual originality is a remarkable gift for imitation, an innate capacity to approximate the tone, the color, and even the fixtures of what he takes to be a significant literary find. This capability of imitation, one of the customary earmarks of genius, nevertheless when encountered in Jeffers is somehow startling, so completely are our minds possessed of his stonelike image. Yet with such talents just under the skin of his fingers we can no longer wonder at his later success in accommodating Greek tragedy to his special purposes. In "The Alpine Christ" he proved to himself he could do it, and then, because it was not enough his own, he set it by.

But though Jeffers abandoned "The Alpine Christ" the impress of *The Dynasts* did not die with it. It would extend far into his future, in fact clear up to "The Inhumanist" of 1948. Its apogee, however, would be reached in "At the Birth of an Age," his great dramatic narrative of 1935. There the elements of Hardy's exemplar and the chastening interval separating him from his subject—the aftermath of the fall of Rome as seen in the closing episodes of the Niebelung Saga—gave him the detachment he needed to convert the form into one of his most exalted statements. If in "The Alpine Christ," hampered by conventional blank verse, his strophes sometimes limp, in "At the Birth of an Age," freed from the Iron Maiden of formalist technique, they will soar in living verse beyond anything Hardy's limitary monism, which denied him the accent of exultation, could permit. In that surging poem Jeffers' debt to *The Dynasts* will finally be paid off, transmuted into the new and vital life that all derivations aspire to be.

[1973]

Notes

1. "The Excesses of God." This strong poem first appeared in Edith Greenan's *Of Una Jeffers* (Los Angeles: Ward Ritchie) in 1939, to be included in Jeffers' lecture-reading tour to the East Coast in 1941. Evidently satisfied with it, he at last incorporated it into his next volume, *Be Angry at the Sun*, 1941.

2. See S. S. Alberts, *A Bibliography of the Works of Robinson Jeffers* (New York: Random House, 1933), 19. Although erroneous in certain inferences, Alberts' account sets the work in place and will give the reader a good idea of the material under survey.

3. William Everson, "Continent's End: The Collected Poems of Robinson Jeffers, A Proposal," *Robinson Jeffers Newsletter*, no. 31 (May 1972): 10.

4. Thus Alberts. But the typescript itself is entitled "The Alpine Christ," and Jeffers, in his published correspondence, never calls it anything else. See Letter 111 in *The Selected Letters of Robinson Jeffers*, edited by Ann N. Ridgeway (Baltimore: Johns Hopkins University Press, 1968), 17.

5. Ibid., 229–30.

6. Of the table of contents listed by Alberts we lack only eight of thirty poems: "To the Girls in my Stories," "Peacock Ranch," "Metempsychosis," "Gypsy Marriage," "Sea-Passions," "Forest Sorrow," "Lamp of the West," and "Confession on Caucasus."

7. Matthew Arnold's "Dover Beach" beautifully captures the mood.

8. Frederic I. Carpenter, *Robinson Jeffers* (New York: Twayne, 1962), 46.

9. I mean, of course, the Protestant Establishment of Western Europe. Rome, having yet to accept the modern world, could neither exult in its triumph nor groan at its fall.

10. Letter 111, *Selected Letters*, 107.

11. Radcliffe Squires, *The Loyalties of Robinson Jeffers* (Ann Arbor: University of Michigan Press, 1956), 16.

12. Melba Berry Bennett, *The Stone Mason of Tor House* (Los Angeles: Ward Ritchie Press, 1966), 74.

13. Ibid., 78.

14. Alberts, *Bibliography of Works of Jeffers*, 17.

15. Squires, *Loyalties of Robinson Jeffers*, 87.

16. If we apply Jeffers' reflex reaction to contemporary events as our dating factor, for what it is worth the latest political instances mentioned in "The Alpine

Christ" occur in the episodes of God rebuking Michael for meddling in the Battle of Jutland, which ended 1 July 1916; and rebuking the Angel Gabriel for interfering in the Graeco-Turkish arena, therefore comparing his own situation to that of Constantine I, whose foreign minister Venizelos violated the king's neutrality by declaring war on Germany 23 November 1916.

17. Here we encounter what would emerge, twenty years later, as one of the basic Jeffersian social tenets, namely that peace corrupts. He first voices it in "Maldrove," from *Californians*, written after the ill-fated Dardanelles campaign, which hence may confidently be dated 1915. It was a fairly widespread idea in the post-Victorian opulence of Europe, popularized by the exponents of naturalism, and must be reckoned partly responsible for the disastrous drift toward war. Jeffers did not gain notoriety for it until the thirties, when the rigors of the Depression made it seem particularly repellent, and it was used to couple him with the Fascists, who had revived it during the "decadent" twenties. Early in "The Alpine Christ" Jeffers canonizes it by putting it in the mouth of God. Throughout his long life he never abandoned it, founded as it was on a more negative view of humanity than even naturalism propounded. But whether it was a popular slogan before World War I or an unpopular one before World War II made little difference to him: he held it as his own.

18. Bennett, *Stone Mason of Tor House*, 81.

19. Carpenter, *Robinson Jeffers*, 47. An anonymous reviewer at the time of my book's publication pointed out that the ostensible model for "The Alpine Christ" was Goethe's *Faust*, which Jeffers and Una studied together when they met in a German class at the University of Southern California in 1907. I have mislaid the citation, compounding my fault. But I am convinced that the operative, truly efficacious influence, was not *Faust* or *Prometheus Unbound*, but *The Dynasts*.

20. *The Oxford Companion to English Literature*, ed. Sir Paul Harvey (Oxford: Oxford University Press, 1932), 247.

III: *BRIDES OF THE SOUTH WIND*

Sometime early in the 1920s an obscure poet in Carmel-by-the-Sea, the little art colony on the central California coast, gathered together a collection of verse and offered it for publication. Whatever the collection was actually called, we know it today as *Brides of the South Wind*. Like many another tentative collection from the pen of an aspiring poet, this one was never published. A New York editor rejected it as being "unpleasant." Its author put it aside; then, in time, he destroyed it. But he kept writing new poems, poems which, overnight, would deliver his name from its accustomed obscurity to that of one of the most celebrated giants of twentieth-century American literature.

That *Brides of the South Wind* was never published is unfortunate, for we know from surviving tables of contents that it contained several poems which are now lost.[1] Even if those poems could add nothing to the ultimate stature of the artist, their existence would aid us in piecing together the link between the immature and the mature verse of one of the most original of poets. And in the study of originality, no matter what the field, all connecting indications are important. Often they serve to chart the underlying psychic movement that is soon to erupt into consequentiality.

The title *Brides of the South Wind* comes to us from S. S. Alberts' *A Bibliography of the Works of Robinson Jeffers,* where it is is given as the name of the interim volume between *Californians* and *Tamar*.[2] Two tentative tables of contents are listed. These are an invaluable clue to the composition of material, some surviving, some lost, which the poet set down between the publication of the two books.

However, when the papers (now at Yale) which Alberts noticed are examined, it is evident that Jeffers himself never had in mind a volume to be called *Brides of the South Wind*, as Alberts mistakenly inferred. That name was for Jeffers merely the section title under which he could group his narratives, as distinct from the lyric and meditative poems he wished to include between the same covers, a practice he had resorted to in *Californians*. This section title, which bears the name, far from being a full title page, is actually numbered page 22. And it cannot apply to either of the tables of contents given, for neither of them groups the narratives together. However, it does apply to the two prose fragments Alberts prints, the "Notes for a Preface" and its sequel, dated June 1922. In both these Jeffers clearly refers to the sectional separation as bearing this name. Furthermore, a third title page surviving at the Humanities Research Center, the University of Texas at Austin, confirms this.

Still, though Jeffers never considered *Brides of the South Wind* as a title for a book, there are reasons for retaining it as such. It is clearly the best of the several tentative ones established from the versos of later work. And since Alberts wrote, the discovery of Jeffers' long lyrical drama "The Alpine Christ" has thrown a deepening light on this whole period. Looking back as it does to *Californians*, its publication has divided the interval under scrutiny by half, so that Alberts' reference to *Brides of the South Wind* makes it a convenient title to designate the remaining pieces which look forward to *Tamar*.

But more than this, there is something suggested in it that applies to this particular interval of the poet's life with special force. In his "Notes for a Preface" Jeffers says: "The south wind brings the rain, it is from this my stories take their title. After months of drought, tempered only by the sea-fogs, our first rainstorm is a moral event like a revolution, a joyful event like a resurrection." Let the reader recall these words when, in my introduction, I take up the poem "Fauna." It will be remembered that the heroine of that tale is specifically identified as "the woman of the south." If my interpretation is correct, then the term *bride,* as Jeffers used it in his section break, has more than symbolic significance for the poet. A moral revolution and a resurrection all at once, clearly it was. But it was also the signature of a joy too poignant for him to forget.

The profound gloom that gripped the soul of Robinson Jeffers following the double deaths of father and daughter at Pasadena in 1914 continued unabated across the next two years.[3] He had found his region that same summer. His bride Una and he had chanced on the central California coast south of Monterey, one of the decisive moments of their lives. Yet, concurring as it did with those deaths, and the impress of widening war in Europe, that very discovery made his own self-finding excessively poignant and somehow guiltful. Perhaps, given peace, his grief could have found assuagement in the blessed beauty of the region he embraced as his own. But eastward, across the Atlantic, the Europe he had known and loved, loved through the formative years of childhood and early adolescence, was eviscerating itself, devouring its guts in a cannibalistic savagery that appalled the civilized world. Historically it is called the First World War.

And it was this that kept the rift of death alive in his heart, smoldering, oppressive and sere, unhealable. We can see the blockage in the various poems he was writing, poems of a profound gratitude for the place he knew to be his own, but also of a throttled and inexpressible grief. Until the discovery of the lost fragment "The Alpine Christ," it has not been possible to estimate how severe the impact of war on his spirit actually was, even before America's entry into it. On the evidence of this newly found fragment, that force was very nearly overwhelming.

"The Alpine Christ" was written, by my reckoning, in Pasadena across the last half of 1916. Jeffers and Una had gone back to the family home, this time to be close to Una's trusted physician for her second pregnancy and the approaching lying-in. They arrived there in June; the twin boys were born in November. Early the next year Jeffers returned to Carmel alone in order to locate a proper home for his suddenly expanded family.[4] It was the first time the young couple had been separated since their marriage. After the long sexual abstinence of pregnancy and the inevitable distancing between man and woman that parturition entails, it was for Jeffers, purely as male, a moment of delicately balanced danger. For Una, wife and new mother, it was a momentary lapse of viligance, an understandably maternal preoccupation with the wonder of twin sons, but nonetheless one of those fateful oversights that once allowed can never be recalled. She should never have let him out of her sight.

Jeffers had conceived "The Alpine Christ" as a long lyrical drama or, as we would say today, dramatic narrative, to be called *Witnesses*. It was to be a work in several parts. With the first part completed in Pasadena, more than likely he looked to the weeks alone in Carmel as a God-given interval of creative expansiveness in which to complete his mighty epic of the war without interruption. And he did attempt it, but of that attempt we possess little. He published only "The Songs of the Dead Men to the Three Dancers," which opens this book.

Creatively expansive Jeffers' return to Carmel certainly was, but something in him had been undergoing deep change. Abiding loyalties were loosening their hold under the impact and imminence of death—death of his daughter, fruit of his loins; death of his father whose seed he was; and the death of Europe, the matrix of his mind in his father's presence. And then began the approach of his own death, the imminence of his personal involvement. On 1 February 1917, while Jeffers was alone in Carmel, Germany, angered by the immense volume of war materiel that America was covertly or brazenly shipping to the Allies, doggedly resumed unrestricted submarine warfare, a fatal mistake. The United States, umbrageous, its ships sinking on the high seas, reacted, and the public, fanned on by the pro-Allied press, clamored for war. When it came on 6 April no one was really surprised, least of all Jeffers himself. Had he not nursed in his heart its obscene fascination across long months of anguish?

But it was not alone the precipitate declaration of war that postponed the completion of *Witnesses*. On the basis of the evolving poetry something personally climactic, an emotional upheaval of soul-shaking abruptness, accompanied the outbreak. And it was a thing the young artist was totally unprepared for, a thing which the happily married husband and new father of sons could hardly have predicted for himself. Jeffers fell in love. Plunging into a fervor of sensuality, first with a stranger and then with a friend, he brought into jeopardy the basic relationship of his life, the centrality of his love for Una. Upon her arrival home she found herself in a situation that took all her tact to salvage.

What the immediate upshot was we have no way of knowing, for these episodes were only the prelude to another, and more bitter, encounter. But rather than dismissing them as merely a dramatic irregularity in the poet's life (though clearly they were that, too) let us look for something deeper. I detect an eruption of the ancient Eros-Thanatos archetype that chimes like a bell down the long corridor of history, one of the prime movers of human destiny. On the evidence of the poetry it produced, this impassioned interval in Jeffers' creative ordeal was precipitated by the approach of death. In order to verify it let us look at the indices of war, the face of Death itself, as it shows in his earlier poems.

As far as his poetry is concerned, Jeffers' first awareness of the war occurs in *Californians*. In "The Year of Mourning," completed, he lets us know, toward the end of 1915, he sees the personal deaths of the year before, first of his daughter, Maeve, and then of his revered father, as cast against the terrible carnage of the European conflict, a carnage that had by that time reached sickening proportions. In the horror of this bloodbath his latent suicidal impulse is stirred and he exclaims:

> And all year through that flood of wrath and fear
> Waxes beyond the flowerings of the morn;
> That sanguine flood, and fills with death the world.
> O rather with those millions, O with them
> Much rather would I bleed and perish, hurled
> Into the monstrous gape
> And ravening maw of war, so thou mightst live![5]

But in "Maldrove" he mentions the war directly, the British disaster at Gallipoli, broaching for the first time the view that would get him in trouble in the thirties, namely that war, given a decadent civilization, has a purifying function. It was, I think, written in 1916, and as a symptom of his drastic reversal of values, is significant of what was to come, both for the nation and for himself.

In the "Ode on Human Destinies," which closes *Californians*, the war is felt not so explicitly, but as a disturbing force precipitating him to attempt an important poetic theme prematurely, revealing thereby his deep apprehension. The ode begins with a meditation on the peacefulness of his newfound region, and an attestation of its use to him in his own development, which he feels incomplete.

But something threatens to shatter the tranquility. He speaks of an approaching "sunderance," something that will destroy his peace, and bring him strife:

> But in my ears a word
> Of sunderance hath been spoken, and I know
> How soon the year of quiet will cease to be,
> How soon from stormy and fiery years my soul
> Yearn back upon her peace of long ago,
> This rare tranquillity.[6]

He is impelled, he says, because of the threat approaching, to take up an important theme he has been mulling over, one not yet fully matured in his thought, his powers being as yet imperfect:

> Therefore, albeit from heart and will most pure,
> Untimely thoughts, a theme not yet mature
> Are mine: but if occasion yield me space
> In any future days,
> Or truce of storm, I shall not fail to speak.
> In full what now in strains unworthy and weak . . .

His theme is the divine essence of beauty, a theme that would serve as his central religious intuition over the years, and which he will again attempt to spell out after the war in the poem "Point Pinos and Point Lobos." For us, however, it is apparent that it is the approaching threat of war that made him prematurely attempt to realize it now.

For this sunderance is something he is in fact clearly drawn to. In "Moral Beauty" from *The Alpine Christ* volume, a sequel to the ode, he writes with something akin to lust of the consuming commitment of the soldier:

> This beauty is with the soldier when he stands
> True-heartedly in hell, no more returning
> From the fire-tortured hollow and hopeless lands;
> This beauty upholds him when the hideous burning
> Like a huge beast's throat full of hot foul breath
> Strangles him, and with clawing and blood-stained hands
> And a great cry of joy he embraces death.[7]

And just as clearly in "The Alpine Christ," the major attempt of the American prewar interval, it is the awful omnipresence of war that makes him situate the action in the Alps. Not only was the high isolatedness of Switzerland a symbol of transcendent peace for the whole world all through the great struggle, as he indicates in a later poem, but that the Alps had a special meaning among his memories of his father is clear. For in "The Year of Mourning," seeing those peaks indeed as a haven above the bloodbath, he associates them as well with the paternal figure:

Bring back to me, O Alpine mountains bleak,
Those years happy forever, when yet whole
I walked with him, and wept not for his sake,
Ere he my father and the better part
Of this diminished heart
Had entrance to the mountain-cave of death!

But "The Alpine Christ," when it came, was a good deal more than the nostalgic retrospection of his boyhood years in Switzerland. In my afterword to that poem I pointed out how Hardy's *The Dynasts* gave Jeffers the lens to bring the European tragedy into focus. In that first attempt at dramatic narrative he reached out with his mind and wrestled intellectually with its problems. He strove to the limits of his learning and his philosophy to get the thing into perspective, and in its writing he was able to clarify for himself the place at which he had arrived. But it was an intellectual effort only. The passion that informs it is the same passion of grief that closed out *Californians*. Had he finished it we might have been able to see more of his mind, but in any case we could have seen it only through the eyes of his sorrow, and that much we have already. Before his work could attain the transcendence we later know, what must occur is the injection of direct passion. And this is the thing that brings us to the work of the present book.

But first the legacy of "The Alpine Christ" is brought forward in "The Songs of the Dead Men to the Three Dancers"[8] to open the book. It might well have been printed as a close for *The Alpine Christ* volume, but its interest is greater than that, for it constitutes the earliest poetry Jeffers chose to retain in his *Selected Poetry,* and therefore may be seen as a kind of fountainhead of what was to come, even though in spirit it is essentially of "The Alpine Christ" impulse. For our immediate purpose here its accent on Desire, Death, and Victory establishes at the outset the primacy of the Eros-Thanatos archetype which holds the key to everything that was soon to follow. But as yet all is still abstract and objective.

It is apparent, then, that in order to touch Jeffers' real poetry of war we must seek for something immediate—something involving a specific intrusion into the personal life. To follow "The Songs of the Dead Men" opening this area of direct consequence I have chosen the poem "Fauna," first published in *Tamar* in 1924. Alberts speaks of it as having been written in 1918,[9] but if my intuition is correct it emerged just before America's entry into the war and signals a radical interior change in the soul of the poet.

And yet at first glance nothing would seem more improbable. This derivative Greek pastoral? Clearly it is based on the classic Daphnis and Chloe love-idyll. Its diction is elaborate and rhetorical, its situations suggestively artificial. From the merely formalistic point of view it is characterized by the same unreality as obtains all through the aloof post-*Californians* period, save for one thing. It is redolent of a lush eroticism that those abstract poems never possess. And it is this very eroticism which enables us to recognize in it the true transitional interval reaching beyond the abstractness that preceded it, the real impact of the war on Jeffers' life. An examination of the text reveals that the eroticism was by no means all that impersonal. It is, rather, erupting out of something in the poet's life so powerful as to be very nearly catastrophic.

First, however, let us look at the references to the war in the poem itself. The conflict is mentioned, but it is still so far away it seems to invoke in him no more than the same suicidal impulse we saw already in the elegy to his father and in "Moral Beauty":

> But to embrace her bodily
> I being thoroughly mad would give myself to torture, or to taste her
>   sweet
> Lie in the windrows bloodily,
> Downed by despicable death in the place where the equal-minded
>   warmen meet,
> And the Mother of Love smiles moodily.

For the poet the causes of conflict are indistinguishable—the equal-minded warmen, German, Englishman, or Frenchman; Russian, Turk, or Bulgar, are all one to him. But he would not introduce the reference save for his own imminent involvement. America was catapulting to war and he knew it. Or rather it was *because* America was plunging into war that he wrote what he wrote.

How is this? A man writes a pseudoclassical love-idyll because his nation is sliding into war? Indeed he does. For that classical love-idyll is about physical passion. And the approach of death, actually or symbolically, incites the uprush of libido, the instinctual urge to survive. This is an archetype so emphatic that its presence, when it occurs, is unmistakable. In moments of great crisis, especially those affecting the whole social life, the broad collectivity of man—such crises as earthquake, floods, epidemics and wars—it erupts with devastating force. Who can forget the episode from the Lisbon earthquake that Voltaire incorporates into *Candide,* the incident of the sailor who, in the midst of disaster, with people dying on every side, roots among the rubble until he finds money, and then runs to enjoy the gratification of a prostitute? As Voltaire intended, our moral sense is affronted; but the very effectiveness testifies to a basic truth.

A more pure and evocative manifestation of the same archetype occurs in Axel Munthe's *The Story of San Michele.* During the plague of Naples he is, as a young doctor, called to the convent of an order of nuns. Death envelops the entire city, and the abbess of the convent is stricken. At her bedside he is assisted by a young nun, and at the abbess's demise Munthe, overcome by he knows not what, suddenly embraces the girl and feels her response. It was for each a movement of unmistaken eroticism, quite out of character for the two people involved, both of whom were bound by the equally iron codes applying to physician and religious. But the archetype has truly spoken, and the wise doctor is not blind to its implications. In a masterly summary he declares:

> In looking back upon my Naples days after a lapse of so many years I can no more excuse my conduct today than I could then, but maybe I can to a certain extent explain it.
>
> I have not been watching during all these years the battle between Life and Death without getting to know something of the two combatants. When I first saw Death at work in the hospital wards it was a mere wrestling match between the two, a mere child's play compared with what I saw later. I saw Him at Naples killing more than a thousand people a day before my very eyes. I saw Him at Messina burying over one hundred thousand men, women and children under the falling houses in a single minute. Later on I saw Him at Verdun, His arms red with blood to the elbows, slaughtering four hundred thousand men, and mowing down the flower of a whole army on the plains of Flanders and of the Somme. It is only since I have seen Him operating on a large scale that I have begun to understand something of the tactics of the warfare. It is a fascinating study, full of mystery

and contradictions. It all seems at first a bewildering chaos, a blind meaningless slaughter full of confusion and blunders. At one moment Life brandishing a new weapon in its hand, advances victoriously, only to retire the next moment, defeated by triumphant Death. It is not so. The battle is regulated in its minutest details by an immutable law of equilibrium between Life and Death. Wherever this equilibrium is upset by some accidental cause, be it pestilence, earthquake or war, vigilant Nature sets to work at once to readjust the balance, to call forth new beings to take the place of the fallen. Compelled by the irresistible force of a Natural Law men and women fall in each other's arms, blindfolded by lust, unaware that it is Death who presides over their mating, his aphrodisiac in one hand, his narcotic in the other. Death, the giver of Live, the slayer of Life, the beginning and the end.[10]

With this statement in hand I ask the reader to take up the poem "Fauna." Read closely—is it not apparent that Death has touched its mutual chord of Eros and Thanatos in the soul of Robinson Jeffers? A suicidal impulse is there, and the love-rush, too, apparently triumphant. Read closely—the poem emerges as no classical love-idyll at all: it is a blunt document from the poet's personal life.

In my introduction to *Californians* I discussed at some length Jeffers' poem "Mal Paso Bridge." I pointed to it as involving the same archetype as informs Dr. Munthe's memorable peroration. I noted that at the approach of the war Jeffers had thrown himself into an extramarital love affair, and in the Mal Paso poem had spelled it out with naked explicitness. When I began the present study I assumed that "Fauna" was simply the imaginative foreplay of a life-movement that surfaced into physical involvement in the latter sequence. But when I returned to the love-idyll in order to compose this introduction it became apparent that, despite the veil of the Greek model, the poet dropped too many clues to doubt that he was narrating an actual liaison. The difference is that in "Fauna" he is still being discreet. The approach of death in the form of war has not yet driven him to recklessly abandon all pretense and state his passion openly. Moreover, the lush imagery and the stilted diction themselves identify "Fauna" as a transitional rather than a terminal piece. It is the interim work between *Witnesses* and the outbreak of war. Were it nothing more, the revival of life-giving eroticism would still make it of deep significance, for this is its real relevance. Given the awful frigidity that grips the verse of *Californians* and *The Alpine Christ*, "Fauna's" breath of passion cracking that lofty stiltedness almost makes one cheer.

For looked at by hindsight, read in the glaring light of "Mal Paso Bridge," the author's involvement, despite the screening of the women under the classical names of Fauna and Nais, is manifest. What the poem is saying, unmistakably, is that Jeffers finds himself smitten by a dark woman from southern California. He is married and honor forbids him to consummate the passion. In his frustration he confides to an unmarried girl, whom he calls Nais, who in contradistinction is "white" and from the North. She mocks his honor and offers herself instead. He is offended, and stumbles down to the sea. But there something overcomes him, something he calls The Mother of Love, and, rushing back to her, he succumbs. Having thus found his honor gainsaid he experiences liberation and does not hesitate to approach his true desire of the southland. Nor does she demur.

Now the important thing for us, I think, is that although these preliminary affairs can be seen, beyond the veil of Greek legend, as quite as actual as the Mal Paso Bridge affair, here the approach of death in the form of the war had not yet forced the poet's artistic sensibility to the ultimate. All remains literary and conventional. But soon, with America's entry, the mask is ripped aside, and he throws himself off Mal Paso Bridge with a suicidal impetus bent on eventual self-destruction.

Thus it is Death, the inexorable approach of the war, that breaks the abstracted stiltedness of all the *Californians* and *The Alpine Christ* writings, and it does so by driving down to the passions. Jeffers has been too dutiful, too much the courteous, diffident, honorable husband. There is too much idealism. It is all correct but unreal. Take the Pasadena poem of 1915, "To U.J." which Edith Greenan quotes in her book *Of Una Jeffers*. The vineyard setting is doubtless actual enough—southern California has its vineyards—but its spirit is not the Jeffers we know. It concludes:

We have met three Gods in our vineyard
Up at the hill's brow.
Iacchus is one and Love is one,
There is a greater still
Here on the brow of the hill
And when, under what sun,
In the world, or how,

> In what extreme day
> Golden or gray,
> Have ever another poet and his bride
> Gone hand in hand, side by side,
> Talking of wonderful gifts and signs,
> Walking with Gods between vines . . .
> O full of Gods is the vineyard,
> And I am silent now.[11]

Silent he might be. But what goes on in the vineyard up Carmel Valley is far different from this decorous wandering in the southland. True, "Fauna" does not yet have the actuality of "Mal Paso Bridge," but at least the libido is once again liberated after the correct rectitude of Jeffers' early married life in Carmel, haunted by the depressing tragedies of their daughter, Maeve, and the poet's father. The telltale stiltedness of all that work is the clear affect of a man who is repressing his instincts in order to conform to something preexistent in his mind, his youthful idealism crystallized in the gaiety and benevolence of his wife's high spirit, plus the authority of his familial training and his moral code—everything that he himself in "Fauna" calls his "honor."

All this is pure conjecture. No published facts whatsoever exist in support of it except the poetry and a few established dates. But certain inferences emerge to suggest its probability. For instance, Melba Bennett in her book *Robinson Jeffers and the Sea* says that after she had gained Una's confidence they once spoke together about this troubled time: "Sitting high up in Hawk Tower while the sea pounded on the point, Una told me that one year of the war—1917—was the most troublous year of her and Jeffers' marriage."[12] And when in the mid-forties Melba Bennett began her work as official biographer she had difficulty getting clarity on the period. Perhaps intuiting Una's hypersensitivity on this point she rather evasively shifted the force of her questioning, speaking not of the life but of the work. Thus both Jeffers and Una could honestly deny any problems regarding his *writing* of that time. And in a follow-up letter to Melba Bennett Una skates with extreme delicacy around the most sensitive area in her married life:

> He has an honest indifference about getting things straight about himself. For instance, your ideas about his suffering during his early verses in Carmel, I said that looking back over our more than thirty years together it seems to me he was during our 1914–1915–early

1916 years here more simply and completely happy and at ease than I ever knew him at any other time and he said "yes, that is true. . . ."[13]

These were the years when Jeffers was the perfect mate, the correct and dutiful husband, preoccupied with the outward adoration of his beautiful wife, the inward grief over his father's death, and the approach of war. What happened? Something snapped. "Mal Paso Bridge" is too searing a document, "Fauna" too transparent a veil to dismiss.

Another incident comes to mind from Edith Greenan's *Of Una Jeffers* that is suggestive. Una's old seamstress *cum* nursemaid from Los Angeles, a woman merely called Fifield, accompanied her and the twins on their return from Pasadena in March 1917.[14] Edith Greenan speaks of Jeffers' morbidity and touchiness at this time, hints at heavy drinking, and remembers his morose nocturnal brooding, muttering over his poems, pouring his wine. Fifield was disturbed. She exclaimed to Una, "I'll testify for you in any court at any time, Mrs. Jeffers."[15] Edith Greenan dismissed it as a joke but it is evident there was talk of divorce in the family. It was a bad time for everyone.

But in the throes of this crisis Jeffers at last found himself, establishing his interior freedom. He might return to the role of dutiful husband, but interiorly his creative life was free. And that freedom carried forward into his witness to the world. Una's insistence that she was the only woman in Jeffers' life is legendary, and he never contested it; but not only did he write "Fauna" and "Mal Paso Bridge," *he published them.* It is with these violational poems that we must place the beginning of his creative independence. For they mean that through excess and moral injury Jeffers carved out the one place within himself to which Una's sovereignty could not penetrate. He defined his own kingship.

With America's declaration of war in April 1917 the long Eros-Thanatos groundswell that had been gathering for years crested and broke over Jeffers' swimming form, and he very nearly went under. How much time actually elapsed between the "Fauna" affair and that of Mal Paso is impossible to say. It could not have been long, but the difference is marked. One gets the feeling that "Fauna" was somehow validated in the poet's heart as a forgivable lapse, a boyish throwback to the eroticism and dandyism of *Flagons and Apples,* with an appropriate emphasis on the carnal to certify the advance beyond adolescence, but for all that essentially adolescent in spirit. "Mal Paso Bridge," however, is a violation of a different stripe: no gallantry excuses it. It is celebrated as an evocative love, certainly, but there is the glint of coldness that lets us know the poet is unashamedly in this one for something more inflexible. Nais had shown him how to gainsay honor in order to gratify Life? Let honor now be gainsaid in order to gratify Death.

Originally, "Mal Paso Bridge" was not a sequence; the various parts appear in early tables of contents as separate pieces, only brought together under the inclusive title several years later.[16] Thus the sequence as a whole cannot be assigned a specific point in time. But the event that precipitated both the love affair and the poem was clearly America's plunge into the war. Nevertheless "Mal Paso Bridge," though comparatively slight, is far and away the most interesting of his wartime verse, the most intensely personal that he had so far written. "Fauna" had been a conventional veil thrown over a conventional lapse. In "Mal Paso Bridge" the veil is torn aside. Celebrating a more naked physical encounter, this time not in the absence of his wife but in her presence, Jeffers is defiant. Melba Bennett notes the tension, the opposition between Jeffers and Una on the matter of going to war.[17] Jeffers speaks of it as a duty, but the Eros-Thanatos archetype, passion and suicide, was there as well, and Una knew it. She fought tooth and nail to save him from himself; then, when she knew she was beaten, and Jeffers moved toward enlistment in 1918, fate itself stepped in to save him. The war ended. But to illustrate how attractive Jeffers found the war, there survives at Austin a poem once included in the "Mal Paso Bridge" sequence. It reads:

> In Monterey I have watched brown-shirted men,
> Young, innocent, and eager, coming down
> From the Presidio; or in happy groups
> Idling along the street. They will fight well,
> And laugh in the wars; and many of them shall know
> The sad and splendid passion of a young death.

Between the great tongs of truth and deception the soul of the poet we know was born. His own need, his wife's anguish, his nation's zeal. And his heart a glob of lava between the three.

After "Mal Paso Bridge" I have placed what remains of the breakthrough narrative "Peacock Ranch." I use the word to specify the radical disseverance in subject and tone from the conventional narratives of *Californians* and the more accomplished, but still derivative, effort of "The Alpine Christ." Of the poem nothing so far survives except four typescript pages, given here for the first time. Yet as late as 1925 we find Jeffers, in a letter to George Sterling, offering it as a possible book for the Grabhorn Press, where he speaks of it in passing as having been written in "Locksley Hall" meter after the famous poem by Tennyson.[18] And in another letter a year later he refers rather nostalgically to it as perhaps never to be published.[19] Clearly he has not rejected it out of hand, as he did "The Alpine Christ." This leads us to conclude that his emphatic rejection of the one, and implicit acceptance of the other, are perhaps our strongest clue to the poet's own deep intuition regarding the dividing line between the past and the future in his evolving work. Thus it is a pity we have no complete text of "Peacock Ranch," for what we do have makes it quite clear that this poem signals the long-deferred transition from the conventional romantic poet of *Californians* to the savage iconoclast of *Tamar*. His first narrative of irrepressible violence, it was conceived by him after the impact of the war changed him from ideality to ruthlessness.

Ruthless? Indeed he is. That alone is the force that buckles the stately "Locksley Hall" meter of "Peacock Ranch" to chaos, making it a travesty of Tennyson's usage. (The threat of incest had shaken the heart of Tennyson's poem; one wonders what, then, was the theme of "Peacock Ranch"?) Even for the early Jeffers the writing is unbelievably bad. Some thirst in the poet's soul, groping forward toward evocation, ruptures from under the burden of content, a lapse difficult to account for except by a loosening of Jeffers' psychological adhesions and a resultant shakiness of technique. If so, this can be blamed directly on the ruthlessness of war. In "Fauna" the war is still remote; in "Peacock Ranch" American troops are already in France. The poet smells blood.

And baring his fangs he swings forward to a more violent asseveration. Ticking off Old McDonald's derelictions, "Folly, adultery, madness, shipwreck, death," he intones that consequential morality is false, and that "God's paths are more / Deeply strange than your [conventional] divinity plumbed yet." And then the crucial, not-to-be-equivocated, assertion: "I am the man, I have dived lower." Thus "Peacock Ranch" joins "Mal Paso Bridge" in Jeffers' impatience with the morality of his immediate past, his need to violate personally and openly the code that shaped him.

Jeffers' next poem, "The Coast Range Christ," while in many
ways as gauche as "Peacock Ranch," is enormously interesting for
the perspective it throws on his creative ordeal. I see it as the work
in which he completed the immolation of his youthful idealism on
the altar of physical passion—not the idealized desire of the early
poems, but the libido of insensible gratification that for him was
symbolized by the war. In the "Mal Paso Bridge" affair he had
touched something ruthless in himself never before known, and
he was shocked into self-understanding, because it was his reaction to the approach of death. For perhaps the first time he
experienced the inflexible sensation that what one finds oneself
doing is wrong, wrong, wrong, but is nevertheless, as a deed,
unmistakably actual—not right, but incontrovertibly *real*, a truth
that is more primal than morality and hence assumes precedence
over it, something which cannot be touched without some awful
contradiction of the guts, the archetypal force that was to emerge
as the source of Jeffers' power. True, in "Fauna" it was indeed
Death who presided over those ardent pagan nuptials, but the
poet obviously did not understand. Death was not yet close
enough to reveal his influence. But in "Mal Paso Bridge" the poet
at last got the message. The struggle between Eros and Thanatos
had advanced to an actuality that begins to directly inform the
verse.

It was Death, he was forced to concede, that made him violate
his marriage vows, Death who made him betray the trust of the
woman dearest in his life—really the only woman of supreme
value he ever recognized—brute Death and brute gratification,
constellated into one image of the Actual, like a gorged eagle that
has used fire for its beater to drive game into its talons, perched
on his shoulder and paralyzing with its presence the acute sensitivity under its remorseless gaze, never again to let him enjoy the
ambience of life lesser mortals know. Whatever a full reading of
"Peacock Ranch" might show us, in "The Coast Range Christ" we
see that visage clear for the first time. Its face is the terror and
ordeal of his long life. Like Prometheus the gash it made as it fed
on his liver reopened eternally the wound from which he could
never recover.

With "Fauna" the libido had been released; with "Peacock
Ranch" the ingredient of violence was introduced; now, out of
that fusion, Peace O'Farrell, the woman of aggressive physicality
in "The Coast Range Christ," emerges to bring the action down
from the classical and the literary to the dynamic and the actual.

She is two steps forward from the amoral Nais of "Fauna," who required neither the legitimacy of marriage nor the glamour of ideal beauty epitomized by Jeffers' own desire, for motivation. I say two steps because the first step, Dove McDonald of "Peacock Ranch," is too fragmentary for us to realize anything about her. In any case, where Nais was significantly a single girl, with Peace O'Farrell Jeffers welds these characteristics into the married woman. He thus brings all the aspects of the archetypal feminine to bear on his own idealism. Let us hold in mind the evolving image of woman, as revealed in the verse we have: the Nais-Fauna duality from "Fauna," Dove McDonald from "Peacock Ranch," and Peace O'Farrell from "The Coast Range Christ." Taken as a composite image they constitute the base for the final projection, the great leap forward.[20] When he makes the jump he will create Tamar Cauldwell from Point Lobos, she who truly possessed her desire.

Jeffers shrank from violence, but there was a part in him, perhaps the deepest part, that exulted in it. The savagery, the mutilations, the gloating in blood, we will know, later on, in abundance. As far as we can now tell it was this part that secured its first triumphant emergence in "The Coast Range Christ." And it was accomplished when Peace O'Farrell, who had seduced the idealist David and been repudiated by him, relapsed into the arms of Sherman Hicks. Jeffers would wait many years, wait for another war, to avenge it. In "The Love and the Hate" from *The Double Axe* (1948) he mates them, man and wife, and the roots of his ambivalence toward each would be terribly stanched in the figures of Reine and the elder Gore. It would take him years to sink to it, and when it came, under the sovereign touch of Death in another war,[21] it would constitute the most unlovely revealment of his heart he would ever consent to show us. But he had to abandon Tamar, the transcendent one, to drink of it.

In "The Coast Range Christ," though, the ethereal and otherworldly aspect of Jeffers' shattered idealism is clearly delineated in the fate of the youthful conscientious objector, David. Compare it with that of his immediate predecessor, Manuel Rüegg, of "The Alpine Christ." Manuel goes off in lofty heroism to meet an unimaginable fate, but here the calculation of Peace O'Farrell smashes David, simply erases him. Is Jeffers getting back at the Nais-Fauna, and her of Mal Paso, for their power over his flesh? In David's death is he accusing them, one and all? I think so. But whatever hostility Jeffers shows toward Peace—and it is everywhere evident—it is clearly she who sets the way for Tamar. The

Greek pastoral milieu of "Fauna," which effects the break from the lofty cosmic "Alpine Christ," is shattered before the direct impact of the ruggedness of place in "The Coast Range Christ" and the woman who typifies it. When it is over, Jeffers has fleshed out enough of the impulse to undertake the exposition of the real thing in his writing. But we must not forget that it was the transcendent archetype, the Eros-Thanatos impulse, which decreed this action, rather than some random and frenetic passion.

For in the Mal Paso Bridge showdown the results of defiant self-assertion were not confined to simple psychological deliverance, efficacious as that cruel therapy proved to be. A true artistry emerged from this crisis. In the evocative transcendence that followed, some of Jeffers' most poignant touches emerged, his first permanent work: famous poems much anthologized later, beautiful lyrics like "The Maid's Thought" and "Divinely Superfluous Beauty." Here we see emerging the religious instincts that would soon constitute the overreaching force of his mind, his singular contribution to religious expression. A special pulse, or vibration, redolent of the blush of the erotic awakening, characterizes these pieces, accounting for their placement here, rather than later on.

I have chosen to close this first section of the book, the section containing work produced under the onslaught of war, with the beautiful short poem "The Excesses of God." The paradox of liberation through violation would be the main tenet in his great work to follow, but now in this short lyric he sums it up with a succinctness that makes it memorable. For he had by then thrown himself beyond the pale of his own morality, tasted a wild freedom, and had seen it—even the freedom purchased through sin—as somehow divine.

> Is it not by his superfluousness we know Our God?

For here he identifies that aspect of divinity with his own humanity, something he would not concede later on; but now, at the threshold of his mature thought, he acknowledges it as true:

> There is the great *humaneness* at the heart of things.

He has discovered it within himself, and become as God through his own excesses, and realized a kind of triumph. But he realizes it as based on a very large "if," life's mightiest problematic, the awesome imponderability of human assent, a mystery he himself would savor for the rest of his days:

If power and desire were perch-mates.

With the Armistice Jeffers' great bid for freedom was dashed and he stalked dutifully back into harness. The verse that immediately follows is clearly a return to the tight-lipped reserve that characterized his poetry before his break with "Fauna." "God's Peace in November" ("The Truce and the Peace"), his major effort of the period, is mostly written in sonnet form, one of the strictest of forms. The determination to shear the rhyme-tassels from his verse, made in the spirit of defiance at Mal Paso Bridge, has come to nothing. In this entire Armistice interval there is not a single open-form poem surviving. The fact that in "God's Peace in November" he once again addresses himself to the problem of his father is significant. Originally composed of twenty-seven pieces, Jeffers eventually published only fourteen; but eleven others survive, only one sonnet and parts of two others being lost. They are printed here for the first time for the light they throw on his attitude at the closing of the war.

Peace to the world would seem to call for rejoicing, but "God's Peace in November" is about the most depressed verse Jeffers ever wrote. Eros is nowhere to be seen. Thanatos is all. But it is not the triumphant death that we saw in "The Songs of the Dead Men to the Three Dancers." It is rather the depression of death denied, the disappointment of one who had hoped for a glorious kind of suicide in war, and was restored to life. He sees ahead nothing but age:

> Just as my father who is dead grew old
> Granted long life I shall grow old at length,
> The temples frosted that white color cold
> Spreads to the beard and crown . . .

And he ponders the vibration of his own defection, seeking to grasp its paradox:

> Is this man's sin, to love God more than Christ,
> Peace more than liberty?
> Only when wine or anger had uniced
> My heart came love to me,
> Came love, rebuke in the deep-brooding eyes,
> And freedom wounded red . . .

It is as if he catches the glimmer of the fact that his passionate bid for apotheosis was one with the world's vast violence, and now quietude has come back to the nations, then peace, dead peace, is to be accepted as his lot.

This recognition is what makes the poem, tight-lipped though it be, so far beyond the more formal stiltedness that preceded "Fauna." There is a toughness here, an intellectual wrestling with the mortal issues involved, that makes this poem memorable. Jeffers did well to prune it down to fourteen sonnets, for as published it has an aloof reserve entirely appropriate and impressively detached. But the finding of the larger poem is fortunate, for it lets us see the probe into his own heart for the truth it was.

It is the presence of this same reserve that leads me to place here most of the extant sonnets that Jeffers published up through the late twenties. As was his wont, when asked for contributions, he reached back and brought forward work from earlier intervals. These sonnets—"Adjustment," "Compensation," "Promise of Peace," "Stars," "To His Father," and "Consciousness"—all have the ring of the somber knelling deep in his soul saying that possibility has died, that life lives on in its own long death.

(As a note of retention of the values gained through violation, I am now convinced that "A Woman Down the Coast," printed in *The Alpine Christ & Other Poems*, was written here. I placed it earlier on the basis of its form and mood, being unprepared at that time for the massive regression this whole Armistice period attests to, something unapparent until the formation of the present book. For sometimes a poet will *reenact* something he has already outlived, repeat it in order to verify what is fully past. In retrospect I now doubt he would have been able to write "A Woman Down the Coast" save in the aftermath of "Fauna" and "Mal Paso Bridge." If so, its trenchant extension of his discovery that *freedom is purchased through violation* is truly impressive.)

That the mood of guiltful and depressed somberness could not long obtain following such open experimentation as the war had produced was obvious. Something must move forward, and Una, with her unerring feminine instinct, put him to work—not callously and vindictively, but wisely and with tact. Instinctively she began to build a more secure foundation for their marriage. They purchased land on Carmel Point and built a house. It was a site at that time quite distant from the village, and must have meant a sacrifice for her, for she was more socially inclined than he. But she recognized that her own gregarious instincts crossed his solitary ones, and she moved to place him beyond the temptation of casual women. Franklin Walker in his *The Sea Coast of Bohemia* gives a glimpse of the life of Carmel in the teens. We catch an insight into the whirl from which Una and Robin retired, and it was just in time:

> I Father having followed other guides
> And oftener to my hurt no leader at all,
> Through years nailed up like dripping panther hides
> For trophies on a savage temple wall . . .[22]

The capability for self-destruction was deep in the nature of Robinson Jeffers. It was Una who saved him from that gross penchant.

Jeffers responded. Moving beyond the role of mere house-buyer, he began actively to build. Helping the masons set rock in the walls he wrote the first of his stone-working poems, "A Barren Foreland." I use it to open the final section. The intonation is Yeatsian, not yet Jeffers' own, but it is not without interest that the inset lines are brought forward from the last page we possess of "Peacock Ranch."

> There are only simple things here,
> Three great people my dear,
> The earth's old hard strength,
> The keen air's messenger power,
> The coiled sea's moving length,
> Immense neighbors of ours.

With this carrying forward he maintains his grip on three elements: earth, air, and sea. The final element needed to complete the quadernity is fire, and he would not touch that till "Tamar." But for now the poem's deepest significance is that it is addressed to Una, and that the erotic libido, so lately lavished on others, is once again flowing back to her.

In choosing the order of the poems of the final section I have relied chiefly on my sense of their developing surety, the sense of following a vein in the granite Jeffers was handling, until the feckless eroticism that had delivered him from the abstract death of "The Alpine Christ" into the pain and dissolution of libidinous passion, was purged in the absolutely austere fire necessary to produce "Tamar." He had to create a crucible in which the incest-impulse so evident in *Californians* could be burned pure in the white-heat passion of that poem, and these stone-working poems provide that crucible. Rock by rock he seemed to be constructing the monumental vessel in which his alchemical transformation could be effected.[23]

But it was not simply the incest-impulse that was annealed there, it was also his quarrel with the world. One of the most important psychological documents to turn up from this period is the unpublished poem "The Beginning of Decadence." In August 1919 Tor House was completed and the Jefferses moved in. In January 1920 the League of Nations was formed, an event which definitely crystallized for the American conscience the revolution against its own participation, a revulsion that had been growing since the Versailles Treaty of the year before. Writing in the awakening springtime of 1920, well-ensconced in his new home, Jeffers is nevertheless furious at the turn of international affairs. I have followed this poem with three fragments culled from the files at Austin. There is no telling their names; they could be from almost any of the poems whose titles survive in extant tables of contents but whose texts are lost. What binds them together with "The Beginning of Decadence" is Jeffers' disgust at the course of the world, and his own self-exasperation at having been sucked into the complicity of wartime involvement.

Taken as a whole these fragments represent a considerable body of effort, and it is curious that he was not able to bring any of it off. The problem is principally a matter of form. His anger was trenchant enough to produce sound verse, but apparently he had not recovered his unrhymed, quantitative-stress measure put by at the Armistice, and these long, metrically slack lines with their weak rhymes simply fail to jell. His use of this form, beginning with "Peacock Ranch," extending through "The Coast Range Christ," and finally petering out in these statements of anger and contempt, suggests that he hoped to forge an instrument rangy enough to accommodate his broadening outlook, but it was not until the work with stone slowed down his pulse and confirmed him in his essential gravity that he turned back to his unrhymed quantitative-stress measure and at last settled on it as his mode.

After these I have placed two self-chastening pieces heretofore unpublished which show the recovery of his basic measure, "To His Sons" and "Of Not Going to War." They were hard poems to write, the admission of self-delusion and of guilt. But they were germane to the process of self-purgation in which he was involved.

Beyond this point the problem of which poems, in terms of actual composition, preceded "Tamar" and which followed it, is not possible to solve. But for our purpose of forming a link between the war-crisis poetry of "The Coast Range Christ" and the transcendence of "Tamar," a gathering weight is discernible. This is probably a considerable oversimplification of Jeffers' actual chronology, and it is frankly undertaken in order to serve our own needs of a viable approach rather than attempt the impossible. The unpublished poetry is given here to fill out the possible range of his interest, but his elimination of it from his canon was sound, for it does nothing, really, to assist in our intuition of the gathering approach to "Tamar." By changing our figure from crucible to path, it is not hard to construct a ramp that can fittingly approach that poem. This is what I have attempted. I will not justify the placement; its consonance must be self-evident and satisfying, or dismissed as presumptuous.

It was purely a sense of fitness that led me to close this book with the evocative ode "Continent's End," but as it happens, through a singular bibliographical boon, intuition for once is verified by positive fact. In the Beinecke Library at Yale there exists an extraordinary document, perhaps the most significant (certainly the most unique) of all the surviving oddments to escape Jeffers' bemused disinterest—a document long accounted for, indeed, but the relevance of its positive date heretofore going unnoticed. It is a 14×24-inch bank statement from the Los Angeles Trust Company listing Jeffers' financial entries for the period 17 January to 17 February 1922.[24] On its reverse side the poet has set down the first, and final, draft of "Continent's End" and beside it, wonder of wonders, he gives terse, suggestively fertile notations to himself for the incipient narrative "Tamar." Among preliminary sketches of Hawk Tower and its interior stairway we see, brought into focus from the confusion of the scribbled page, the poet's emergent destiny. Here, early in 1922, Ode, Tower, and Narrative float in tremulous suspension, quickening in the cloudy alchemy of creative truth. It is a document almost too naked to touch. A poet's torturous evolution coils on its breakover moment. In its depths we gaze on an astounding birth.

[1974]

NOTES

1. Three early tables of contents survive, two at the Beinecke Library at Yale and one in the Tor House Collection at the Humanities Research Library of the

University of Texas at Austin. For the Yale specimens see Alberts, *A Bibliography of the Works of Robinson Jeffers*, 17–18; for the specimen at Austin, see Appendix 4.

2. Ibid., 17n and 19.

3. See my introduction to *The Alpine Christ & Other Poems* (Cayucos, Calif.: Cayucos Books, 1974).

4. Bennett, *Stone Mason of Tor House*, 82.

5. "The Year of Mourning," in *Californians* (Aromas, Calif.: Cayucos Books, 1971), 145.

6. "Ode on Human Destinies," ibid., 151.

7. "Moral Beauty," in *The Alpine Christ*, 12.

8. See the note to this poem.

9. Alberts, *Bibliography of Works of Jeffers*, 17.

10. Axel Munthe, *The Story of San Michele* (New York: E. P. Dutton, 1929), 177.

11. Greenan, *Of Una Jeffers*, 16.

12. Melba Bennett, *Robinson Jeffers and the Sea* (San Francisco: Gelber, Lilienthal, Inc., 1936), 54.

13. Bennett, *Stone Mason of Tor House*, 84.

14. Ibid., 83.

15. Greenan, *Of Una Jeffers*, 45. Edith Greenan describes the incident as a night in which Jeffers stayed up till dawn, crashing into the bedroom to retrieve the jug Una had stashed beside the bed. Apparently a tussle ensued. If Una convinced Edith Greenan that this was indeed the night Jeffers wrote "The Excesses of God," it has to be our choicest example of her robust humor.

16. Alberts, *Bibliography of Works of Jeffers*, 18.

17. Bennett, *Stone Mason of Tor House*, 83.

18. Ridgeway, *Selected Letters*, 38.

19. Ibid., 63.

20. It now appears that Myrtle Cartwright of "A Woman Down the Coast" stands between Peace O'Farrell and Tamar Cauldwell. Conceived in Jeffers' depressed Armistice Period she does not have the crystallized character of the emerging archetype, yet she does serve witness to it. Where Peace is all erotic articulation, Myrtle Cartwright is mute. But this muteness deepens Jeffers' delineation of the force he is seeking to isolate, for she is as powerless before it as was Peace. However, both women are largely unconscious. The difference with Tamar is that she *knows* what she does.

21. My belief that the activation of the Eros-Thanatos archetype in Jeffers' mind on the approach of World War I found its confirmation in the reactivation of the same archetype on the approach of World War II is based on the following facts: At Easter of 1938, Hamilton, the poet's brother, an accomplished pilot, flew Jeffers to Death Valley. Jeffers brooded beforehand on his own death, and left a holograph will to Una in case of a crash (Melba Bennett, *Stone Mason of Tor House*, 169). In April of that year he wrote "Contemplation of the Sword," in which these lines occur:

> Dear God, who are the whole splendor of things and the sacred stars, but also the
>   cruelty and the greed, the treacheries
> And violence, insanities and filth and anguish: now that this thing comes near us again
>   I am finding it hard
> To praise you with a whole heart.

In the summer of that same year Jeffers, under the very eyes of Una, plunged into a casual affair with a houseguest of Mabel Dodge Luhan at her Taos ranch.

This time Una attempted suicide (Bennett, *Stone Mason of Tor House*, 171). These facts seem particularly indicative. But whoever desires further evidence should read in sequence all the short poems that make up the close of *Be Angry at the Sun*. They are shot through with the cry of Eros confronting the imminence of Death.

22. "To His Father."

23. "Fortressed in stone and silence," he was to say of the dead President Harding, sheltered in the vessel of the tomb (Appendix VI).

24. In a letter to Donald Friede dated 25 November 1925, Jeffers describes this "great sheet" and notes its contents. (*The Selected Letters*, 52). On the following page Ann Ridgeway transcribes the notes for "Tamar," but I decipher them somewhat differently than she does. "The conflict is in Will's mind chiefly. He is protagonist. He is going to punish Lee, his own and his father's equal failings are finally unfolded to him." In this initial plan the role of Tamar is curiously undeveloped. Then in a sudden interjection to one side Jeffers notes: "Tamar's rape by Lee happened before Lee went to the war. Now on the eve of his return she is strangely excited. Stella advises her. She confesses to Stella." It would seem that herein lies the germ of the story that Jeffers was soon to develop. It must have been after this seminal intrusion of the feminine into his masculine plot that Jeffers stroked in the name TAMAR at the head of the column, a shift in the locus of his psychic energy that impelled him to add the rueful adumbration, "Tho this is my last tale." Actually it was his first, relegating those that preceded it to insignificance. In our end is our beginning.

"Something New Is Made": *Bricolage* and Jeffers' Narrative Poems of the 1920s

Arthur B. Coffin

In the introduction to Random House's 1935 edition of *Roan Stallion, Tamar and Other Poems,* Robinson Jeffers wrote that he had decided as early as 1914 to follow his own lights with respect to poetry (*RST* vii).[1] He wanted to be original, he said, not imitative of Shelley and Milton (as he had been), nor "slight and fantastic, abstract and unintelligible" (vii, x), as he feared his contemporaries were fast becoming. The "more advanced contemporary poets," Jeffers contended, seemed to be following the example of Mallarmé, consequently "divorcing poetry from reason and ideas, bringing it nearer to music" (viii).

In Jeffers' view, modern poetry in 1914 "had turned off the road into a narrowing lane" in pursuit of aesthetic concerns at the expense of ideas and content. Eventually "nothing [would] be left but musical syllables," he believed. If that were to be the direction of modern poetry, Jeffers was reluctant to follow. Yet everything seemed already to have been said, he mused, and that realization seemed to suggest that one might follow the example of the Chinese: "eliminate one's own words from the poem, use quotations from books as the elder poets used imagery from life and nature, make something new by putting together a mosaic of the old." Perhaps, writing in 1935 about this earlier decision, Jeffers had in mind Eliot's *The Waste Land* when he observed of the "mosaic" process that "one or two noble things might be done that way" (ix), but to him that prospect appeared no more promising than Mallarméan musicality.

Jeffers recalled that he saw himself "making [his] final decision not to become a 'modern'." He continued:

> I was doomed to go on imitating dead men, unless some impossible wind should blow me emotions or ideas, or a point of view, or even

mere rhythms, that had not occurred to them. There was nothing to do about it. (x)

As he defined the term in this introduction, Jeffers did not become a "modern," but by the time he had written and published "Tamar," it was evident that, like such modernists as T. S. Eliot, Wallace Stevens, Robert Lowell, and Theodore Roethke, he was trying to create poetic structures that would bring order and integrity to his vision of the world (which was nature *and* God) and that would reestablish the reality he believed Mallarméan "moderns" had forsaken.

In a variety of ways, these modernists and others responded to the profound sense of loss or abandonment that Matthew Arnold described poignantly in "Dover Beach." As inheritors of an intellectual world remarkably altered by such nineteenth-century figures as Lyell, Darwin, and Nietzsche—of a world in which, as Arnold stressed, the "Sea of Faith" had retreated—they sought new structures of order that would help reestablish authentic relationships between themselves and the world. Many of them discovered that, deprived of tradition, they could look only to their own resources; others turned again to the classics after the example of T. E. Hulme, Irving Babbitt, or Paul Elmer More.

In the quest for ways to structure the powerfully integrated vision of God, nature, and humanity that he eventually articulated, Jeffers had an uncommonly wide range of intellectual resources at his command. Thus in addition to his own imaginative reserves, he drew upon the classics, literary tradition, and even on the science and philosophy that themselves appeared to have destabilized the failed legacy of traditional institutions. By 1948, Jeffers called this sought-for vision Inhumanism, a "philosophical attitude . . . a shifting of emphasis and significance from man to not-man; the rejection of human solipsism and recognition of the transhuman magnificence [of nature]."[2] To achieve Inhumanism, Jeffers, following his early decision to be original, conducted a complicated exploratory process that involved interesting strategies of inquiry.

Elsewhere, apologizing for bad dreams, Jeffers wrote that, by imagining "victims" and "phantoms" who would be our "salvation," he tried to displace suffering that he might otherwise have had to endure himself (*CP* 209–10). And in the Prelude to "The Women at Point Sur," an early version of it having been published as "Preface" in 1926 (*SL* 81), Jeffers looked back on "Tamar" and "Roan Stallion" and declared:

Culture's outlived, art's root-cut, discovery's
The way to walk in. Only remains to invent the language to tell it.
   Match-ends of burnt experience
Human enough to be understood,
Scraps and metaphors will serve.

                                                                                    (*CP* 240–41)

From these comments, it is clear that Jeffers had resolved to
explore the relationship of humanity to nature and to God by
employing fictive constructs ("imagined victims") in a somewhat
systematic process, beginning with "Tamar." Jeffers himself saw
"Tamar," "Roan Stallion," "The Women at Point Sur," and
"Cawdor" as forming a progression—an exploratory progression
in which he altered particular variables and judged the consequences (*SL* 144).

In these statements, furthermore, Jeffers described a methodology, using the "Match-ends of burnt experience" and "scraps
and metaphors [that] will serve," which resembles the concept of
bricolage set forth by Claude Lévi-Strauss. Trying to identify the
difference between two types of scientific knowledge in *The Savage
Mind*, Lévi-Strauss contrasts two intellectual methods—those of
the *bricoleur* and the "engineer." The engineer he views as one
whose scientific mind leads him to proceed with specific tasks by
attempting to create events and thereby change his world. The
engineer is limited, however, by his need to use tools and materials designed to complete a particular project. Without a plan, for
example, the engineer cannot proceed with his work. From the
perspective of the use of language, Lévi-Strauss's engineer, according to Jacques Derrida, "should be the one to construct the
totality of his language, syntax, and lexicon."[3] The engineer
would be "the absolute origin of his own discourse" (256–57).

Unlike the engineer, the *bricoleur* attempts to address only the
immediate needs of his situation, as he finds it, for the *bricoleur* "is
adept at performing a large number of diverse tasks" and "making
do with 'whatever is at hand.'"[4] Thus the *bricoleur* (who functions
like a Jack-of-all-trades, as the word implies) uses elements defined by and from the projects of others to produce constructs to
meet immediate needs, and he feels free to use "whatever is at
hand."

Lévi-Strauss contends that "the engineer works by means of
concepts and the 'bricoleur' by means of signs" (19–20) and that
the *bricoleur*, unlike the engineer, must interpret the results of his
restructuring of the received elements, for each redistribution

represents the displacement of conventional meanings. Not having a clear conception of the "final" structure, however, the *bricoleur* must rely on uncertain knowledge.

The engineer succeeds because he can depend upon the reliability of his materials; he *believes* a certain object is itself and nothing else. The *bricoleur,* however, succeeds because of the number of substitutions of meaning he can assign to a given collection of objects. His discourse assumes what Derrida calls "free play . . . a field of infinite substitutions in the closure of a finite ensemble." Derrida warns that this "field permits these infinite substitutions [because] there is something missing from it: a center which arrests and founds the free play of substitutions." The play of signification, therefore, becomes an attempt to *supplement* the lack of center or fixed origin with the interpretive activity itself. As Derrida observes, the "superabundance" of the signifier, "its supplementary character, is thus the result of a finitude, that is to say, the result of a lack which must be *supplemented*" (260–62).

Certainly Jeffers grew intellectually beyond "Tamar," but it is reasonable to assume that by the time he wrote this poem he already possessed most of the matter of science, astronomy, psychology, myth, the classics, and philosophy that would become evident in his work. While he attempted to clarify his vision of humanity and the world, Jeffers placed more or less emphasis on these intellectual elements as he tested his invented victims in different assemblages.

Taking our cue from Jeffers' acknowledgment that he saw "Tamar," "Roan Stallion," "The Woman at Point Sur," and "Cawdor" as representing a specific line of development in his work and keeping in mind the process of *bricolage*, it would be instructive to examine these poems by focusing principally on some of the ideas most often mentioned with respect to Jeffers: those of Schopenhauer; Nietzsche; the cyclists Vico, Spengler, Petrie, and Ellis; Lucretius; and Spinoza.[5] In this paper, however, I shall focus chiefly on the elements from Nietzsche that Robinson Jeffers tried, accepted, or rejected, and shall include as well a brief look at Schopenhauer and the Roman poet Lucretius, the former because there was no place for him in Inhumanism and the latter because his Epicurean materialism replaced the earlier Nietzschean components of Jeffers' verse.

One expects to find evidence of Schopenhauer in Jeffers' *bricolages*, but analysis proves the expectation to be illusory. Although Jeffers knew Schopenhauer,[6] the point in an examination of his work from the perspective of the process of *bricolage* is that he chose *not* to use any of Schopenhauer's ideas. We recall that for Schopenhauer the world existed as the objectification of his will; the world existed because he willed it to exist; without his willing, it did not exist. For Jeffers, however, there is no such causal relationship between the individual and the world. In "Credo," for example, he contrasts his view with that of his "friend from Asia." The poem concludes: "The beauty of things was born before eyes and sufficient to itself; the heart-breaking beauty / Will remain when there is no heart to break for it" (*CP* 239).

In his essay "A Few Words on Pantheism," Schopenhauer wrote, "The chief objection I have to Pantheism is that it says nothing. To call the world 'God' is not to explain it; it is only to enrich our language with a superfluous synonym for the word 'world.'" Furthermore, he added, "it must be a very ill-advised god who knows no better way of diverting himself than by turning into such a world as ours. . . ."[7] Clearly there are great differences between the views of Schopenhauer and those of Jeffers, who repeatedly attested that the beauty of the things he saw in nature was the visible manifestation of the presence of God and who found thereby that he could not utilize Schopenhauerian ideas in the development of Inhumanism.

Nietzsche, like Jeffers, wanted to discover how one could achieve new beginnings in a world of intellect that had become tradition-bound and lifeless: How could one escape nihilism? The first step, he believed, was to acknowledge the necessity of the revaluation of values, which he described in *Ecce Homo* as "an act of supreme self-examination on the part of humanity" that would result in the contradiction or destruction of received values but not necessarily in the institution of new values in their place (*BWN* 782). For Nietzsche, the will to power functions as a method of evaluation, and, to the extent that one can overcome the struggle of the opposed forces of the Apollonian and the Dionysian within oneself and achieve balance, that person exercises the principle of the will to power. Nietzsche also recognized a connection between the will to power and sexuality, which he described as the principle of sublimation. Through the mechanism of sublimation, sex was a means to an end—not to sexual fulfillment but to the will to power.

The will to power, which leads to self-mastery, calls forth the principle of the Overman, whom Nietzsche's Zarathustra had introduced:

Man is something that shall be overcome. . . . Behold, I teach you the overman. The overman is the meaning of the earth. Let your will say:

the overman *shall* be the meaning of the earth! I beseech you, my brothers, *remain faithful to the earth,* and do not believe those who speak to you of otherworldly hopes! (*PN* 124, 125)

Agreeing with Hegel that the idea of infinite progress was pernicious, Nietzsche rejected it in favor of the principle of eternal recurrence, that all events recur in great cycles of time. The last of Nietzsche's principles to be considered here is Antichrist, which he viewed as the original revaluation of values. Antichrist meant the repudiation of orthodox, institutionalized Christianity because it obscured its own good and protected its weaknesses. It should be remembered, too, that for Nietzsche the adroit use of power led eventually to kindness and goodness, even if the means to achieve these ends meant violence and pain.

With this skeletal summary of Nietzsche's concepts in mind, let us turn to Jeffers' narratives, in which, responding to Nietzsche's dictum that "the poets lie too much," Jeffers says he "decided not to tell lies in verse" (*SP* xv).

"Tamar" (1924) is the first published result of Jeffers' decisions to be original and to be truthful in his verse. It is a bold poem about a young woman who is the first of Jeffers' characters to attempt the revaluation of values by an implicit attack on conventional Christian morality. In a brash attempt to overcome herself and her surroundings, she seeks power, but she is thwarted by the recurrence of events that she cannot escape.

When Tamar, who feels "trapped" by life, seduces her brother, Lee, she overtly uses sex in a violent (or incestuous) way to create change: her "bright smooth body seemed to have suffered pain, not love" (*CP* 27). And when Tamar discovers her father's incestuous love for his sister, Helen, Tamar reflects at once on her own incest: "[this information] makes me nothing, / My darling sin a shadow and me a doll on wires" (*CP* 30). The narrative emphasizes the cyclical recurrence of events.

Later Tamar is permitted to communicate with Helen, her predecessor in incest, and Tamar boasts to her of the Nietzschean empowerment she now feels:

> I have so passed nature
> That God himself, who's dead or all these devils
> Would never have broken hell, might speak out of you
> Last season thunder and not scare me.
>
> (*CP* 49)

Having seduced her brother and the innocent Will Andrews, Tamar focuses her wiles on her father, David Cauldwell, who, obsessed with his sinful relationship with his sister and now constantly with Bible in hand, is the symbol of corrupted religious orthodoxy. After she seduces Cauldwell, Tamar declares that she, not the old man, will have power in the household, but her newly gained power fails her and the poem ends in violence and death. While Tamar gathers her three lovers in her bedroom, the idiot Jinny, left momentarily alone downstairs, torches the household.

In "Tamar" there are several identifiable Nietzschean elements. The will to power is sexually sublimated in Tamar; she has no other means of asserting her will. Eternal recurrence is brought home to Tamar when she discovers that her "darling sin" brings her no gain. In a transvaluation of values that approaches the Nietzschean Antichrist, Tamar repudiates the laws to which her hypocritical father still clings. The aging David Cauldwell, seeking shelter in Christian tradition nevertheless, remains false. And, feeling ironically like God, the feeble-minded Jinny brings the whole adventure to nothing. It is important to note that both the outworn traditions and Tamar's mode of rebellion are annulled: as the Nietzschean elements were deployed in the poem, they proved unsatisfactory. Tamar's will to power is humbled before decrepit orthodoxy which retains an undeniable, though disappointing, superiority.

The story of California, the young woman in "Roan Stallion" (1925), is probably the best of Jeffers' narratives. It is the first to articulate Jeffers' position that

> Humanity is the
> start of the race; I say
> Humanity is the mould to break away from, the crust to break
> through, the coal to break into fire,
> The atom to be split.

> (*CP* 189)

California, a one-quarter Indian married to Johnny, an "outcast Hollander," lives in mountain isolation with her young daughter, Christine. Returning from a Christmas shopping trip to Monterey, California sees the child Jesus "afloat on radiance" after she prays for help in crossing a rain-swollen stream. Profoundly moved by this revelation, California tries to communicate its significance for her to Christine, but she feels that she does not succeed. Furthermore, by Easter (when the narrative reaches its climax), California finds herself substituting the words "roan stallion" for "God," as she tries to translate the abstract power of divinity into concrete terms for both herself and her daughter.

While Johnny is away drinking in the valley, California celebrates in secular terms her own sense of the resurrected God. In a
remarkable scene, the stallion, symbol of sexual power, and God
conjoin for California, and the narrator intrudes to tell us that she
has become "more incredibly conjugate / With the other extreme
and greatness; passionately perceptive of identity" (CP 194). As
California prostrates herself before the stallion/God, the narrator
tells us directly what is happening within her head:

> The fire threw up figures
> And symbols, meanwhile, racial myths formed and dissolved in it,
>   the phantom rulers of humanity
> That without being are yet more real than what they are born of,
>   and without shape, shape that which makes them:
> The nerves and the flesh go by shadowlike, the limbs and the lives
>   shadowlike, these shadows remain, these shadows
> To whom temples, to whom churches, to whom labors and wars,
>   visions and dreams are dedicate:
> Out of the fire in the small round stone that black moss covered, a
>   crucified man writhed up in anguish. . . .
>
> (CP 194)

When Johnny returns home and lustfully pursues California,
she runs to the corral, where unafraid she stations herself beside
the stallion. As Johnny enters the corral to follow California, the
horse attacks him, California shoots their dog, which has momentarily stalled the stallion, and the horse tramples the man to
death, appearing afterwards to express "obscene disgust" for the
"smear" of him left on the ground. Then, "moved by some
obscure human fidelity," California shoots the stallion. After the
"beautiful strength [of the stallion] settled to earth," she turns to
her daughter the "mask of a woman / Who has killed God" (CP
198).

From the beginning of the poem, California is carefully drawn
as "a nobly formed woman; erect and strong as a new tower" (CP
179) and Johnny as a dissolute, drunken gambler. Jeffers' California and Johnny embody the Apollo and the Dionysus
Nietzsche described in The Birth of Tragedy. For Nietzsche,
Dionysus represented destructive fury—unformed energy—and
Apollo was "the god of all plastic energies," which sought to
impose shape and control on the rebellious Dionysus (BWN 35).
The relationship between these gods was never static; they were
always in dynamic flux or tension, the one seeking release and the
other control.

While California struggles to preserve some of the forms of

Christianity (the metaphysics of which are beyond her intellect) in her world, Johnny is the irresolute, potentially disruptive force in it. As Dionysus, Johnny is ungodlike. In his attitude toward the roan stallion, Johnny is insensitive and irreverent. Jeffers contrasts the prurient Johnny with the "shining and the power" of the stallion, which symbolizes both worthy sexual power and divinity, the false Dionysus with the genuine. California's struggle to assert Apollonian control over Johnny, the degenerate Dionysus, however, is neutralized by her "obscure human fidelity" to institutionalized Christianity.

In "Roan Stallion," Jeffers gave convincing artistic shape to the revaluation of values and to the concept of the Overman, but this deployment of Nietzsche's concepts also fails. California found no escape from her tawdry and valueless life.

Although Jeffers was pleased with "The Women at Point Sur" (1927), this long, turbulent poem raised problems for its reviewers. If the critics did not understand his poem, Jeffers wrote to James Rorty (*SL* 115–17), perhaps it needed further explanation. " 'Tamar,' he wrote, "seemed to my later thought to romanticize unmoral freedom [but]. . . . that way lies destruction of course, often for the individual but always for the social organism. . . ." He went on to say that one of his primary intentions in "Point Sur" was to dramatize the "Roan Stallion" idea of "breaking out of humanity," if it were misinterpreted in the mind of a fool or lunatic. "Point Sur," he contended, "was meant to be a warning; but at the same time a reassertion," and he listed six other "intentions" he had in mind as he wrote the poem.[8] Admitting that these were "too many intentions" for the reader, Jeffers underscored the emphasis on the ideological content of the poem with which the critics found fault. At one point, Jeffers considered using the title "Metaphors Will Serve" (line 21 of the Prelude[9]), and in the early summer of 1926, he provisionally entitled the second draft "Antichrist."[10] Clearly, Jeffers' concern in the Prelude is with the ideological content of the poem and with how it could best be expressed.

Having abandoned his congregation because "Christianity is false," the Reverend Arthur Barclay, the protagonist of "Point Sur," says "God thinks through action, how shall a man but through action?" (*CP* 253). Consequently, he proceeds to free himself from the authority of traditional sanctions, saying "I have come to establish you / Over the last deception, to make you like God / Beyond good and evil" (*CP* 282). Barclay is Jeffers' Zarathustra, but the poet has intentionally changed the shrewd, severe, and supremely ironical Zarathustra of Nietzsche into an insane mimic who is incapable of fulfilling the role to which he aspires.

Continuing his explanation of the poem to Rorty, Jeffers wrote, "It is a matter of trans-valuing values, to use the phrase of somebody that local people accuse me quite falsely of deriving from" (*SL* 116). Of course, Jeffers referred to Nietzsche, but what was the point he was making to Rorty? More, perhaps, than any other of his poems, "The Women at Point Sur" is laden with Nietzschean material. Is this statement a repudiation of Nietzsche? Jeffers' point to Rorty is that although the poem contains Nietzschean elements, Jeffers himself does not derive from (become the advocate of) Nietzsche's philosophy. Although the reading of "The Women at Point Sur" offered here is certainly not a comprehensive one, it does point out Jeffers' self-conscious experimentation with Nietzschean materials such as the concept of the Antichrist, the Overman, and the revaluation of values.

In his "Note on 'The Women at Point Sur'" (later published as "Mediation on Saviors"), Jeffers wrote:

> But while he lives let each man make his health in his mind, to love
>   the coast opposite humanity
> And so be freed of love, laying it like bread on the waters; it is worst
>   turned inward, it is best shot farthest.
>
> (*CP* 401)

"Meditation on Saviors" underscores the point Jeffers made to Rorty when he wrote that "Point Sur" "was meant to be a warning; but at the same time a reassertion" (*SL* 115–17). With respect to *bricolage,* however, we should return to section XII of "Point Sur" where the poet again speaks directly to the reader:

> Here were new idols again to praise [God];
> I made them alive; but when they looked up at the face before they
>   had seen it they were drunken and fell down.
> I have seen and not fallen, I am stronger than the idols,
> But my tongue is stone how could I speak him? My blood in my
>   veins is sea-water how could it catch fire?
>
> (*CP* 288)

Jeffers continues:

> I made glass puppets to speak of him, they splintered in my hand
>   and have cut me, they are heavy with my blood.
>
> (*CP* 289)

and he concludes the section:

> I sometime
> Shall fashion images great enough to face him
> A moment and speak while they die. These here have gone mad: but
> stammer the tragedy you crackled vessels.

(*CP* 289)

Here Jeffers acknowledges that he will have to continue to make substitutions until he assembles a satisfactory *bricolage*.

Trying to put "Cawdor" (1928) into perspective for his publisher, Horace Liveright, Jeffers wrote, "I think of *Cawdor* as making a third with *Tamar* and *The Women at Point Sur,* as if in *Tamar* human affairs had been seen looking westward, against the ocean; in *Point Sur* looking upward, minimized to ridicule against the stars; in *Cawdor* looking eastward, against the earth, reclaiming a little dignity from that association."[11] After the errant saviorism of "Point Sur," Jeffers turned in "Cawdor" to the role of the individual who must come to terms with life as it is on earth and thereby earn self-dignity.

On his farm, isolated by canyon walls and sea, Cawdor is the unquestioned ruler of his land and its inhabitants. His sons, Hood and George, and his daughter, Michal, children of a previous marriage, live in awe of their father's tremendous physical strength and severe self-control. However, Fera Martial, who arrives seeking refuge from a range fire, challenges Cawdor's self-possession. When Cawdor properly proposes marriage to her, Fera accepts with the pointed observation that "There is nothing under the sun worth loving but strength" (*CP* 416).

In this poem based on Euripides' *Hippolytus*, Jeffers' Fera has none of Phaedra's dread of sexual energy gone awry, and she deliberately pursues Hood (Hippolytus) once she is married to Cawdor (Theseus). Using *her* power, she competes with Cawdor for the son, but Hood, fiercely loyal to his father, resists her assaults. Realizing that she cannot penetrate Hood's defenses, Fera deceives Cawdor about Hood's chasteness and leads him to murder his son. When Fera visits Hood's grave, she says, "It was I that killed you. The old man / Who lives in hell for it was only my hands" (*CP* 500). As another embodiment of the Overman, Fera proves to be a bizarre failure, but, though she achieves little for herself, she drives Cawdor to see himself in starkly realistic terms.

Opposed to this turbulent human drama stands the figure of Michal's wounded and caged eagle, implacable in its subjugation.

This proud symbol of nature is balanced against the futile exertions of the humans in the narrative. By the end of the poem, Cawdor, laden with grief and guilt, perceives a kinship between himself and the eagle, and he refuses consolation or judgment other than his own. In his final act of the poem, Cawdor, facing the hill on which Hood met his death, cuts out his eyes with the points of flints. When his son, George, with "sudden / Ungovernable pity thrusts the revolver / Into his hand," Cawdor, in renewed self-control, rejects it (*CP* 521). By thus grafting the conclusion of Sophocles' *Oedipus Rex* to his version of *Hippolytus*, Jeffers suggests that Cawdor, like Oedipus, finally knows who he is, that in blindness he will see better than he did with his faulty vision. He fully accepts his identity and the costs that accompany it.

In Hood and Cawdor, Jeffers fashioned characters whom he valued over the recklessness and deceit of the ineffectual Fera, despite her struggle for power, because she failed to know what she wanted the power for. Nietzsche, too, would have judged Fera defective for the same reason.

As Jeffers explored Nietzschean and other materials in his poetry of the 1920s, he also used images and ideas from Lucretius, whose materialist views resemble at several points those of Nietzsche. The abstractions of Nietzsche had proved useful in the early narratives, but, as Jeffers moved toward defining the Inhumanism of his later work, he turned to the Epicurean materialism presented in Lucretius's *On the Nature of Things*, which Jeffers mentions several times in his work.[12] It is abundantly evident that Jeffers was drawn to Lucretius's view that once man sets aside the ill-founded anxieties engendered by religion and superstition, he can achieve a serene life and enjoy the simple beauty of nature. By the time Jeffers explicitly described Inhumanism, he had completed his exploration of Nietzschean materials and had turned to the more compatible Lucretius, whose presence is clear in Jeffers' remaining work.

After the manner of the *bricoleur*, Jeffers fashioned his poems from "whatever [was] at hand." It is clear in this sequence of narratives, which Jeffers identified as a set, that he, like the *bricoleur* of Lévi-Strauss, preferred to work by means of signs, rather than by concepts. He was explicit in his desire to assemble poetic structures that would permit the interpretive function of *bricolage*. Because the field of "free play" lacked a center, the play of signification became an attempt to supplement it with the interpretive activity itself. For Jeffers, it is obvious, "whatever [was] at hand" included an immense variety of materials ranging from the literature of the ancients to twentieth-century medical science, from myth and ritual to Freudian and Jungian psychology, from biblical lore to astronomy, from the Norse sagas to modern philosophy. He tried and fitted the pieces together; some of them matched his purposes handily, but others he honed to fit or discarded. Poetry is "a means of discovery, as well as a means of expression," Jeffers affirmed in the last paragraph of *Themes in My Poems*. He continued: "Science usually takes things to pieces in order to discover them; it dissects and analyzes; poetry puts things together, producing equally valid discovery, and actual creation. Something new is found out, something that the author himself did not know before he wrote it; and something new is made."

That Jeffers possessed a clear and passionately held view of the world does not contradict the argument presented here about the way he sought to fabricate poetic structures, constructs like those of the *bricoleur,* that addressed the immediate needs of his situation—even though these needs were subject to change. Indeed, he sought change. Derrida observed that the engineer, unlike the *bricoleur,* would be "the absolute origin of his own discourse."[13] Jeffers was not and knew that he could not be that absolute origin. Instead, as Lévi-Strauss defined the *bricoleur,*[14] Jeffers remained within the "constraints" of "a particular state of civilization," which is the contingency he discovered in the process of restructuring the received elements of traditional discourse in his poetry. Jeffers stressed the interpretive activity of his *bricolage;* that is, he "supplemented" the materials he used with the interpretive activity. His habit of intruding in his poems to comment on the narratives—as we have seen in the poems discussed here—is the overt manifestation of this activity.

NOTES

1. In this paper I have used the following abbreviations and given parenthetical page citations in the text:

BWN Friedrich Nietzsche, *Basic Writings of Nietzsche,* trans. and ed. Walter Kaufmann (New York: Modern Library, 1968)

CP Robinson Jeffers, *The Collected Poetry of Robinson Jeffers. Vol. 1 (1920–1928),* ed. Tim Hunt (Stanford: Stanford University Press, 1988)

PN Friedrich Nietzsche, *The Portable Nietzsche,* trans. and ed. Walter Kaufmann (New York: Viking Press, 1954)

RST Robinson Jeffers, *Roan Stallion, Tamar and Other Poems* (New York: Random House, 1935)

SL Robinson Jeffers, *The Selected Letters of Robinson Jeffers, 1897–1962,* ed. Ann N. Ridgeway (Baltimore: Johns Hopkins University Press, 1968)

SP   Robinson Jeffers, *The Selected Poetry of Robinson Jeffers* (New York: Random House, 1938)
WP   Friedrich Nietzsche, *The Will to Power*, trans. W. Kaufmann and R. J. Hollingdale (New York: Random House, 1968)
    2. In "Original Preface to 'The Double Axe,'" which is included in the 1977 edition of *The Double Axe and Other Poems*, Jeffers describes the inception of Inhumanism:

> But this book is not mainly concerned with the war [World War II], and perhaps it ought to be called "The Inhumanist" rather than "The Double Axe." It presents, more explicitly than previous poems of mine, a new attitude, a new manner of thought and feeling, which came to me at the end of the war of 1914, and has since been tested in the confusions of peace and a second world-war, and the hateful approach of a third; and I believe it has truth and value. (171–72)

It is noteworthy that Jeffers himself felt that Inhumanism had been "tested."
    3. Jacques Derrida, "Structure, Sign, and Play in the Discourse of the Human Sciences," in *The Languages of Criticism and the Sciences of Man: The Structuralist Controversy*, ed. Richard Macksey and Eugenio Donato (Baltimore: Johns Hopkins University Press, 1970): 247–72.
    4. Cf. Lévi-Strauss's description of the "bricoleur." From *The Savage Mind* (Chicago: University of Chicago Press, 1966), 17–18.
    5. For extended discussions of these ideological components, see Arthur B Coffin, *Robinson Jeffers: Poet of Inhumanism* (Madison: University of Wisconsin Press, 1971).
    6. Ibid., 34–59.
    7. From *Parerga und Paralipomena*, in *Religion: A Dialogue and Other Essays*, trans. T. Bailey Saunders. Schopenhauer Series, vol. 3. (London: S. Sonnenschein, 1891).
    8. Continuing with the other "intentions," Jeffers wrote that "The Women at Point Sur" was (1) "an attempt to uncenter the human mind from itself," for there is "no health" for the individual or society that is "introverted" upon itself. The poet meant the poem to be a "tragedy," (2) "that is, an exhibition of essential elements by the burning away through pain and ruin of inertia and the unessential." It was (3) "a valid study in psychology . . . sketching the growth of a whole system of emotional delusion from a 'private impurity' that was quite hidden from consciousness until insanity brought it to the surface." Therefore, Jeffers believed, the poem was (4) "a partial and fragmentary study of the origin of religions; which have been necessary to society in the past . . . yet they derive from a 'private impurity' of some kind in their originators." As a satire (5) "on human self-importance," the poem related back to the first intention. Finally, the poem was (6) "a judgment of the tendencies of our civilization, which has evidently turned the corner down hill" (*SL* 115–17).
    9. Lawrence Clark Powell, *Robinson Jeffers: The Man and His Work* (Pasadena: San Pasqual Press, 1940), 59.
    10. David A. Plott, "Feasting Gods: The Early Narrative Poems of Robinson Jeffers." Ph.D. diss., Harvard University, 1984, 123.
    11. Powell, *Robinson Jeffers*, 46.
    12. Coffin, *Robinson Jeffers*, 242–52.
    13. Jacques Derrida, "Structure, Sign, and Play in the Discourse of the Human Sciences."
    14. Lévi-Strauss, *Savage Mind*, 19–20.

Loving to Death: A Consideration of "The Loving Shepherdess"

R. W. (Herbie) Butterfield

An intellectually precocious child and a youthful poet who was publishing verses at the age of sixteen,[1] Robinson Jeffers thereafter through his twenties and early thirties developed only slowly towards the possession of a self-confident and distinctive voice, so that it was not until he was thirty-seven that his first mature, independent volume appeared. However, so fecund and powerful was the genius he had by then revealed that by the end of the decade, when *Dear Judas and Other Poems* was published, he already had the reputation of a major contemporary poet, albeit one thoroughly and divisively controversial. In this he shared the fate of two antecedent figures who were to minister closely to different facets of Jeffers himself: Poe and Whitman.

Like the preceding volumes from *Tamar* onwards, *Dear Judas* had among its wide notice mixed reviews; but what was new and in a backhanded way a testimony to Jeffers' eminence was an onslaught—sustained, virtually unqualified, and intendedly devastating—by a fellow-resident of California, the young Yvor Winters.[2] Though not yet thirty, Winters had already covered over every trace of the modernist, Imagist poet he had earlier been, and now, subscribing to values that were formalist, rationalist, classicist, and humanist, he was ready to find Jeffers in almost every respect deficient, formless, irrational, romantic, and inhumane. (Poe and Whitman were of course to come off little better at his hands.) Winters' critique set the pattern for the low opinion in which Jeffers' work would generally be held by those who became known as the New Critics,[3] which in turn led to what e e cummings called the "immensely scandalous" neglect of him[4] in most academic and established literary circles. The publication of this essay was thus a crucial event in the history of Jeffers' reputation.

Although Winters chose to survey a number of Jeffers' writings, his immediate brief was to respond to *Dear Judas and Other Poems*.

This volume represented Jeffers broadly, featuring most of the poetic genres he employed: the dramatic poem with an ancient setting, "Dear Judas"; the contemporary, locally situated narrative, "The Loving Shepherdess"; two variations on classical themes; and a handful of short poems, descriptive or meditative. "Dear Judas" Winters dismissed, in his characteristic, mock-precise manner, as having "no quotable lines, save, possibly, the last three, which are, however, heavy with dross." In the case of that provocative, risk-taking poem, Winters was not altogether out of line with the evaluation of other early readers,[5] but "The Loving Shepherdess," which was thematically related to "Dear Judas" and which Winters also ridiculed and disdained, was generally well received,[6] and it has remained one of the more happily considered of his narratives, if also one of the less frequently examined.

"The Loving Shepherdess" is conspicuous among Jeffers' longer poems for the sweetness and gentleness of its major character, for the predominance within it of her natural faith, and for its pervasion by a spirit of selfless love, or by love, as Jeffers himself expressed it, "nearly pure, therefore undeluded, but quite inefficient." This love was in turn opposed to the "pitying" love he felt was embodied in his Judas, and the "possessive" love in his Jesus.[7] In barest outline it is the story of the shepherdess Clare Walker, who wanders the back roads and hills around Carmel and Point Sur with her small and dwindling flock of sheep, variously rebuffed and abused, but befriended in particular by the untutored visionary, Onorio Vasquez. Clare's lover has previously shot dead her father in an argument over her; and she has afterwards miscarried and learned from the doctor that she will not survive any future childbirth. Now, in autumn, and pregnant as a result of her inclination never to refuse love offered, she knows that in April she will come to term and die—as indeed she does, at last alone, bereft even of her sheep.

The story was derived from a lengthy footnote to Scott's *Heart of Midlothian*, in which the author reports the legend of Feckless Fannie, who was famous in southern Scotland and the Border regions between 1767 and 1775, and from whom the "first conception" of his novel's heroine, Madge Wildfire, was taken.[8] Jeffers of course imbues his shepherdess with an emotional and philosophical significance nowhere so much as hinted at in Scott's footnote, while at the same time he sticks closely to many of the basic details of the story he found there. Fannie, who "carried always in her hand a shepherd's crook," is initially "attended by twelve or thirteen sheep"; Clare, with "a bent staff of rosy-barked madrone wood" in her hand, by a flock of ten. The two both feel a total commitment to their individually named sheep, desiring never to be parted from them and preferring to sleep among them rather than indoors. In turn, the sheep are utterly dependent upon them and in their momentary absence barely able even to graze contentedly. Soon escaping from hospitality and eschewing comfort, each of the shepherdesses has an inner need to press on in the open in all weathers. Fannie's old ram is named Charlie, who

> always claimed the sole right of assisting her; pushing any that stood in his way aside, until he arrived right before his mistress; he then bowed his head nearly to the ground that she might lay her hands on his horns, which were very large; he then lifted her gently from the ground by raising his head.

Clare's "patriarch ram," who "close at her side dipped his coiled horns," is named after the biblical Saul, rather than Charlie; but Charlie's name is not lost, being transferred, along with his masculine strength and service, to Clare's lover. Fannie's wanderings, like Clare's, were the product of a fatal conflict between father and lover, though Jeffers reverses the original outcome in which it had been her father who had killed the suitor. Just as Clare is taunted by the local schoolchildren, so too was Fannie "tormented" by "a crowd of idle boys" to the extent that she was "actually stoned to death between Glasgow and Anderton" among her sheep. If such was not Clare's fate, another legend, however, had Fannie "last seen, about the skirts of the Cheviot Hills, but without her little flock," much in the manner of Clare. As for Fannie's fecklessness, the Oxford English Dictionary in its concise edition defines "feckless" in the third instance as "inefficient"; and we are reminded of Jeffers' description of Clare's kind of love as being "quite inefficient." The similarities between the personalities and conditions of Fannie and Clare are such that we may say that Jeffers in effect recreated Scott's shepherdess and transported her, spiritually enhanced and articulated, to wander 150 years later the uplands and lowlands of his own California coast.[9]

We must attend briefly to Clare Walker's name. "Clare" is clear, bright: "Her thin young face / Seemed joyful and lighted from inside." (And she will give herself to a young cowboy, suggestively named Will Brighton.) "Walker" refers to the substance and shape of her life; ever walking with "broken shoes" or bare feet upon the earth, towards her destiny. We know from the beginning that what strength she possesses must have been painfully discovered, for she is naturally sensitive and vulnerable, with her features "formed too finely to be so wind-burnt," and, amid the jeering schoolchildren, with her "delicate lips moving." Here she differs from Fannie, who furiously laid about her; for Clare, being mobbed, is "meek as one of her ewes," mingling with and inseparable from them, sharing her bread with them, as they their milk with her. Each of the flock of ten has from her not only its individual name[10] but also for her its individual personality, yet each is part of the beautiful whole that she perceives. Looking after her flock is her life's purpose; there is no other, as she tells Onorio Vasquez: "I'm taking care of my sheep / I'm doing like most other people; taking care of those that need me and go on till I die."

Clare's passage to this wise simplicity has been a hard one. Her mother had died in giving birth, as she, we are constantly warned, will likewise do. Her father, a farmer "kind and cruel," had raised her until she had fallen in love with a neighbor, Charlie Maurice, with whom she had first experienced the "lovely way" of sexual love. This idyll is brief. Charlie shoots Clare's father dead, and she, torn between love-loyalty and truth-telling, affirms that her father had committed suicide "because the sheep had a sickness and I was pregnant." She is rewarded with imprisonment on suspicion of murder, abandonment by Charlie, and at last the loss of her child through miscarriage. Afterwards she returns home, wanting only to do penance and to tend to what remained of her father's flock. But shipwrecked sailors, struggling inland in search of food and shelter, kill one of her sheep, forcing her to flee to save the rest. Homeless from this point on, she understands that her life's mission is to be "the loving shepherdess," tending to all who may need her. Despite her knowledge that to conceive a child after her miscarriage would be fatal, she gives herself to a man who cares for her during a spell of illness, so that "the spring and summer were full of pleasure and happiness"; but "When the moon filled my blood failed to be moved, / The life that will make death began in my body."

Clare's impulse of love had once been of a conventional kind, romantically concentrated upon one person, Charlie. Now, blasted and chastened by experience, and under sentence of death,[11] it has become general, indiscriminate, and offered to all. "A shell broke and truly I love all people. . . . I am now so changed: every one's lovely in my eyes / Whether he's brown or white or that poor old man." Her affections are quite impersonal.

She is simply a vehicle of unmoored love, without emotional attachment: "He looked at her face, / His own burning, but in hers nor fear nor laughter, / Nor desire nor aversion showed." She cries out the lesson she embodies to Onorio Vasquez: "I hardly ever remember in the nick o' time / What ought to be said. You must tell him / That all our pain comes from restraint of love." And the love here, although by no means limited to the sexual, very much includes it.

We would not, though, expect from Jeffers an entirely or even largely humanist conception of love; and so of course Clare's generous promiscuity is but a partial expression of a larger vision that extends beyond the human to embrace all beings, all things, all deeds even. "You love all creatures alike," says Onorio. And Clare rapturously elaborates:

> ". . . The beetle beside my hand in the
>   grass and the little brown bird tilted on a stone,
> The short sad grass, burnt on the gable of the world with near sun
>   and all winds: there was nothing there that I didn't
> Love with my heart, yes the hill though drunk with dear blood: I
>   looked far over the valley at the patch of oaks
> At the head of a field, where Charlie's people had lived (they had
>   moved away) and loved them, although they'd been
> Always unfriendly I never thought of it."

Within such a comprehensive pantheism, her individual body might readily be sacrificed, given away, or literally incorporated elsewhere:

> "There was one of those great owly hawks
> That soar for hours, turning and turning below me along the bottom
>   of the slope: I so loved it
> I thought if it were hungry I'd give it my hand for meat."

(Thus Jeffers himself in a poem of his old age would desire to be consumed by a vulture:

> To be eaten.
> by that beak and become part of him, to share those wings and those
>   eyes—
>   What a sublime end of one's body, what an enskyment;
> What a life after death.[12])

There is about Clare a Franciscan quality as she moves through her peaceful kingdom, where "All the deer knew me; / They'd walk in my flock." For her in this context, life alone is the measure of good. As, moreover, "all our pain comes from restraint of love," so all that is evil is restraint of life. Suicide is therefore hideous to her. On hearing of the suicide of April Barclay (like Onorio, a character from Jeffers' "The Women at Point Sur"), she responds with a shiver of revulsion. "'What, spill / Her own one precious life,' she said trembling, 'She'd nothing but that? Ah! no! / No matter how miserable. . . .'" Similarly, abortion horrifies her, all the more so because of the obvious temptation it offers of escape from her own approaching doom. When Onorio broaches the subject, his face appears to her "like a devil's in the steamy glimmer." Women who resort to such a course, she considers, "have small round stones / Instead of hearts."

This love of various and abundant life, this absorbing and celebratory pantheism, is countered, however, by an altogether more bitter knowledge of the ubiquity of pain, suffering, and cruelty. Clare's sheep, the recipients of her most constant and spiritually symbolic devotion, often die violent deaths. She takes these in anguished sympathy upon herself, as likewise she has borne for and with them every lesser pain: "When they coughed, / Clare shook with pain. Her pity poisoned her strength." Furthermore, she is also possessed of a Calvinistic sense of sin—we must surely take her family heritage to be Protestant—and of the fear of an agonizing retribution and damnation. It is such a remnant of Calvinism that for the most part alternates rather than integrates with her pantheism, and she is described as "always either joyful or weeping."

Jeffers himself has been said to have subscribed to a similar Calvinistic pantheism,[13] and there is a clear connection between transgression and punishment in "The Loving Shepherdess." Thus Clare's first lovemaking leads directly to the murder of her father, while loss of her favorite sheep is a consequence of a later dalliance with Will Brighton. Clare herself reflects on "the death I must die / Drawn out and dreadful like the dream of hell" for giving herself to her last love. Against the insight that "all our pain comes from restraint of love" is set the dark, opposing premonition "that some dreadful pain would pay for so much joy."

Eventually Clare's light side, the boundless capacity for love and joy, mingles with the dark, her pervasive awareness of worldly pain and stress. This leads her to a vision of a paradise that is both of and not of this world, "the place [that] was my mother's body before I was born."

> "Have you never seen in your visions
> The golden country that our souls came from,

Before we looked at the moon and stars and knew
They are not perfect? We came from a purer peace
In a more perfect heaven; where there was nothing
But calm delight, no cold, no sickness, no sharp hail,
The haven of neither hunger nor sorrow,
But all-enfolding love and unchangeable joy
Near the heart of life."

To abort the child she herself carries would thus be not only to deprive it of future life but to cast it from its present perfect painless heaven:

"When I was in my worst trouble
I knew that the child was feeding on peace and happiness. I had
    happiness here in my body. It is not mine.
But I am its world and the sky around it, its loving God. It is having
    the prime and perfect of life,
The nine months that are better than the ninety years. I'd not steal
    one of its days to save my life. . . ."

Clare imparts her own willed prenatal memory ("I've thought and remembered"), her retrieved experience of the blessedness of fetal life,[14] to the one figure who shadows her throughout, Onorio Vasquez. Onorio, who treats Clare with a constant, attentive, practical kindness and who responds to her with something of her own kind of disinterested love, is Indian-Spanish. (The first person in the poem to be kind to Clare is remembered as "a brown-skinned Spanish-Indian boy.") In "The Women at Point Sur,"[15] Onorio had been introduced as a follower of the false prophet Barclay, whom "he had taken for incarnate God." Emerging chastened from this experience, he wants "to hear nothing / of what there was at Point Sur."

Onorio is a visionary, but a visionary without the power of understanding or interpretation. The eyes that see his visions for him are like those of some nonhuman creature from another element: thus, listening to Clare, "the dark eyes / Gave no sign whether they understood, gazing through her with a blue light across them / Like the sea-lions' eyes." We have come upon these sea lions a little before, in lines of subtly modulating vocalic and consonantal music that are among the most delicately beautiful in "The Loving Shepherdess":

The bleating of sheep answered the barking of sea-lions and Clare
    awoke

Dazzled in the broad dawn. The land-wind lifted in the light-spun
   manes of the waves, a drift of sea-lions
Swung in the surf and looked at the shore, sleek heads uplifted and
   great brown eyes with a glaze of blind
Blue sea-light in them.

Through such eyes Onorio sees such sights as these:

"I've watched, the whole night of a full moon, an array of centaurs
Come out of the ocean, plunging on Sovranes reef
In wide splendors of silver water,
And swim with their broad hooves between the reef and the shore
   and go up
Over the mountain. . . ."

But what Onorio sees is an image rather than a sign: "I never
knew why." Though his visions are "the jewels and value of his
life," and though when "they failed / And were not seen for a year,
he'd hungered to die," they have no spiritual application for him.
The knowledge he has to convey is merely of an unbridgeable gap
between the physical world and the world whence visions ema-
nate, a conviction that humanity is shut off from higher meaning:

      "Oh, never
Let visions nor voices fool you.
They are wonderful but we see them by chance; I think they mean
   something in their own country but they mean
Nothing in this; they have nothing to do with our lives and deaths."

The most protracted of his trance states is that in which his
faltering attempt to recall the name of the life-saving operation of
which he had heard long ago, the Caesarean section, leads by
verbal association to a visionary image of Caesarism, Roman imperial power at its summit. Such power may stand generally for the
triumph of anthropocentric arrogance, "the pride of the earth,"
which in turn is subverted and brought into the perspective of
modern astrophysics, according to which "the earth was a grain of
dust circling the fire, / And the fire itself but a spark, among
innumerable sparks." But that lengthy vision too ends for Onorio
as one that is untranslatable, as he gazes solipsistically at "his own
eye / In the darkness of his own face," yearning from his fragmented psyche for cosmic unity: "We kill . . . God / To be atoned
[at-oned] with him. But I remain from myself divided. . . ."
   Onorio fades from the narrative at the close of the penultimate

section, leaving Clare to walk alone the last stages of her life's journey. He has had one final brief vision that turned him back from accompanying Clare further,

> another vision on the road, that waved
> Impatient white hands against his passage, saying
> "If I go up to Calvary ten million times: what is that to you?
> Let me go up."

It is one of several references to the Christ story in "The Loving Shepherdess," and one of the several associations of Clare with Christ that parallels the action of "Dear Judas."

Jeffers himself in a letter had pointed out "The relationship between the two longer poems of [*Dear Judas*]," and in "Dear Judas," Jesus as much as Judas himself had been the protagonist. In that poem the facet of Jesus presented was exclusively that of Christ the King, Christ the tiger, or, in Jeffers' typology, Christ the hawk, on whose soaring magnificence the pitying, pathetic Judas would be "for many centuries" parasitic:

> you enter
> his kingdom with him, as the hawk's lice with the hawk
> Climb the blue towers of the sky under the down of the feathers.

In "The Loving Shepherdess" the facet of the Christ presented in the guise of Clare is entirely that of gentle Jesus, meek and mild, of Christ the Shepherd, Christ the lamb, or Christ the fisherman-heron who is hunted out of the sky by "the heavy, dark hawk" of power and ferocity. So Clare, standing in the midst of her flock "wore a pallor of starlight woven in her hair" for halo; or, elsewhere, bearing the burden of sin, and in delirium addressing her father (dead, in heaven), she speaks at one and the same time as Christ crucified and as one of Christ's tormentors:

> Sleep and her fever confused her brain,
> One heard phrases in the running babble, across a new burst of hail.
> "Forgive me, father, for I didn't
> Know what I was doing." And, "Why have you forsaken me, father?"
> Her mind was living again the bare south hilltop
> And the bitter penitence among the sheep.

As one by one, the members of her flock, the subjects of her pastoral care, fall away, she is left to her lonely Calvary between thieves and outcasts, with a "toothless tramp" on one side and "the sickly sullen boy on the other." Easter may not be named—for this is not a story of resurrection—but all along she has known that the month of her preordained fate is April.

There is no consistent or programmatic equation of Clare with Christ, however; the connections are intermittent and sometimes quite casual. It is more a case of the Christ story being one of the forms that Clare's self-sacrificing, universally sympathetic love may take. For Jeffers, the man steeped in Christian tradition, it is a principal form; but for Jeffers, the non- or anti-Christian Inhumanist, it is also only one of the forms.

Clare may not be a specifically Christian pilgrim, engaged on the Pilgrim's Progress; but hers is a pilgrimage and a progress nonetheless. If one recalls her surname, Walker, hers becomes the human or, more broadly, natural journey through life, impelled by love, towards the death that is the organic destiny. There is no avoidance of that final port; "we can't escape it," Clare knows. And in the nature of things, there can be no arguing with the movement of life; so "we have to go on," she says, and repeats, and presses on, always northwards. The northerly direction of Clare's journey is marked at least a dozen times. North, the bare, cold place of extinction? Or, to the culturally "hyperborean"[17] Jeffers, the direction towards which natural virtue gravitates? Both perhaps, in the way of the salmon striving upstream to its naturally appointed place, an analogy that Jeffers has Clare rather superfluously point out to us:

> Far up the Carmel Valley
> The river became a brook, she watched a salmon
> Row its worn body up-stream over the stones
> And struck by a thwart current expose the bruised
> White belly to the white of the sky, gashed with red wounds, but
> > right itself
> And wriggle up-stream, having that within it, spirit or desire,
> Will spend all its dear flesh and all the power it has gathered, in the
> > sweet salt pastures and fostering ocean,
> To find the appointed high-place and perish. Clare Walker, in a
> > bright moment's passage of anxious feeling,
> Knowing nothing of its fate saw her own fate reflected.

As the salmon swims, so Clare trudges on, spending her own dear flesh, pursuing upstream against the current of things her own natural mission, as she expresses it with lovely, monosyllabic plainness, to "take care of those that need me and go on till I die." Her appointed perishing comes not in a "high-place" nor her agony in a garden, but amid a thicket of willows, those trees anciently emblematic of sorrow and desolation:

> She crept down to the river and hid her body
> In a willow thicket. In the evening, between the rapid
> Summits of agony before exhaustion, she called
> The sheep about her and perceived that none came.

If Clare thus meets her individual death, having walked the path of her individual life, there are times in the poem when she seems to shed her particular, personal, contemporary humanity and generally to embody the world—the planet earth, Whitman's "vast Rondure, swimming in space"—and to encompass its time-span, as it too moves through a journey, eons-long, from explosive origins to whatever destiny awaits it. Jeffers is very much a poet of origins and destinations, of first and last things, of genesis and apocalypse, of *The Beginning and the End,* to quote his appropriately titled final volume of poems. So in "The Loving Shepherdess," when "Clare stood and trembled in the simple morning of the world," it is indeed in the morning of the world that she seems to stand, not in the morning of a twentieth-century day. Or, when the visionary Onorio tells of "her old enormous father / Who rode the furrows full tilt, sowing with both hands / The high field above the hills, and the ocean," it is not her actual Californian father that we see so much as a huge, primitive, godlike shape in the morning of the world. Or again, when in her abstracted wandering she is said to resemble "some random immortal wish of the solitary hills," she is for that moment less a person than an essence or metaphor of the world's body. And at last, she would seem in her infinitely extensive love to have absorbed the whole of human history and to carry the species with her towards the summation of its account,

> Walking with numbed and cut feet
> Along the last ridge of migration
> On the last coast above the not-to-be-colonized
> Ocean, across the streams of the people
> Drawing a faint pilgrimage
> As if you were drawing a line at the end of the world
> Under the columns of ancestral figures:
> So many generations in Asia,
> So many in Europe, so many in America:
> To sum the whole.

She has become the world—"And Clare loves all things / Because all things are herself"—so that in one aspect the story of her is the story of the struggle of all life, nonhuman and human alike, the salmon's and the shepherdess's, from the haven of egg or womb to the appointed high-place or willow thicket. As Jeffers had commented a few years before, in praise of seabirds and celestial planets, but also of human endeavor:

> all the arts lose virtue
> Against the essential reality
> Of creatures going about their business among the equally
> Earnest elements of nature.[18]

"The Loving Shepherdess" is Jeffers' most fully developed treatment of a character ruled through life until death by love. Insofar as Jeffers himself, the classically educated, westwards-venturing scion of a deeply Protestant line, was a complex amalgam of the stoic, the libertarian, the Whitmanian pantheist, and the Calvinist, so Clare is likewise variously derived. She passes the test of at least a popularly understood stoicism; she frequently speaks the language of pantheistic adoration; in her sexual ethics she is unrestrainedly libertarian; yet at the same time in her selfless, pastoral mission she is archetypally Christian. Her love is both charitable and erotic, but for all the impersonal generosity that she has learned for the last year or so of her life, she is perhaps, in Jeffers' terms, on the one hand too full of pity and too self-sacrificing, and on the other hand, too romantic and self-destructive to be properly wise and self-sustaining, to be other than "quite inefficient." Nearly two decades later Jeffers would put into the mouth of his exemplary Inhumanist his most considered, summary words on an "efficient love" and a sufficient care:

> "Moderate kindness
> Is oil on a crying wheel: use it. Mutual help
> Is necessary: use it when it is necessary.
> And as to love: make love when need drives.
> And as to love: love God. He is rock, earth and water, and the beasts
>   and stars; and the night that contains them.
> And as to love: whoever loves or hates man is fooled in a mirror."[19]

All is not love in "The Loving Shepherdess," of course. There is violence as well, the killing of man by man, the devouring of beast by beast; there is sexual catastrophe; and there is horror, ghastly images like the still-life portrait of family hatred around the kitchen table that Clare spies through a farmhouse window, haunting moments of insight such as the old farmer gives us, muttering "meekly" in his abject despair: "My wife and my sister have hated each other for thirty years / And I between them." In these respects the poem is of a piece with Jeffers' other narratives and dramas. Yet in its prevailing character, in the spell of sweetness that Clare casts over the whole poem, it is quite untypical of Jeffers' oeuvre; indeed it is, as has often been remarked, in that respect unique.

Being unique, it lacks for the most part both the typical virtues and the typical faults of Jeffers' other long poems. While there is less bathos and less rhetorical strain, there is also less resonance in the language, less grandeur. And while there is less horror, there is also, thereby perhaps, less awe. Nevertheless, "The Loving Shepherdess" remains a poem to which any Jeffers admirer should turn or return, both for its intrinsic beauty and for the balance it provides, to "Dear Judas" specifically and programmatically, and to Jeffers' narrative and dramatic work generally. It does not represent Jeffers at his greatest stretch, but it does show him at his most tender and truly charitable, moved, so painfully, by the spirit of love.[20]

NOTES

1. "The Measure" was published in *The Aurora*, December 1903.

2. Yvor Winters, "Robinson Jeffers," *Poetry* 35 (February 1930): 279–86.

3. Allen Tate is largely an exception to this general rule. See, for instance, his remarks in *Sixty American Poets 1894–1944* (Washington, D.C.: Library of Congress, 1945), 55–59.

4. F. W. Dupee and George Stade, eds., *Selected Letters of E. E. Cummings* (London: Andre Deutsch, 1972), 273.

5. The poem latterly has been discussed at length and represented as an important work by, among others, Frederic I. Carpenter, *Robinson Jeffers* (New York: Twayne, 1962), 80–81; Arthur B. Coffin, *Robinson Jeffers: Poet of Inhumanism* (Madison: University of Wisconsin Press, 1971), 106–11; and Robert Zaller, *The Cliffs of Solitude: A Reading of Robinson Jeffers* (New York: Cambridge University Press, 1983), 131–43.

6. See Alex A. Vardamis, *The Critical Reputation of Robinson Jeffers* (Hamden, Conn.: Archon Books, 1972), 71–78.

7. See Lawrence Clark Powell, *Robinson Jeffers: The Man and His Work* (1940; reprint, Haskell House, 1970), 47.

8. See *Heart of Midlothian*, note to chap. 14.

9. Many of the principal characters in Jeffers' narratives have either Scottish blood or names with Scottish associations. Though this is not the case with "The Loving Shepherdess," we should recall that Clare's original, Fannie, is Scottish.

10. For the record, Saul must be the "patriarch ram"; Butt and Ben are "the two old wethers"; Leader, Fay, Fern, Frannie, Nosie, and probably Tiny are ewes; and little Hornie, the single lamb.

11. Though Coffin's comment is apt, that "for ill-disguised dramatic purposes,

Jeffers, the former medical student, fails to provide [Clare's] doctor with information about Caesarean delivery" (Coffin, *Robinson Jeffers*, 112).

12. "Vulture," in *The Beginning and the End and Other Poems* (New York: Random House, 1963), 62.

13. By Albert Gelpi, in *The Tenth Muse: The Psyche of the American Poet* (Cambridge: Harvard University Press, 1975). Jeffers' Calvinistic pantheism is in contrast, at times only slight, with the often pantheistic Calvinism of his ancestor Jonathan Edwards.

14. This nostalgia for the heavenly positive of the womb that Jeffers attributes to Clare is to be distinguished therefore from the exemplary negations of Ecclesiastes ("Yes, better is he . . . which hath not yet been") and of the chorus in Sophocles' *Oedipus at Colonus* ("Not to be born is best").

15. "The Women at Point Sur" is not the only earlier narrative of which we are reminded in "The Loving Shepherdess." We also pass by "the mouth of Cawdor's canyon," where "Japanese tenants / Now kept the house," and a little later "by a gate / Where Tamar Cauldwell used to lean from her white pony / To swing the bars."

16. As Zaller, for instance, has pointed out in *The Cliffs of Solitude,* several of Jeffers' longer poems are "paired," balanced or contrasted, in the same volume.

17. The word *hyperborean,* the right word surely, is Kenneth White's, in *The Coast Opposite Humanity: An Essay on the Poetry of Robinson Jeffers* (Llanfyndd, Carmarthen, Dyfed: Unicorn Bookshop, 1975), 19.

18. "Boats in a Fog," *Roan Stallion, Tamar and Other Poems* (New York: Random House, 1935), 89.

19. "The Inhumanist," in *The Double Axe and Other Poems* (New York: Random House, 1948), 106.

20. That he is without doubt a great poet other contributors to this volume will surely attest. I have myself made two attempts to demonstrate and acclaim this greatness, in two general treatments: a monograph, "Robinson Jeffers," in *American Writers,* Supplement 2, part 2 (New York: Charles Scribners' Sons, 1981), and an essay, " 'The Dark Magnificence of Things': The Poetry of Robinson Jeffers," in R. W. (Herbie) Butterfield, ed., *Modern American Poetry* (London: Vision Press, and Totowa, N.J.: Barnes & Noble, 1984).

The Emasculation Syndrome among Jeffers' Protagonists

Robert J. Brophy

The casual reader of Jeffers will be puzzled by patterns that repeat themselves in his narratives. The reader who pursues story content and realistic detail will particularly be struck by an insistent trauma inflicted upon many if not most of Jeffers' male characters—the leg-wound-with-limp that either predates the plot's opening or develops as part of the story's structure.

Consider the following examples:

David Carrow, in Jeffers' "The Coast-Range Christ," suffers a gunshot wound in his thigh inflicted by his would-be lover Peace O'Farrell, who, in trying to seduce him in his hill refuge, has been repulsed and rejected. He then dies in a Christlike transfiguration.

At the opening of "Tamar," Lee Cauldwell, Tamar's brother, fractures his leg by spurring his pony over a sea cliff. The leg scar lingers throughout the story, figuring as a kind of incitement to sexual involvement, but at the same time as an inhibition. It is highlighted at the moment Lee pauses before entering the pool at Mal Paso Creek, on the brink of his fall into incest with his sister. In his death at the story's end, Lee takes with him his double, Will Andrews, Tamar's second lover, by stabbing him in the groin with a hunting knife. The effect is to inflict a wound upon a surrogate.

At the close of Jeffers' "The Tower Beyond Tragedy," the patricide Orestes uses a graphic emasculation symbol to describe how he cuts his ties with humanity, as he remembers "the knife in the stalk of my humanity," which "I drew and it broke." Orestes thereby frees himself from incestuous family involvement in order to wander high Arcadia till killed by a serpent.

In Jeffers' tragic reenactment of the drama based on the legend of Theseus and Phaedra, "Cawdor," Hood Cawdor escapes the seductions of his father's new young wife by stabbing himself in the thigh, an act that Jeffers calls the "Attis-gesture." Hood thereby incites Fera's vindictive lie, thus sending his father to the high rock to which Hood has fled and from which the agonized father hurls him to his death. Cawdor himself ends the drama by gouging out his eyes with Indian flints taken from the ground—an Oedipal gesture that psychoanalysts typically identify as a substitute for self-castration.

Reave, the tragically arrogant protagonist of "Thurso's Landing," is crippled and emasculated in cutting down his father's conveyor-cable, the remnant of the family's bankrupt lime-kiln business, which has come to epitomize the father as failure and enemy. Reave's brother, Mark, comes to the story crippled by a war-related leg wound. His limp seems to symbolize an acute sensitivity and suppressed sexual desires. He finally hangs himself.

In "Such Counsels You Gave To Me," Howard Howren's crippling appears to be more psychological, yet it manifests itself in a physical staggering (*SC* 11) as well as in a traumatized mind that "crawls blindly about his body like a numbed spider" (*SC* 17).[1] In a dream he experiences himself as crucified. Later, while clumsily cutting away the skin of the "monstrous crucified phallus" of a wild pig, he wounds himself with a knife. The "crucified phallus" is identified both with his father and with him. Finally confessing that he does not want other women but has always desired his mother, he rejects that mother and goes to society's judgment and his own psychic crucifixion, having effected his father's death by strychnine.

Bull Gore in Jeffers' "The Love and the Hate" is shot in the loins by his soldier son, Hoult, who leaves him dragging his legs impotently behind him as he futilely scrambles from an all-consuming forest fire.

The leg wound, the thigh wound, and the groin wound are a recurring syndrome in Jeffers' stories. The wound in each case is related in some way to the sexual realm. It is an infallible sign of debility and doom, leading always to a tragic death. If one surveys modern literature for parallels, one is hard put to find imagery employed for comparable purposes or with comparable frequency. Hemingway's hero Jake Barnes has suffered an incapacitating groin wound, but Jake is not a tragic hero and does not die as a result of any fatality implicit in the trauma. The mysterious physical-psychic wounding that emerges in other Hemingway stories (in Frederic Henry, Nick Adams, and others) seems to another purpose and not particularly helpful toward understanding Jeffers' pattern. The same can be said for the leg injury of

Tennessee Williams's Brick Pollitt in "Cat on a Hot Tin Roof."
There may be some initial similarities, but the story's direction is
opposite to Jeffers'. Nor is Little Lee Roy, the club-footed Negro
in Eudora Welty's "Keela, The Outcast Indian Maiden," much
help, although some of the symbolic resonances are interesting.
Eliot's impotent Fisher King of "The Waste Land" might be more
apropos, but that poem is in the satiric mode and not a tragic
narrative. Clearly no single author uses the groin trauma or its
variants in a way remotely parallel to Jeffers, and certainly none
uses the pattern so repeatedly, as though it were a necessary part
of each story-telling.

What follows are two possible readings of this pattern, one
psychoanalytic, the other in terms of myth ritual. Jeffers' own
mother-father-sibling pattern fits the Freudian mold. There is
significant literature to the effect that his writing reflects a coming
to terms with Oedipal conflicts.[2] On the other hand, Jeffers'
outspoken desire to recast myth in his time, his fascination for the
monomyth of eternal return, and his frequent invocation of sacramental rituals such as baptism, purgation, communion, priest-
hood, divine nuptials, and various rites of passage can be readily
substantiated. Both critical approaches seem to account for the
emasculation phenomenon in distinctly different ways.

Freudian critics will readily interpret Jeffers' preoccupation
with groin wounds and emasculation. Jeffers' stories, they would
say, are the dreams (Jeffers himself calls his narratives "bad
dreams") in which the author attempts to kill his father in order to
sexually possess his mother, but, finding himself unable to do so,
admits defeat, symbolically and guiltily castrating himself.

In such a reading, the character of Lee Cauldwell in "Tamar"
can be thus identified as Jeffers, the drunken profligate of
postcollege days; David, Lee's father, becomes the reincarnation
of Jeffers' clergyman father, teaching, preaching, and wielding a
traditional authority. Tamar would represent Jeffers' mother
(William Everson suggests this analysis in his introduction to the
reissue of Jeffers' *Californians*[3]), to whom he is incestuously attached and attracted. In the showdown that results, Lee (Jeffers)
has neither the courage to stand up to his father nor the ability to
renounce incest for freer, more mature liaisons. Lee's limp, like
his hesitancy and regression, becomes a self-fulfilling prophecy.
His castration urge is consummated when he symbolically emascu-
lates himself by stabbing his double, Will Andrews, as the story
ends.

David Carrow projects merely another variation on the same

theme. David, in the Freudian view, is Jeffers' troubled persona attempting to deny his hatred and aggression by a philosophy of pacifism (see, again, Everson in his edition of Jeffers' *The Alpine Christ,* for suggested connections between Jeffers' ambivalence over war and his father complex).[4] Peace O'Farrell is Jeffers' mother, the temptress and destroyer, to whom he is fatally attracted (the Hamlet-Gertrude pattern in the Freudian scheme). David resists consummation, however, and therefore precipitates Peace's Phaedralike vengeance against himself. Confronted by the crisis of his guilty desire, instead of working through the guilt to a freer sexuality, he has her emasculate him, thus restoring him to the innocence of withdrawal and regression. He can then gladly allow his father, who is in turn a double for Jaime O'Farrell, Peace's husband, to shoot him.

Likewise, Orestes, who has struggled throughout "The Tower Beyond Tragedy" to extricate himself from complicity in his father's death (which, according to the Freudian schema, he secretly desired and projected upon his mother), finds that his final desperate matricide, which is both vengeance and sexual renunciation, is not enough. Plagued in his mountain hysteria by fantasies of sister incest, he chooses not to take his father's place and marry his sister-mother, but to renounce sexuality. Thence, after the self-castration mentioned above, which may be interpreted physically or psychologically, he returns to the womb of nature where he is eventaully destroyed by the serpent, phallic representative of his father.

Once we break through the superficial layer of familial relationships, we find in Hood Cawdor yet another variation of the Oedipal pattern. His new stepmother represents the forbidden sexual preserve of his father; to this extent Fera personates Hood's mother, although there is actually no blood relationship between Hood and Fera but only the legal one. The sexual lure of mother-stepmother is prefigured in the shellfish hunt of section 3. Already strangely moved by Fera, Hood is suddenly confronted with a vulvalike cut in her hand and, as Jeffers describes his response, "He saw the white everted lips of the cut and suffered a pain / Like a stab, in a peculiar place" (*C* 24). His thigh wounding is thus anticipated. Hood, too, is unable either to challenge his father by sexually possessing his mother-surrogate or to resolve his Oedipal conflict and be free. Instead he chooses symbolically to castrate himself, and, in rejecting his stepmother, to invoke her wrath with its deadly threat of paternal vengeance. It is no consolation to the son that he is posthumously vindicated in his father's symbolic self-emasculation. Hood has already chosen death rather than resolve his father problem.

In "Thurso's Landing" we find doubles acting again. Mark and Reave can be seen as different manifestations of Jeffers' Oedipal urge or as different strategies for resolution, equally foredoomed. Mark, the weaker and more passive of the two, sensitive and psychic, is already signed by the emasculation limp. Self-destruction is his response, his only solution to the conflict. His reaction to his dead father is not as well articulated as his brother Reave's. Mark is raw-nerved, frail of ego, self-censored to an extreme. Perhaps finding his Oedipal block transferred from his father to his brother, his attraction is for Helen, his brother's wife. Realizing the incestuous nature of this longing, perhaps on a deeper level than the legally defined incest implied, he despairs of resolution. Unable to murder his father and marry his mother, he completes the castration implicit in his wound by destroying himself. Reave, Mark's double in this hypothesis, is fixed on a fatal hatred of his father who cannot be reached beyond death. If Helen is conceived as a mother-surrogate for him, he may find his father a marital obstacle, for he is unable to achieve an adequate sexual relationship with his wife. Yet he cannot let her go to his friend, Rick Armstrong, for reasons evidently explainable only in terms of a refusal to suffer defeat like his father—that is, by his father. Enter therefore a second surrogate, Esther, a weak creature with no personality and no sexuality, who can assure Reave temporarily that he is not defeated at this profound level of his being.

Reave attempts to cut the cord that ties him to his past, a cord representing his relationship with both his father and mother. He tries to erase memory and symbolically to castrate his father. But his own fatality is implicit in the reckless need to erase history. Possibly seeking self-obliteration in the temerity of cutting his father's skip cable, he is emasculated and hopelessly crippled by the collapse of the rotted tree that holds it. Thence he is condemned to a life of self-punishing expiation, as Freudians might say, for his consciously unadmitted but guilty desires. Till the story's end Reave lies in unremitting pain, bedridden, paralyzed from the waist down. Yet he will not accept release in any form, or even drugs to ease the pain. Indeed he breaks the gun that Helen brings to kill him, in what may be a second symbolic act of self-emasculation. He finally gains surcease, if not self-forgiveness, when his wife-mother, Helen, sacrifices him in ritual splendor on the dramatic Pacific headland that is Thurso's Landing.

"Such Counsels You Gave to Me" seems to have been conceived openly as a drama of the Oedipal complex. Howren and Howard, father and son, despise each other and vie for the mother, Barbara, who has remained enmeshed in the sexual contest of father and son. She has long ago transferred her sexual desires from husband to son and has manipulated the son through this. Unable to love other women, Howard has lived, studied, and striven only to be able to return and possess the mother. But he stops short of admitting that desire to possess; he demands only the right to stare at and fondle her nakedness. As he seems to confess, he has returned not to the womb but to the breast (*SC* 70). With his doppelgänger (the hallucinated self whom he meets after killing his father), he considers an Oedipal self-blinding (71), but judges it a futile gesture. He then decides to return to the ranch, wait for the authorities, and accept judgment and punishment. If Howard is Jeffers' self-projection, the story is a confession of inner desires that may direct and consume his life but that cannot be sated or resolved. Again the cripple fails either to consummate union or to resolve the conflict by moving beyond it. The sainted mother has become the mother-whore; the son can only choose guilt, atonement, and death.

Hoult Gore, the protagonist of Jeffers' "The Love and the Hate," so closely parallels Howard Howren that one may be distracted by the points of repetition. A casualty of the Pacific Theater of World War II, where he has had an island burial, Hoult breaks out of the grave from sheer hatred of his father and comes home to confront the heavy-handed, single-minded Bull Gore, who has manipulated him, not by loathing and financial threat as in the case of Howard, but by jingoistic patriotism. Howard's tuberculosis is paralleled in Hoult's chest-shattering war-wound. The figure of the mother in both stories is almost the same. Reine Gore and Barbara Howren have both taken young lovers; both are fatally attractive to their sons; both have heavy, crude, bulllike husbands. The means of vengeance against Hoult's father is not poison but bullets. It may seem too that the son in both cases succeeds in resolving the Oedipal conflict by killing the father. Hoult symbolically castrates Bull Gore by shooting him in the loins and then possesses his mother before letting death reclaim him. But this apparent triumph is acted out from the foredefeated vantage of death. The story thus seems a fantasy wish-fulfillment. The soldier son has already been killed, having unquestioningly submitted to his father's power and suppressed his mother love. In his return to the Gore ranch there is no real victory for him. Upon his Oedipal consummation, his body immediately disintegrates.

The foregoing analyses are tentative and conjectural, but they illustrate the type of patterning a Freudian analyst and critic might find in the turbid narratives of sexual jealousy, emotional impotence, hatred, and violence that permeate Jeffers' story-telling. But fascinating as it is, for many this Freudian pattern is not satisfying; it does not explain enough. Jeffers may have been pursuing the death of his father and union with his mother throughout his life and may have unconsciously revealed it in his writing. Who is to say? The fact that in "Hungerfield," Jeffers' last narrative, we find him using the protagonist's struggle with his mother Alcmena's death by cancer as a strategy to deal with Jeffers' own wife Una's death by the same disease is no doubt significant in this regard. The limping hero of his narratives may well reflect a subliminal embodiment of Jeffers' unresolved Oedipal conflicts. The argument seems uncontrovertible but also unprovable. More to the point, it is aesthetically limited, as Freudian criticism generally tends to be. The insinuations must be faced, sorted, weighed, and probably left behind, if one is to deal with the story further as a work of art and not as a clinical foray into biography.

More promising and rewarding would be an elucidation of the castration-limp pattern as a conscious artistic choice, part of an image and symbol complex that is meant to carry the stories' meaning. The reader is led to ask, therefore, what else might a fatal limp and emasculation syndrome portend? In what artistically articulated system of gesture and symbol does it convey tragic resonances and fatal forebodings?

As I have done elsewhere,[5] I would turn for my answer to the origins of Greek tragedy—to the world-view and symbol-system of primitive myth and ritual such as that which surrounded the ancient Dionysian festival. Cultural anthropologists at the turn of the century, as Jeffers entered college, were already offering this revolutionary insight as an opening upon the history and literary dynamic of Greek tragic drama.[6] According to this view, the matrix of tragedy lay in the fatal career of the year-god, whose life pattern was proposed as a paradigm for the life/death process of all things. The hero's human traits, his choices, his progressive self-destructiveness, were seen as symbols of a momentum that was deeper than human choice, more universal than human sexuality. In the god's death was mourned the corruption and death of all that could be corrupted and die. In his promised resurrection was foretold the resurrection of all that must be renewed. Emasculation, which Attis, Adonis, Osiris, and so many other year-god figures suffered, was reductively not a sexual happening but a manifestation of the world's sacrificial nature. In this primitive, sacramental world, all things must be fragmented so they might be reassimilated and renewed. Here castration symbolized the end of one fertility cycle, foreboding seasonal barrenness that would insure renewal, refecundation, and spring's prolific seed-scattering.

In the dithyramb, the primitive rituals that were the root of the tragic dramas, the year-god, variously personified but always recognizably the same, was subjected to one of a cluster of narrowly patterned and closely interrelated symbolic rites of passage that are reductively the same: all signal the end of the fertility cycle and the need for apocalyptic forces to reduce the old world to fragments that can then be reassimilated into new beginnings. In the sacred time and space that is myth and ritual's realm, fall-winter marks the end of the world: spring is creation *ab initio*. Within this system, castration symbolizes the harvest scythe's finality, the terrible severing of fecundating forces; leg and thigh-woundings are substitute gestures for castration. Fragmentation, stoning, and holocaust portend the reduction of the old world to a seed state, a sacrificing of old life forms so that new forms may take up the building blocks thus yielded. Heel wounds suggests all life's vulnerability, the heel touching earth and death. Serpent or scorpion or dragon or boar is the agent of winter darkness and absolute cold. Crucifixion and hanging are a hopeful offering to the ultimate source of life and in themselves are a promise of renewal, a black fruit that will yield green. Crucifixion is a peculiar variation of tree-hanging, pierced limbs reflecting the castration trauma, side wounds suggesting either the groin injury or the beginnings of a dismemberment that anticipates the sacred feast on the victim's flesh. The cross symbolizes the universality of immolation, the perennial constrictions of life (space and time, matter and spirit).

It seems instructive in this context to survey the overall patterns of death in Jeffers' narratives. They fall into each and all of the categories identified above, and almost all are ritually accomplished. Some of the death processes involve double or triple use of these symbolic modes (leg wound, groin wound, and holocaust, for instance, in "Tamar"; Attis gesture and scapegoat fragmentation in "Cawdor").

Among those who will die (or are marked for death) we may number: (1) by holocaust: Lee and David Cauldwell and Will Andrews in "Tamar," Bull Gore in "The Love and the Hate," Hawl Hungerfield in "Hungerfield"; (2) by fragmentation: Johnny in

"Roan Stallion," Pentheus in "The Humanist's Tragedy," Lance Fraser in "Give Your Heart to the Hawks," Creon and Jason in "Medea"; (3) by hanging: Jaime O'Farrell in "The Coast-Range Christ," Judas in "Dear Judas," Mark Thurso in "Thurso's Landing," Margrave in "Margrave," Odin, Prometheus, and the Hanged God in "At the Birth of an Age," and Bruce Ferguson in "Mara"; (4) by piercing/shooting/stabbing: Agamemnon and Aegisthus in "The Tower Beyond Tragedy," Hood and Cawdor in "Cawdor," Gunnar, Carling, Sigurd, and Hoegni in "At the Birth of an Age," Thurso Senior in "Thurso's Landing," Hoult and Bull Gore, and David Larson, Reine's lover, in "The Love and the Hate"; (5) by crucifixion (or being marked for death by Christlike stigmata): Arthur Barclay in "The Women at Point Sur," Lance Fraser in "Give Your Heart to the Hawks," and Carling in "At the Birth of an Age"; and (6) by emasculation-gesture: David Carrow in "The Coast-Range Christ," Hood Cawdor and Cawdor Senior in "Cawdor," Reave Thurso in "Thurso's Landing," and Howard Howren in "Such Counsels You Gave to Me."

In this paralleling of year-god figures and Jeffers' characters, the ritual manner of death, and the mutual reinforcement of symbols are particularly important to note. After all, recalling the categories above, one might object: how many other ways of violent death are available? The point is, however, the manner and import of the dyings. The year-gold's death is related to the vegetation cycle. From his blood seasonal flowers arise—iris, anemone, campion, hyacinth, and lily. His hanged body is pelted with pine cones or other seeds; his tree form is burned and the ashes spread as seed on the fields. When David Carrow dies, it is amid a compounded Christ-imagery of death and transfiguration. Jaime O'Farrell dies seeking a treasure hoard (the sun's rays?) in the tunneled ground; in his hanging, Jaime is a "black fruit," propitiation for spring blossoming. Lee Cauldwell's laming is directly related to withered vegetation; he attacks the serpent (winter), acts the ritual fool (the sun-god's mad phase), and is burned to ashes for the reseeding of earth (his name means meadow, and "grass grows where flame flowered" are the poem's final lines). The withered Johnny in "Roan Stallion" is Actaeon-like in his trespass on women's realm (his irreverence toward the mysteries of fertility); he is fawn and satyr, a sacrificing priest and a sacramental victim. Agamemnon in "The Tower Beyond Tragedy" is immolated as a bull-offering to the gods; Aegisthus dies under chariot wheels, Hippolytus-like and with Dionysian overtones. Orestes' death from the serpent (winter) suggests that the new king of

ritual succession must in his turn become the old king and die.
Barclay in "The Women at Point Sur" expires in a cave-tomb after
a ritualistic three days, his hands scarred with stigmata, his body
like a "burial pillar smeared with the blood of sacrifice," his last
intention apocalyptic ("shepherd my devouring fire. . . . north on
the cities"). Cawdor reenacts not only the Oedipal gesture but the
Orion myth, finding sight in blindness and atoning for his arrogance. Thurso takes his "house" like a ship on a mythic voyage
to destruction upon the last shore, a Viking demigod last seen on
his unlit funeral pyre. Lance Fraser, Prometheus-like in his torture by birds of prey, Christ-like in his stigmata, Oedipus-like in his
mistaken oracle, goes to his death as a scapegoat, the old king
dying for the new (his wife, Fayne's baby), and as an immolation to
bring rain to purge the guilt-plagued forelands. And so the stories
go, another half dozen or more, in the same pattern, immersed in
sacrificial imagery, myth patterns, and Greek and biblical allusions.
     As in the early Greek drama, in which the year-god's repre-
sentative was given a buskin to highlight his limp and to signify his
coming demise, so in Jeffers' narratives the limping hero is the
marked man, foredoomed to sacrificial death. No Jeffers limper
survives a story. The groin trauma of his heroes, which alludes to
the harvest scythe, symbol of the autumn's death-fixation, anticipates the inevitable consummation—the final piercing, rock-dash-
ing, or house-burning that closes the ritual.
     Jeffers was not without his artistic faults, and he indulged in
some pointless repetitions, especially late in his career. But he can
for the most part be seen as a careful craftsman in a peculiar
genre that might be designated as a ritual drama. He chose his
symbols and wove them tightly. If so many of his heroes limp, it is
not out of lack of authorial invention but because the limp places
his protagonist within a special realm of ceremonial gesture and
raises his fatality to the level of universal immolation by which the
world lives.
     Certainly this myth-ritual approach to reading Jeffers can be
vulnerable to the charge of reductive analysis often leveled at
Freudian criticism, and the protagonists seen as being reduced to
sacrificial analogues of the year-god, mimicking certain theories
of cultural anthropology familiar to the poet. However, several
points should be noted. Jeffers' poetry is intent on the very issues
that myth-ritual emphasizes—the inevitability of pain and death,
the cycle of life that rules all things, great and small, the relative
unimportance of any part within the whole of nature, the universality of sacrifice as a means to enable rebirth, and the divinity at

the heart of things, God slaying himself so that existence may remain dynamic and the refulgence of beauty be enhanced.

Jeffers' conscious concerns are rarely, if ever, with human psychology or individual fate. He tells us that the "mountain and ocean, rock, water and beasts and trees / Are the protagonists, the human people are only symbolic interpreters" (B&E 50). In an early letter to Donald Friede, his Liveright editor, he speaks of his attempt to get clear of the human so that "the dancer becomes a rain-cloud, or a leopard, or a God."[7] He describes the episodes in his narratives as "a sort of essential ritual, from which the real action develops on another plane." That other plane would seem to be Jeffers' central concern; it is the cosmic stage on which the drama of transhuman beauty is played out, the tragic platform on which all protagonists die in autumn sacrifice that the heart may live.[8] If we would hear Jeffers rightly, we must be receptive to mythic resonances and keep ourselves open to experiences of ritual. The cosmic dance must be danced. Characters' masks and costumes change but the gestures remain the same. A limp, self-mutilation, a heel-, thigh-, or groin-piercing is essential to that cosmic dance that continues, with or without humanity.

NOTES

1. Abbreviations of Jeffers' volumes are as follows:
SC   *Such Counsels You Gave to Me and Other Poems* (New York: Random House, 1937)
C   *Cawdor and Other Poems* (New York: Liveright, 1928)
DJ   *Dear Judas and Other Poems* (New York: Liveright, 1929, 1977)
S   *Solstice and Other Poems* (New York: Random House, 1935)
B&E   *The Beginning and the End* (New York: Random House, 1963)
2. The most comprehensive and persuasive handling of the Freudian element in Jeffers is Robert Zaller's *The Cliffs of Solitude: A Reading of Robinson Jeffers* (New York: Cambridge University Press, 1983).
3. *Californians*, ed. William Everson (Cayucos, Calif.: Cayucos Press, 1971), vii–xxvi, also reprinted in this volume.
4. *The Alpine Christ and Other Poems*, ed. William Everson (Cayucos, Calif.: Cayucos Books, 1974), ix–xxxiii, also reprinted in this volume.
5. Robert J. Brophy, *Robinson Jeffers: Myth, Ritual, and Symbol in his Narrative Poems* (Cleveland, Ohio: Case Western Reserve University Press, 1973).
6. Jeffers' reading throughout his long career is haphazardly recorded at present. He was certainly familiar with Sir James Frazer's *The Golden Bough*. Whether he read Gaster, Cornford, Harrison, Campbell, Eliade, and others still remains conjectural, though this question might yield to further research, as more of his and Una Jeffers' letters are recovered.
7. *The Selected Letters of Robinson Jeffers*, ed. Ann N. Ridgeway (Baltimore: Johns Hopkins University Press, 1968), 68.

8. This limping figure is, of course, not the only sacrificial type through which Jeffers explores the nature of being. The cosmic horse in "Roan Stallion," "in whose mane the stars were netted, sun and moon were his eyeballs" (*RS* 24), is immolated in its earthly surrogate. The Hanged God in "At the Birth of an Age" cries out: "I am the agony . . . I torture myself / To discover myself; trying with little or extreme experiment each nerve and fibril, all forms / Of being" (*S* 89). The Christ apparition in "The Loving Shepherdess" protests Onorio's belated interference in Clare's final agony: "If I go up to Calvary ten million times: what is that to you? Let me go up" (*DJ* 112), Calvary being every sacrificial death, every end of the cycle. The wounded eagle of "Cawdor," in the death dream that identifies it with the life of the cosmos, represents, says Jeffers, "the archetype body of life," "maimed and bleeding, caged or in blindness"; "Yet the great Life continued; yet the great Life was beautiful" (*C* 117).

Jeffers' Artistry of Line

Dell Hymes

For almost a half-century it has been known that Jeffers did not write what is loosely called "free verse," but had a "metrical intention."[1] Since Herbert Klein's pioneering work, the nature of that metrical intention has not been much studied or well understood. William Everson rightly argues that recognition of Jeffers' true stature requires attention not only to Jeffers' ideas but also to his craft.[2] Close study will show that Jeffers was resourceful and inventive in technique. Indeed, when Everson writes that a critic who rejects Jeffers' metric in the name of aesthetic norms of "clarity and precision and vigor" has to be shown that there are other norms, whose "uses are vital to the life and well-being of language and hence of civilization,"[3] he concedes too much. Such a critic can be shown that Jeffers himself achieves clarity and precision and vigor.

LINE RELATIONS IN JEFFERS

The New Measure

Most critics agree that "Tamar" is the beginning not only of Jeffers' fame, but of his greatness as a poet. It marks a dramatic change in the creative vigor both of story and style from what he had published previously. The two changes go together. Robert Zaller observes of Jeffers earliest narratives:

> The elements of the mature narratives—balladlike dramas of passion played out against the somber beauty of the California coast—were already present in these first works. But the characters remain curiously unrealized, figures of a pastoral idiom as stilted as the meters they are cast in.[4]

What if "Tamar" had been written in the rhymed couplets of the "The Coast-Range Christ," a predecessor that accompanies it in the volume that made Jeffers' reputation?

Zaller has analyzed the development that led to "Tamar" in terms of Jeffers' self-understanding:

> Not until Jeffers could see in human passion a worthy analogue of natural process was he able to transcend melodrama and create fully realized characters in a dialectically conceived relation to the external world. But that would not occur until he had come to terms with passion in himself and confronted the Oedipal sources of his art. (p. 5)

To tell his truth

> he could hope to do so only through a female protagonist. . . . What Jeffers found in search of his father's spirit was Tamar, who sought the father through the flesh. If Tamar herself could not resolve Jeffers' conflict, she would provide him with a way of objectifying it, of suggesting transcendence not through self-immolation but through carnality and violence. And if for her the end would still be a holocaust, it would not be until she had won through—and survived—the very limits of human experience. (14, 15)

To my surprise I agree with Zaller. Freudian interpretations of literature usually had seemed to me misleading, missing the actuality of a story in a selective and arbitrary grasping at preestablished symbols. Not in Zaller. His readings of Jeffers' narratives make point-for-point sense of their unfolding. The Oedipal dialectic penetrates and clarifies.

The problem of tragic art, as posed by Nietzsche, is that great works require a balance between a Dionysian foundation and an Apollonian order imposed upon it. A summary of the argument of *The Birth of Tragedy* reads as if written with Jeffers in mind:

> Its epitome is mastered energy, its poles are chaos and epic harmony. When the Dionysian element rules, ecstasy and inchoateness threaten: when the Apollonian predominates, the tragic feeling recedes.[5]

A feminine protagonist releases the energy in "Tamar," and a new measure masters it. Zaller explains the Dionysian pole: the Apollonian requires explanation as well.

In this essay I particularly want to extend investigation of Jeffers' new measure. Attention has gone mostly to the scansion of the lines themselves, to the bases and sources of their patterning as lines. Relations between lines have not, so far as I know, been much attended.[6] It is this aspect on which I will concentrate.

Narrative: An Ending as Beginning

"The Coast-Range Christ," written about 1917 (*RST* 175–204, *ML*186–219),[7] is the only major narrative between *Californians* and "Tamar" that Jeffers published. To Zaller it is central to his development: "Perhaps more than any other single work . . . [it] reveals the mind and art of Jeffers in crisis" (14, 6). Speaking, however, of the dialectic of characters, Zaller comments, [it] "is a static, not to say stillborn, work, and in it Robinson Jeffers is still a poet stepping . . . on the throat of his own song" (12). Frederic Carpenter observes:

> The long and irregular but sometimes monotonously rhymed couplets illustrate the poet's transitional experiments with verse; they are interesting, but contrast sharply with the wholly original and skilfully modulated versification of "Tamar" . . . although the narrative remains somewhat pedestrian, the concluding strophes and antistrophes of choros and antichoros seem, by contrast, to take wings and soar.[7]

Soaring there is, but the narrative is not over. These final lines complete it within the perspective of God, dawn, and the breadth of the world, in a partial departure from rhyme and a thoroughgoing alternation of length of lines. Here is a sketch of the grouping and scansion of the lines. (Space indicates pairing of lines; numbers indicate beats.)

Choros	(1)	8 4 10 6 9 5 10 4	[unrhymed]
Antichoros	(1a)	10 5 10 6 9 5	[unrhymed]
	(1b)	8 7 8 7 8 8 8 7 7 7	[couplets]
Choros	(2)	10 6 12 6 12 4 9 5	[quatrains]
Antichoros	(2a)	10 5 10 4 10 6	[unrhymed]
	(2b)	7 8 7 8 7 9 8 9 7 7	[couplets]
Choros	(3)	9 7 12 5 12 6 11 6 9 10	[quatrains couplet]
Antichoros	(3a)	(9)6 8 8 8(9) 8 9	[couplets]
	(3b)	(8)7 7 7 6 8 7 7	[couplets]

The nine parts move from unrhymed (1, 2, 5) to rhymed couplets (3, 6, 8, 9 and the couplet ending Choros 3) with rhymed quatrains *(abab)* intervening (4, 7). The one regularity is alternation of longer and shorter lines. This holds for the first and every subsequent choros, and for the first part of each antichoros except the last. Length of line is not fixed, but alternation of long and short is constant. The second part of each antichoros, and the first of part of the last as well, keep close to an intermediate length, commonly 8 or 7. Each antichoros appears to end with a pair of 7-beat lines.

The soaring at the end of "The Coast-Range Christ" thus goes together with a new relation among lines.

Matrix for Lyric

The shorter poems in the breakthrough volumes of 1924 and 1925 *(Tamar, Roan Stallion)* show the new relation in full flight. It is the pattern for most of them, a pattern for experiment.

"Mal Paso Bridge" *(Tamar,* 171–74 in *RST)* is the poem with the often-quoted clause, "To shear the rhyme-tassels from verse," and the shearing goes with sheer exuberance of invention. There is no rhyme, but there are eight sections, no two alike: twenty-six lines all of 5 beats (1); ten lines of alternating 5 and 4 (2); three tristichs, all of 4 beats (3); two unrhymed quatrains, both 4444 (if the last two syllables of each last line can be taken as metrically unmarked) (4); seven distichs of alternating 5 and 3 (5); six distichs of alternating 6 and 4 (6); two unrhymed quatrains of the pattern 5553 (7); four tristichs of the pattern 442 (8).

In "Mal Paso Bridge" there is not the variety of foot and patterning of line that the mature style will soon display, but the breakthrough is broached. The shorter poems of *Tamar* and *Roan Stallion* show a development that makes rhyme virtually impossible as a structural element, a marker of equivalence.[9] Jeffers "masters energy" in three respects: with a variety of types of feet within a line; with a variety of lengths of line; with lines grouped in a variety of ways. In each respect he invents novel relationships. The relations within a line allow both a variety of unfamiliar feet, notably the ionic and the paeon, and juxtapositions of feet whose metrical stresses are adjacent. Lines have an unfamiliar variety of lengths and unfamiliar length altogether. Lines are related to each other in novel, varied ways.

Patterns of relation. The shorter poems of *Tamar* and *Roan Stal-*

lion show Jeffers experimenting with relations among lines. The experimentation involves three dimensions: patterns of grouping line lengths; variability in the length of lines that correspond within a pattern; the range of difference between lines of contrasting length.

Grouping: All the poems group lines. There are no poems with seriatim, ungrouped lines. Line length may be constant; it is then long, or normatively so, and such lines are grouped as distichs ("Point Joe" [*RST* 233–34, *SP* 78], "Continent's End" [*RST* 252–53, *SP* 87–88], "Shine, Perishing Republic" [*RST* 95, *SP* 168]). The common pattern is to have lines of two different lengths alternate. The triadic pattern of "Divinely Superfluous Beauty" (*RST* 205, *SP* 65) is a lovely extension. In later volumes one finds inventive larger groupings of lines. "Be Angry at the Sun" (*BA* 152–53) has sets of four, in which a variety of short lengths are brought round each time to a yet shorter concluding line, 3 beats in the second stanza, two in all others. "The Bloody Sire" (*BA* 151) has sets of five, in which three stanzas of the form 4 4 4 4 6 are completed by a summative 4 6 pair. "The Excesses of God" (*BA* 104) is sonnetlike, with fourteen lines in which five alternations of 5 3 are concluded by four summative lines that alternate 63 63.[10] Some more extended shorter poems, meditative in character, have different line-lengths between one sequence and another: "Point Pinos and Point Lobos" (*RST* 235–41); "Night" (*SP* 158–60).

Variability: In a given pattern of relationship, lines may be constant in their differences of length. Such is the case with "Natural Music" (*RST* 245, *SP* 77), where the six distichs are uniformly 7 4 (seven beats, four beats), and "To the House" (*RST* 246, *SP* 82), where six distichs are uniformly 4 5. As noted, "The Bloody Sire" has three regular pentastichs: 44446, followed by a final pair, 4 6, and "The Excesses of God" has five alternations of 5 3, followed by two of 6 3. (Of course a poem whose lines are of constant length has constancy in the lack of difference.)

Where lines alternate, the odd-numbered are usually long, the even numbered short. Sometimes, however, a poem begins with the shorter line. Such is the case with "To the House" and "To the Rock That Will Be a Cornerstone of the House," and also "Wise Men in Their Bad Hours" and "Science." The marked, concluding line of each stanza of "The Bloody Sire" has 6 beats, following four 4-beat lines.

Corresponding line-lengths within a pattern commonly vary around a norm. Sometimes the variation is quite localized, a single line or two. Such is the case with "Divinely Superfluous Beauty," whose four triplets are 633 743 633 633; "To the Rock That Will Be a Cornerstone of the House" (*RST* 247, *SP* 83), whose two stanzas show 47 47 57 47 46 47 4, and 64 64 64 65 64 6, respectively,[5] and "Joy" (*RST* 97, *SP* 170), whose ten lines show 54 63 63 63 63.

In other cases variation is more frequent, but a norm still evident. Such is the case with "Salmon-Fishing" (*RST* 245, *SP* 81), whose lines alternate as 63 53 53 53 53 54 63 553 (the additional longer line at the end [553] may be another closing device); "To the Stone-Cutters" (*RST* 249, *SP* 84), where the lines may be scanned as 64 73 64 74 64); "Wise Men in Their Bad Hours" (*RST* 251, *SP* 86), where a rather steady alternation of 4-beat lines is interrupted by a sequence of four with 5 beats, 46 45 45 46 46 46 46 5555 46 45; "Birds" (*RST* 86, *SP* 161), with 84 74 76 86 84 84 86 75; "Fog" (*RST* 87, *SP* 162), with almost constant alternation of 3-beat lines, 72 53 33 52 53 53 73 63 73; "Boats in a Fog" (*RST* 88, *SP* 163), which settles into alternating 4-beat lines at the end, 73 83 74 63 64 73 64 64 74 74 64; "Granite and Cypress" (*RST* 89, *SP* 164), with clearly polarized lines of 92 103 93 93 102 92 93; "People and Heron" (*RST* 92, *SP* 166), with a constant 8-beat in odd-numbered lines (83 84 84 85 84); "Science" (*RST* 101, *SP* 173), with 49 59 49 49 48 58; "Post Mortem" (*SP* 179), with clearly polarized lines of 93 93 103 103 103 83 94 83 84 93 84 104; "Summer Holiday" (*SP* 181), with 46 57 46 56 56, where the almost constant length of the even-numbered lines seems defining, but where a different picture emerges when one groups the lines into the two five-line verse paragraphs of the syntax: 46574 65656. Note also the clearly, but contrastingly marked short/long of "Ante Mortem" (*SP* 178), with 48 48 59 58 59 48; and the long/ short of "Post Mortem," with 93 93 103 104 103 84 94 83 84 93 84 104.

Range: The examples just given show that alternating lines, contrasting lines, differ in the amount of difference that obtains between them. Let us call this a matter of range. There are three types, which can be dubbed *polar, double,* and *adjacent.* (Obviously if lines have the same length their relation is constant.) Mixing occurs, but one of the three types appears to frame a poem.

"Granite and Cypress" and "Post Mortem" are examples of a polar relation. In both the odd-numbered lines are in the upper range of a Jeffers line (9, 10, and some 8 in "Post Mortem"), while the even-numbered lines are in the lower range (2, 3, some 4 in "Post Mortem"). The interval of difference is great.

Many poems are examples of a doubled relation. The beats of

adjacent lines may not be precisely in a 2 : 1 relationship, but fall within a range close to that. The interval of difference is at least three beats. Such are "Divinely Superfluous Beauty" (6 3), "Natural Music" (7 4), "Salmon-Fishing" (taking the opening and closing 6 3 as norm); probably "To the Rock That Will Be a Cornerstone of the House," which seems defined by 4 7; "People and a Heron" (83 84); "Joy," almost entirely 6 3; "Science," with 49 59 48 58; "Ante Mortem" with 4 8, 5 9; "Cassandra," with almost entirely 6 3; "To the Stone-Cutters" (6 4, 7 3); "Boats in a Fog," with 7 3 (four times), 7 4 (three times), 8 2, and 6 3 dominating 6 4 (four times).

Sometimes lines alternate in the relations 6 : 4 and 5 : 3. Each is one step from 6 : 3 and can be considered akin to doubled relations. "To the Rock That Will Be a Cornerstone of the House" seems to belong here, 4 7 dominating the first stanza and 6 4 the second. "Fog" fits here, while noting its exceptional pair of 3-beat lines early on, as does "Boats in a Fog" and also "The Excesses of God," almost entirely 5 3, ending as it does with 6363.

In "Birds" there is a steady maintenance of a long odd-numbered line (8 or 7), and half the even-numbered lines are 4, but half of them 6 or 5. Maintenance of an interval of at least two beats appears to constitute a pattern in such a case.

A few poems show an adjacent relation. Lines alternate in length but the difference is entirely or preponderantly a single beat. Such are "To the House," 4 5 throughout; and "Wise Men in Their Bad Hours," predominantly 4 6 and 4 5.

Line Length as Device (1)

Study of any individual poem may show significance for any of these dimensions in relation to its thrust. Groups of poems may show one or more of these dimensions to have recurrent significance, and instances will be taken up below. There is a great need for study of all of Jeffers' poems with attention to both his evident inventiveness of form and his recurrent, prosodic practices. There is more than the presence of a measure; there is its varied deployment.

It does seem likely that much of the variation in Jeffers' verse is ad hoc. A poem got started and began to take shape in a certain way, and a feeling for pattern carried it out. It seems likely that in the short poems of the initial breakthrough it is the pervasive alternation of lines of different length itself that is meaningful. There is often little connection between a line of a given length and particular content. Sentences and clauses hardly coincide with lines. One ends, another begins, in the midst of a line. Syntactic units continue from a line of one length to a line of another like water escaping down a wheel (cf. "Divinely Superfluous Beauty" and "Natural Music").

Such alternation of lines allows a dialectic of movement on the page, a way of getting away from confining, a priori form, a way of keeping open the relation on the page between the movement of language and the movement of the world. If this statement seems one that might be made about William Carlos Williams, the parallel is intentional. Jeffers and Williams both achieved a pattern of freedom, a measure alert to the emerging thrust of a poem, open to continuing experimentation.[11] The difference is that Williams is famous for doing so while Jeffers is not. Williams announced a program, Jeffers left it to the chance of another to discover his metrical intention, and even then remained reticent. He did not wish to found a school, but perhaps over time others still will adopt and extend his discoveries as a distinctive tradition.

Line-length as Device (2)

Significant connotations for length of line do emerge within individual poems. Sometimes the position of a difference in length seems significant. At the end of the last sequence In "Point Pinos and Point Lobos," for example, the summative expression at the end (111) has six lines of 10 beats, followed by a split line of eleven beats in all (8 + 3, with space and indentation preceding the 3) and two lines of 12 beats. The enhancement seems intended. One might call it simple augmentation, somewhat like a concluding alexandrine. Especially perhaps in later poems, the longer line of an alternating pair may be lengthened at the end. In "The Excesses of God" (*BA* 104) five regular distichs of 5 and 3 beats are completed by a pair of distichs that are 6 3, and in "Cassandra" (*DA* 117) five regular distichs (6 3) are completed by one whose lines are 7 5. Again, the augmentation seems a device (sonnetlike in the case of the fourteen lines of "The Excesss of God"). On the other hand, framing lines may be shorter. In "Be Angry at the Sun" (*BA* 152–53) it seems no accident that in each quatrain the first and last line are shorter than the second and third, and the fourth line always shortest of all: 3562 4653 3652 4562 3562.

It may be possible to discover that particular lengths of line, and particular patterns of alternation, have meaningful associations, at least in certain sets of poems. The long lines at the end of "Point Pinos and Point Lobos" and in the ten-line distichs of "Continents End" both reach toward the sublime. It seems striking that both "To the House" and "To the Rock That Will Be a Cornerstone of the House" have the less common pattern of shorter line first. Other cases will be discussed below. Only a comprehensive study can tell the full story.

Whether or not associations of meaning between lengths of line and patterns of alternation of line-length prove pervasive in the shorter poems, it can be shown that such connections may emerge in the course of a particular poem. Three short poems from *Solstice* provide a demonstration.

In "Rock and Hawk" (*Solstice* 133, *SP* 563) the seven stanzas have each three lines, and the first two lines of a stanza have invariably three beats.[5] The third line has two beats, or so the first three stanzas establish. In the fourth stanza the third line may tempt one to hear a pair of amphimacers, "Not the cross, not the hive," but is easily taken as having just two beats (cross, hive). In the fifth stanza the third line, "Disinterestedness," might be taken as two beats, with elision of the third vowel ("Disint(e)restedness"), but may read more easily as three: "Disinteréstednéss." In the sixth stanza the third line is inescapably three beats: "Márried tó the mássive (/Mysticisms of stone)." The seventh, final stanza renews the predominant pattern: 3, 3, 2. One has then 332 332 332 33(2) 33(3) 333 332.

The possibility of added beats in the fourth, fifth, and sixth stanzas, increasing to certainty in the sixth, penultimate stanza, seems intentional. Otherwise the final lines of the stanzas could have been made to conform: "Not cross, not hive"; "Disinterést"; "Márried to mássive." The intention seems a formal one of arousing, suspending, and fulfilling an expectation. The two-beat line has a sense of ending in stanzas one and three: the return to it in the final stanza brings a sense of affirmative conclusion.

There is a similar effect in the modified sonnet "The Cruel Falcon" (*Solstice* 93, *SP* 562). The fourteen lines are grouped 4, 4, 2, 4 and rhymed (mostly with assonance) *abab cdcd ee fff*. The first four explore and qualify the theme "Contemplation would make a good life," the second four a contrary assertion, "Pure action would make a good life," each with corresponding imagery as to how that life should be (strict, sharp). The third stanza states briefly, without imagery, something lacking the good of either:

In pleasant peace and security
How suddenly the soul in a man begins to die.

In the fourth stanza the inevitable consequence is stated, the need and necessity of intensity:

He shall lóok up abóve the stálled óxen
Envying the cruel fálcon,
And dig únder the straw for a stone
To brúise himself ón.[13]

For the most part, there is no regularity of line length within stanzas, nor of corresponding lines across stanzas. (I scan the poem as follows: 6534; 5432; 46; 4442). One stanza, the last, does have a sequence of lines of the same length (444), and the second and fourth stanzas both end with two-beat lines, the one bringing the octet to a conclusion, the other the poem as a whole. The intervening stanza, the third, seems a pivot and contrast, having only two lines and going as it does from 4 to 6 beats, thus reversing the movement of other stanzas, all of which end with a line shorter than that with which they began. In the context, six beats is expansive. Thus patterning of line length supports meaning; regularity following variation and the return of a two-beat end line after departure fit a sense of inevitable consequence in the final stanza.

"Life from the Lifeless" (*Solstice* 134, *SP* 564) is in yet a different pattern of stanza and line length, yet also with an emergent connection between alternation of line length and meaning, and one that has analogy to the two others from *Solstice* just discussed. There are five stanzas, each of three lines. None are identical. (I scan the poem as follows: 424; 622; 333; 363; 444). The fifth and final stanza gathers the poem together, as it were, stating the outward-pointing moral in three lines all of four beats. It is the only stanza to have all its lines of the same length. Moreover, in the stanzas that precede, lines of two and four beats almost always coincide with positive meanings, lines of three and six beats with negative meanings:

Spirits ánd illúsions have died,
The náked mind lives
In the béauty óf inánimate thíngs.

Flówers wíther, gráss fádes, trées wilt,
The fórest is búrnt;
The róck is nót burnt.

The déer stárve, the winter birds
Díe on their twigs and lie
In the blúe dawns in the snów.

Mén suffer wánt and becóme
Cúriously ignóble; ás prospérity
Máde them cúriously vile.

But lóok how nóble the world is,
The lónely-flówing wáters, the sécret-
Kéeping stónes, the flówing sky.

The connection between length of line and kind of meaning is not perfect: "The deer starve, the winter birds" is part of the negative imagery, but with four beats (following "grass fades, trees wilt," "deer starve" can only be taken in the same way). The positive assertion "The rock is not burnt" might be read with three beats, although that seems less likely than two. Not everyone would find a fourth stress on "is" in the last stanza, although Jeffers' regular use of ionic feet, and the weight of the word at this point, convince me that it is to be taken so. But clearly the poem opens and closes with positive assertions and images in its first and fifth stanzas, set off against negative images in the three stanzas between; clearly the opening and closing stanzas are dominated by four-beat lines; clearly the negative imagery is introduced with a six-beat line ("Flowers wither . . ."); clearly the negative descriptions are concentrated and accumulate in three- and six-beat lines just preceding the closing stanza.[14]

These three poems published in 1935 show a certain consistency, a use of two- and four-beat lines, as opposed to three and six, for a sense of conclusion, and, sometimes, of positive statement. The poems themselves are of quite varied shape—four stanzas of four, four, two, four lines; seven stanzas of three lines each; five stanzas of three lines each, and show quite varied relation among line-lengths within and across stanzas. There is always pattern and measure, yet they emerge individually in each case.

Again, the sense of form adapted to the emerging thrust of the poem in hand, of continuing experimentation with form, is parallel to the work of William Carlos Williams. That Williams and Jeffers were contemporaries is important to remember, despite the difference in the way each broke from the "tassels of rhyme."

Line-length as Device (3)

Given that pattern and measure emerge individually and that Jeffers continued to experiment with form throughout his career, it is not possible to say that the meanings of line-length found in these three poems hold for other poems. Only a study of Jeffers' short poems as a whole could tell. But it is possible to suggest recurrent kinds of meaning for broad contrasts of line-length in the sequences of his longer poems. There alternation of length occurs, not line to line, but section to section. Let me explore this with two meditations, "Point Pinos and Point Lobos" and "Night," and then take up "Tamar."

In his sensitive assessment of "Night" Brophy calls it

> Jeffers' pivotal lyric . . . simply and effectively structured in classic meditation form—a natural scene is offered for contemplation, followed by the considerations arising from it.[15]

Length of line enters into the structuring in a subtle way.[16] How it does so can usefully be assessed against the background of another early meditative poem, "Point Pinos and Point Lobos" (*RST* 235–41).

"Point Pinos and Point Lobos" anticipates the lovely second stanza of "Night" in its lines of invocation—

> . . . O shining of night, O eloquence of silence,
>   the mother of the stars, the beauty beyond beauty,
> The sea that the stars and the sea and the mountain bones
>   of the earth and men's souls are the foam on, the opening
> Of the womb of that ocean.
>
> (RST 236)

and in lines that say of the Buddha:

> . . . and to meditate again under the sacred tree, and again
> Vanquish desire will be no evil.

The form also remembers "Tamar": the Buddha, found here as well as in Asia, smiles his immortal peace, commanding Point Lobos

> And the burnt place where that wild girl whose soul was
>   fire died with her house.
>
> (RST 240)

"Point Pinos and Point Lobos" has intrinsic interest as a sympathetic meditation and address on and to Jesus and Gautama as complementary teachers of men whose messages fall short. Part I addresses Jesus in relation to Point Pinos; Part II addresses

Gautama in relation to Point Lobos. Before doing so it opens with a panorama of the mountains of the world that Jeffers' spirit has visited (reminiscent of the panoramic view within which the action of "The Coast-Range Christ" concludes in choros and antichoros). It then says of the coastal point

> . . . there is no place
> Taken like this. . . .
> . . . Our race nor the great springs we draw from,
> · · · · · · · · · · · · · · · · ·
> . . . has known this place nor its like nor suffered
> The air of its religion.

This is to imply a third religion, native to the continent's end. Part I ends depicting its nature in the case of Jesus, Part II in regard to Gautama. Part III proclaims it generally. The two men whom "wisdom made Gods" tell nothing so wise or sweet as the eternal recurrences of nature. They foolishly rebelled against the laws of the instinctive God, the essence and the end of whose labor is beauty, for whom life and death, darkness and light, are one beauty, one rhythm.

Like "Night," "Point Pinos and Point Lobos" envisages acceptance, but of recurrence and beauty, not, as in "Night," of personal death. It ends with exultance, the other poem with tenderness.

Like "Night," this meditation has sections associated with length of line. Let me show the lengths, then briefly discuss them.

1	A	88888 8888[17] [Point Pinos]
	B	66666 66666 66666 66666 66 4 (split line) [To Jesus]
	C	2 11 12 10 12 11 12 10 3 (split line) [To ocean and night]
	D	5 66666 68666 66666 666 4 (split line) [To Jesus]
	E	2 55655 55555 655 [To Jesus]
II	A	88878 86768 97989 98886 88988 88888 8888
		6 (split line) [Mountains, Point Lobos, Buddha here also]
	B	2 88988 98888 8884 (split line) [To Gautama]
	C	2 877888 [Of Gautama and here]
III		10 10 10 10 10 8 (split line) [Recurrence vs. Jesus, Gautama]
		3 12 12 [invocation of praise]

There are three typical lengths of line. Lines of 8 beats are used for the opening description (IA), the catalogue of mountains

(IIA), and the rest of the part concerned with Buddha (IIB) and the character of the coast (IIC). Lines of 6 or 5 beats are used for Jesus. Lines of invocation of the true nature of the world are lines of 10 beats and more.

The differences in typical length of line go together with their content here and with their uses in other poems. The 8-beat line is one Jeffers uses in distichs (or another poem describing a point, "Point Joe," a poem that immediately precedes "Point Pinos and Point Lobos" in the volumes *Tamar* and *Roan Stallion, Tamar and Other Poems* (*RST* 233–34, *SP* 78–79). Evidently Jeffers found the 8-beat line suitable for such odelike description and reflection. He uses distichs of 10-beat lines in the hymnlike invocations and adjurations of "Continent's End" and "Shine, Perishing Republic" just as he uses 10-beat lines in the early moment of invocation and the concluding evocation here. The use of shorter lines with regard to Jesus goes together with a more intense personal focus on Jesus. Jesus is personally and passionately addressed several times, Gautama barely once (and then as his smile).

> Which tortured trunk will you choose, Lord, to be hewn to a cross?
> I am not among the mockers Master, I am one of your lovers,
> Ah weariest spirit in all the world, we all have rest
> Being dead but you still strive . . .
>
> . . . .
> . . . Unhappy brother
> That high imagination mating mine
> Has gazed deeper than graves: is it unendurable
> To know that the huge season and wheel of things
> Turns on itself forever . . .
>
> (*RST* 235, 237)

In this poem, then, an intermediate level of length (dominantly 8 beats) serves for accounts of nature and Buddha. It lies between two poles of line-length used for heightening intensity. One (10 and more beats) invokes the sublime, the other (6 and 5) personal identification and pain.

Lines that are long and lines that are short, often lines of 10 beats and lines of 5, are prominent in Jeffers, but "Point Pinos and Point Lobos" shows that a simple dichotomy is unable to do justice to his virtuosity, or indeed, to one indication of explicit intention. His notes for an early version of "Tamar," while they do not describe the final poem either as to plot or verse, do state a plan to distinguish three lengths of line, 5, 10, and 8.[18]

There is a special significance to the patterning of line-length in

"Night." As in "Point Pinos and Point Lobos" there are degrees of length of line. These degrees function within a strict pattern.

As previously stated, length of line enters into the structuring of "Night" in a subtle way. First of all, it is stanzas that alternate, not lines except as part of stanzas. There are three contrasts among the stanzas as to length: (a) in number of lines, (b) in typical length of line, and (c) in form of ending. All are consistently maintained.

(a) The seven stanzas alternate as to number of lines: 7 12 7 12 7 12 7. Odd-numbered stanzas, including the first and last, have fewer lines; even-numbered stanzas (ii, iv, vi) more.

(b) Shorter stanzas have a shorter range of lines in terms of length. Here is a scansion of them:

[i]	4 3 4 4 2	**4 2**	
[ii]	6 6 6 8 6	7 6 6 6 6	**7 7**
[iii]	3 3 3 4 3	**4 2**	
[iv]	6 7 6 6 7	7 7 7 7 7	**7 10**
[v]	3 3 3 3 3	**4 2**	
[vi]	6 6 6 6 6	6 6 6 7 6	**7 7**
[vii]	2 7 5 4 6	**7 2**	

(The last two lines of each stanza are given in bold face to call attention to the third relationship form of ending.)

(c) Each of the shorter stanzas ends with a 2-beat line, all but the last with the same pattern (4 2). In each of the shorter stanzas the final cadence is a fall from the longest to the shortest of its lines: 4 2 in (i, iii, v), 7 2 in (vii). Two of the longer stanzas (ii, vi) end with 7 7, the other (iv) with 7 10. In each of the longer stanzas the final cadence is a continuation or an augmentation of its dominant longest length of line. In (ii, vi) 6-beat lines have dominated and the ending is 7 7. In (iv) 7-beat lines have dominated and the ending is 7 10.

Let me take up the connotations of differing lengths of line and then the significance of the form of ending.

Like "Point Pinos and Point Lobos," "Night" makes use of three typical lengths of line, but the quantities are scaled down. That is appropriate to the tone in which the subject is treated. In "Night" the longest lines are commonly of 6 and 7 beats. It is these lines that are associated with the intensity of reaching toward the universe, the sublime. Their twelve-line stanzas (ii, iv, vi) invoke "Night" ("O soul worshipful of her," "O passionately at peace," "O passionately at peace"), while vividly depicting sources of light (the sun, human fires, stars, and planets). The one longer (longest) line, 10 beats, is the last line of a stanza of 6 and 7 beats, and in its position as last line of the middle stanza (iv) and in its content, linking cliff and tide, is a pivotal line:

> . . . To us the near-hand mountain
> Be a measure of height, the tide-worn cliff at the sea-gate a measure
>   of continuance.

It marks the point at which the poem turns to make explicit the respect in which it articulates the idea of the turning of the tide (see discussion of the final stanza below).

The middle range has lines of 4 and 3 beats. Like the middle-range lines of 8 beats in "Point Pinos and Point Lobos," these lines are associated with descriptive calm. The three short stanzas before the last, dominantly of 4 and 3 beats (i, iii, v) assert nothing but simply depict movements of return—to darkness, to water, to land—tide ebbing from rocks, sun setting, and a ship's light far out on the ocean (i); deer moving to a mountain stream (iii);[19] the tide turning toward the land (v).

The lowest range in "Night" is in the 2-beat lines. Each seven-line stanza ends with one, as does, of course, the poem. But where in "Point Pinos and Point Lobos" the lower range is associated with intensity of personal feeling and pain, here the lower range is associated with quietness and, in the end, peace.

Initially the association is a formal one, a function of cadence that provides a sense of closure. In the initial stanza, after lines of 434 beats, the fourth line pictures light that is fading or faint:

>   . . . the slow west
> Sombering its torch; a ship's light
> Shows faintly, far out,
> Over the weight of the prone ocean
> On the low cloud.

With the image of a ship's light the initial stanza moves twice to closure in the 42 42 cadence.

In the next short stanza (iii), after lines of 333 beats, there is an analogous movement of 43 42, with quietness in movement to the stream (no twigs crackling) and darkness (ferns) about the water.

In the third short verse (v), after lines of 33333 beats, there is a single 42 cadence, and the ultimate quietness is addressed, anticipating the theme and prophecy of the last long stanza (vi) and the premise of the ending (vii):

. . . you Night will resume
The stars in your time.

The association of a 2-beat line with quietness and peace is a
function of overt statement in the final short stanza, framing the
rest of the stanza with an opening question ("Have men's minds
changed") and closing answer ("And death is no evil"), but also of
form in the relation of these lines to the other lines of the stanza
and to lines of other length in the poem as a whole.

The final stanza, itself renewing the pattern of shorter length of
stanza and line, at the same time encompasses the longer line
length of the longer stanzas. It begins and ends with 2-beat lines
and has a 4-beat line at its center, yet incorporates lengths (767)
found otherwise only in the long stanzas. In its own ending it falls
from 7, its own longest length and the longest normal length of
line in the poem as a whole, to 2, its shortest and the shortest in
the poem.

These relationships indicate an opposition, or polarity, that is
resolved in the final stanza in favor of that which such shorter
stanzas and their shorter lines or final cadences express. In "Point
Pinos and Point Lobos" the longest lines invoke and hail the
discovery of eternal recurrence and return. In "Night" the shortest lines accept it. In the meditation on the two Points, the discovery is developed by imagining Jesus and Gautama as ultimately
subject to it (I, II), and then asserting the inadequacy of the two in
comparison to it in a grand expansive tutti (III). In "Night" there
is final assertion too, but as quiet recognition. All is natural process, and its description begins, mediates, and ends the passionate
contemplation and reflection of the intervening longer stanzas.
Recurrence is not a lesson learned, but implicit in the governing
image of tide, now enlarged beyond the human world. It means
not only "alternation of white sunlight and brown night" (*RST*
241), day and night, seasons and "fierce renewals," as in the
meditations at the Points, but also a world eventually again without sun ("he will die" ["Night" (ii)]) and human beings. The penultimate short stanza ends: ". . . you Night will resume / The stars
in your time." To be sure, the deeper fountain, Night, immortal, is
the grandest tide, and might be imagined ultimately to recede and
to be followed by another lighted world. But the poem itself ends
with the acceptance of personal death and universal dark. Following the one 10-beat line at the end of the middle stanza the tide
turns to the land and Night will resume the stars (v). Life is said to
remember quietness and to live ready for harbor (death) (vi). A

rock hidden deep in the waters of the soul breaks the surface (vii). (The passage is framed as a question, but the preceding lines make clear the positive answer.) The tide-rocks (i) and the grave depths of the poet's soul in which the splendor without rays dwells always (ii) are identified and generalized to humankind, for whom the darkness beyond the stars now is empty of harps and habitations and death is no evil.

The contraries of the longer stanzas—on the one hand, Night, on the other, human delight, effort, passion, and consciousness, recognizing, addressing, and invoking Night—are formally absorbed and framed within the shorter stanzas. Until the end of the third of the shorter stanzas (v) they assert nothing, but simply describe. The natural processes of the short stanzas are identified with the human history of the long stanzas through the image of the tide-rock.[20] And the pattern of return to quietness is enacted as a conclusion.

The final transcendence is formally prepared from the start. To accept the opening stanzas as description in the pattern given in each is to be prepared for accepting the end. Each of the preceding seven-line stanzas is associated with the description of natural process, and in each the length of line associated with such description falls to 2 beats, associating natural process with rest and peace. In its position, framing, and lengths of line, the final seven-line stanza connotes a natural process, but now one that occurs in men's minds ("Have men's minds changed") and encompasses in its long penultimate line their most passionate quest:

But now, dear is the truth. Life is grown sweeter and lonelier,

and the recognition that "Death is no evil" is of a piece with the low cloud, dark ferns, and Night resuming the stars.

The foregoing observations may be useful in regard to other of Jeffers' shorter poems. No single conclusion should be proposed on the basis of the few poems considered here. Quite possibly Jeffers' concern and practice varied over time, responsive to expressive concerns, an internal evolution, or the sheer desire to experiment with possibilities.

The shorter poems, however, are the lesser challenge. To show a further dimension of artistry may commend them to a wider readership. Still, they have never lacked for admirers. It is the long narratives, which are central to Jeffers' own purpose and effort, that have most suffered neglect.[21] The work of Brophy,

Everson, Zaller, and others is doing much to restore their place. In a further study I hope to show how the principle of relations among types of lines enters into the organization of the long narratives, adding a level of organization, indeed, whose recognition enters into the interpretation of their form and foci of intensity.

BIBLIOGRAPHY

Brophy, Robert J. *Robinson Jeffers: Myth, Ritual and Symbol in His Narrative Poems.* Cleveland: Case Western Reserve University Press, 1973; Hamden, Conn.: Archon Books, 1976.

———. "Night: A Prayerful Reconciliation." *Robinson Jeffers Newsletter* 37 (December): 6–7, 1973(b).

Burke, Kenneth. "Psychology and Form." *The Dial* (July) 79(1): 34–46 (1925). Reprinted as "The Psychology of Form" in his *Counter-Statement* (New York: Harcourt, Brace, 1931; 2nd ed., Chicago: University of Chicago Press, 1957.)

Cushman, Stephen, *William Carlos Williams and the Meanings of Measure* (Yale Studies in English, 163). New Haven, Conn.: Yale University Press, 1985.

[Everson, William] Brother Antoninus, *Robinson Jeffers: Fragments of an Older Fury.* Berkeley, Calif.: Oyez, 1968.

Everson, William. *Archetype West: The Pacific Coast as a Literary Region.* Berkeley, Calif.: Oyez, 1976.

Hymes, Dell. *'In Vain I Tried to Tell You'.* Philadelphia: University of Pennsylvania Press, 1981.

———. "Anthologies and Narrators." *Recovering the Word,* edited by Brian Swann and Arnold Krupat. Berkeley and Los Angeles: University of California Press, 1987.

———. *"Now I Know Only So Far."* Philadelphia: University of Pennsylvania Press, forthcoming.

Jeffers, Robinson, *Roan Stallion, Tamar and Other Poems.* New York: Boni & Liveright, 1925. New York: Random House, twelfth printing, 1934 [RST]. New York: Modern Library, 1935. [ML]

———. *Solstice and Other Poems.* New York: Random House, 1935.

———. *The Selected Poetry of Robinson Jeffers.* New York: Random House, 1938. [SP]

———. *Be Angry at the Sun.* New York: Random House, 1941. [BA]

———. *The Double Axe and Other Poems.* New York: Random House, 1948. [DA]

Klein, H[erbert] Arthur. *The Prosody of Robinson Jeffers.* M.A. thesis, Occidental College, 1930 [So cited in Powell 1940]. [Ridgeway 173 cites as "A Study of the Prosody of R.J."]

Lévi-Strauss, Claude. *The Naked Man.* (Introduction to *A Science of Mythology,* 4). New York: Harper & Row, 1981. [Translation of *L'Homme Nu* (Paris: Librairie Plon, 1971)]

Nickerson, Edward. "Return to Rhyme." *Robinson Jeffers Newsletter* 39 (July 1974), 12–20.

———. "Robinson Jeffers and the Paeon." *Western American Literature* 10 (November 1975): 189–93.

Powell, Lawrence Clark. *Robinson Jeffers. The Man and his Work.* Pasadena, Calif.: San Pasqual Press, 1940.

Scott, Robert Ian. "Robinson Jeffers as an Anti-Imagist." *Robinson Jeffers Newsletter* 63 (June 1983): 8–12.

Stern, J. P. *Friedrich Nietzsche.* Edited by Frank Kermode. New York: Penguin Books, 1978.

Zaller, Robert. *The Cliffs of Solitude: A Reading of Robinson Jeffers.* New York: Cambridge University Press, 1983.

NOTES

This study is part of a larger one. In the larger study the conclusions reached as to Jeffers' use of types of line are used to explore the organization of "Tamar" in some detail, and the whole is framed by a concern to place Jeffers as a narrative poet of the West in relation to American Indian narrative poets who preceded him. On the one hand it appears that both Jeffers and American Indian narrators have assigned meaning to contrast and alternation of types of line. The ways in which they do so are different, but the common principle points to what may be a universal basis of poetry. On the other hand there are links between Indian myths and Jeffers in the handling of character as an abstract calculus of motives, and in a sacramental sense of the relation between their world and those who live in it. Indeed, certain Indian myths express that relation in the light of experienced destruction and loss, analogous to Jeffers' response to the devastation of the lives and expectations of a generation in the First World War. There is in particular a myth of the sun, told by the last narrator of a people who lived on the coast at the mouth of the Columbia River, of which "Tamar" seems in many points a transformation—so much so that if "Tamar" had been found, couched in Indian style, in a text collection from northern California, someone practicing the structural approach of Claude Lévi-Strauss could hardly fail to count it and the Chinookan "Sun's myth" as part of the same series. William Everson (*Archetype West: The Pacific Coast as a Literary Region* [Berkeley, Calif.: Oyez, 1976], 71–74) has also pointed out a striking parallel between "Tamar" and a California-Oregon myth, Loon Woman, in regard to sister-brother incest and death by fire. Cf. Lévi-Strauss, *The Naked Man* (New York: Harper and Row, 1981), introduction.

1. H[erbert] Arthur Klein, "The Prosody of Robinson Jeffers," M.A. thesis, Occidental College, 1930, as reported in Lawrence Clark Powell, *Robinson Jeffers: The Man and His Work* (Pasadena, Calif.: San Pasqual Press, 1940), 118ff.

2. Brother Antoninus [William Everson], *Robinson Jeffers: Fragments of an Older Fury* (Berkeley, Calif.: Oyez, 1968), 29.

3. Ibid., 29–30.

4. *The Cliffs of Solitude: A Reading of Robinson Jeffers* (New York: Cambridge University Press, 1983), 3–4, 5.

5. Within each stanza all the lines are adjacent on the page. I separate pairs of lines to make the patterning of length more perceptible.

6. Regrettably I have not seen the 1930 master's thesis by Klein. What I know

of it through quotation and published letters (Ann N. Ridgeway, ed., *The Selected Letters of Robinson Jeffers, 1897–1962* [Baltimore: Johns Hopkins University Press, 1968]) seems generally correct and sensible. I very much hope that the further inquiry he had undertaken before his death will become available. If what I say should duplicate any of his work, I hope it will be regarded as independent confirmation. In a fuller study I want to offer my own sense of the scansion of Jeffers' lines and the bases of his practice with regard to stress, types of feet, and types of line.

7. Abbreviations for Jeffers' works used in this essay are:

BA *Be Angry at the Sun* (New York: Random House, 1941)

DA *The Double Axe and Other Poems* (New York: Random House, 1948)

ML Modern Library edition of *RST* (New York, 1935)

RST *Roan Stallion, Tamar and Other Poems* (New York: Boni & Liveright, 1925)

SP *Selected Poetry of Robinson Jeffers* (New York: Random House, 1938)

Solstice *Solstice and Other Poems* (New York: Random House, 1935)

8. Frederic I. Carpenter, *Robinson Jeffers* (New York: Twayne Books, 1962), 65.

9. Not entirely impossible. The English poet Paul Muldoon is currently exploiting rhyme as a marker of equivalence within a great diversity of serious poems, as did Ogden Nash in light. Edward Nickerson ("Return to Rhyme," *Robinson Jeffers Newsletter* 39 [July 1974]: 12–20) has discussed Jeffers' renewed experiments with rhyme and stanza form in later years as an indication of his lifelong experimental interest in craft.

10. Where there are only two figures to indicate a pattern of beats, they are separated by space in order to distinguish them clearly from citations of page numbers or other figures. Where there is a series of numbers for beats, its reference seems clear enough and intervening spacing unnecessary. Thus in the preceding sentence, 5 3, but 63 63.

11. On Williams see Stephen Cushman, *William Carlos Williams and the Meanings of Measure*, Yale Studies in English 163 (New Haven: Yale University Press, 1985).

12. Within each stanza all the lines are adjacent on the page. I separate pairs of lines to make the patterning of length more perceptible.

13. In terms of types of feet, anapest anapest antispast / trochee trochee trochee trochee / iamb choriamb anapest / iamb anapest. The conjunction of iamb and choriamb in the third quoted line illustrates a common Jeffers practice, following a foot that ends with stress by a phrase that begins with "under," "over," or "out," and so requires initial stress.

14. I take "curiously" in the fourth stanza as having three syllables, with "ious" representing a single syllable. "Curiously" has metrical stress on its last syllable in the second line, followed by an unstressed syllable, but not in the third line, which is followed by a syllable that is stressed. Alternatively, "curiously" might be taken as having a second syllabification in its second occurrence and the line scanned as "Made them cúrióusly víle," but that seems quite unlikely, especially because it detracts from the intended contrast between "ignoble" and "vile."

All three lines of the stanza are taken as stressed on the initial syllable. "Men súffer . . ." is unlikely; "Mén" takes stress because of its place in the series (flowers, grass, trees, deer, birds).

15. Robert J. Brophy, *Robinson Jeffers: Myth, Ritual, and Symbol in His Narrative Poems* (1973; reprint, Hamden, Conn.: Archon Books, 1976).

16. Not previously noted, so far as I know. I have not yet seen the dissertation

by Kiley, which includes attention to prosody, and a study of "Night" (*Robinson Jeffers Newsletter* 24 [1969]).

17. The separation into groups of five is entirely for convenience of perception. The lines represented by a line of numbers for a section (A B C D E) are continuous on the page.

18. In a letter to Donald Friede of 25 November 1925, Jeffers explains his inability to provide the typewritten manuscript of "Tamar," but does report finding a great sheet containing "1) The first germ of the Tamar story, dramatis personae (several of whom were lost or changed in the telling), incidents, metrical indications" (Ridgeway, *Selected Letters*, 53). Section 1 of the notesheet is reproduced by Ridgeway (ibid.), and has at the bottom:

```
5 beats to the line
   doubled in a few passages to [?] 10s
   quickened to anapests, [?] anapestic
ᴗᴗᴗ  —lyrical passages, [?]
        to 8s
```

The markings are 3 breves and a raised line of equal length, perhaps intended to represent the fourth paeon, a foot of four syllables, with three unstressed syllables followed by a stressed fourth.

Notice that although subsequent writers often refer to Jeffers as having rejected meter, he himself uses the term here ("metrical indications"); five years later in writing to Klein ("metrical intention"), and eight years later writing to Keppel ("All my verses are metrical, or imagine themselves to be") (Ridgeway, *Selected Letters*, 173, 206).

19. One so readily recognizes that this stanza has to do with deer that it may come as a surprise to realize that deer are not named. Perhaps that assists a focus on natural inanimate process, making salient a quiet movement toward water.

20. Presumably the rock in the soul (vii, line 2) breaks the surface at a turning point. What has risen with the withdrawal of the tide in human life will be covered again, just as the tide-rock whose streaming shoulders emerge from the slack at the outset of the poem will be covered with the incoming tide. (In stanza v the coming of [general] Night is associated with the tide turning toward the land.)

21. There is a parallel to another reader of Nietszche's *Also Sprach Zarathustra*, the composer and contemporary Frederick Delius, who is mostly known for his short orchestral pieces, while his major works in opera and for chorus and orchestra (*Appalachia, Sea-Drift, A Mass of Life, Requiem "To the memory of all young artists fallen in the war"*) are seldom performed.

The Verbal Magnificence of Robinson Jeffers

Frederic I. Carpenter

In the late 1920s the tragic poetry of Robinson Jeffers and the tragic drama of Eugene O'Neill challenged and excited the literary audiences of the time. When *Strange Interlude* was first performed in 1928, I was struck by the strange power of the climactic scene in which Nina gathers "my three men" about her, "*thinking*: husband! lover! father! . . . I am pregnant with the three," and as the others watch, kisses each in turn. For me this recalled the final scene of Jeffers' "Tamar," in which his heroine gathers "my three lovers . . . under one roof" and later explains: "I have my three lovers / Here in one room / How can I help being happy?"

In 1932 I wrote O'Neill suggesting this parallel. He replied: "No, there's no contrast with "Tamar." As a matter of fact, though I know and like most of Jeffers' other work, I have never read 'Tamar.'" At the time this disclaimer of interest in "Tamar" seemed disappointing—perhaps even doubtful. But over the years many readers who have admired Jeffers' shorter poems have also shared O'Neill's distrust of "Tamar" and the longer narratives. They have felt that the ancient myths of incest, which had suggested Freud's Electra and Oedipus complexes, should have been allowed to remain in the realm of the literary subconscious. And the explicit sexual violence that recurs in many of Jeffers' long poems has continued to repel many.

Of course, the mythical violence of the long narrative poems can be—and has been—justified and interpreted. The best modern critics of Jeffers have devoted themselves to this task. In *Robinson Jeffers: Myth, Ritual, and Symbol in His Narrative Poems* (1973), Robert Brophy pioneered the study of Jeffers' narratives, emphasizing the background of primitive myth. In *Fragments of an Older Fury*, Brother Antoninus (William Everson) used Carl Jung's theory of archetypes to explain the extreme violence of "Tamar" and of *The Women at Point Sur*. Robert Zaller, in *The Cliffs of*

Solitude, interpreted Jeffers' longer narratives in terms of Freudian psychology. Clearly, the narratives present a challenge that goes beyond the limits of mere poetic explication.

But of course Jeffers was primarily the poet, and his power has manifested itself most clearly in the shorter poems where the complexities of myth do not intrude. To me this power has always seemed self-evident. But even the self-evident may need emphasis and interpretation, and the macrocosmic criticism of myth finds its complement in the microcosmic criticism of the single-line phrase. Narrowing the focus still further, we may consider the single word, which sometimes goes beyond meaning to achieve a kind of verbal perfection, or magnificence.

Let us consider three short poems in some detail, emphasizing the words that transcend their dictionary definitions to achieve new artistic power. One of the most popular and often anthologized is "To the Stone-Cutters" (1924): its brief ten lines seem simple, but suggest infinitely more than they say. A longer poem of three pages, "An Artist" (1928), includes passages of sheer verbal magnificence, although this very magnificence seems to call attention to itself. Finally, the first quatrain of a later poem, "For Una" (1941), is one of the most perfect that Jeffers ever wrote.

To the Stone-Cutters

Stone-cutters fighting time with marble, you foredefeated
Challengers of oblivion
Eat cynical earnings, knowing rock splits, records fall down,
The square-limbed Roman letters
Scale in the thaws, wear in the rain. The poet as well
Builds his monument mockingly;
For man will be blotted out, the blithe earth die, the brave sun
Die blind and blacken to the heart:
Yet stones have stood for a thousand years, and pained thoughts
    found
The honey of peace in old poems.

The theme of this poem is a traditional one—Edmund Spenser called it "Mutabilitie"—the struggle to achieve permanence in an impermanent world. Now Jeffers addresses his stone-cutters directly and realizes their struggle concretely by dramatizing it in action. They "fight" against "time," an all-powerful adversary. But they also "Eat cynical earnings": they are really mercenaries who chisel out "square-limbed Roman letters" to do battle for them. Meanwhile the adjective "square-limbed" humanizes these stone artifacts, while the simple word "letters" suggests the identity of stone-cutting with poetry-making, for the poet also uses letters as the building blocks of his literature. Again, however, he does so "mockingly," for the modern poet has also become cynical, recognizing as he does the omnipotence of his cosmic antagonist. Not only will time blot out man, but also the "blithe" earth that he inhabits. The adjective "blithe" humanizes the planet earth, grouping it with the "cynical" stone-cutters and their "square-limbed letters" as "foredefeated" antagonists of "time." The new theme suggested by these adjectives is the essential unity of the human and the nonhuman in their common fights against time.

"An Artist" is a much longer poem that includes a framework of narrative together with descriptions of nature and dialogue by the artist explaining his motivation. But despite its greater variety and length, its theme is much the same as that of the "Stone-Cutters." This artist is a sculptor—a stone-cutter who now chisels the rock face of a desert canyon into human forms. But because he has accepted his inevitable defeat by time, he is no longer "cynical." He now strives only against "chaos," to create not "square-limbed letters," but actual bodies out of natural stone.

The poet-narrator stumbles upon the entrance to a strange canyon in desert country:

> There were stones of strange form under a cleft in the far hill;
>   I tethered the horse to a rock
> And scrambled over. A heap like a stone torrent, a moraine,
> But monstrously formed limbs of broken carving appeared in
>   the rock-fall, enormous breasts, defaced heads
> Of giants, the eyes calm through the brute veils of fracture. . . .
> . . . .
> The walls grew dreadful with stone giants, presences growing
>   out of the rigid precipice, that strove
> In dream between stone and life, intense to cast their chaos . . .
>   or to enter and return . . . stone-fleshed, nerve-stretched
> Great bodies ever more beautiful and more heavy with pain,
>   they seemed leading to some unbearable
> Consummation of the ecstasy . . .

The repetition of "stone" and "rock" make this vivid description seem wholly natural: "stones of strange form" in "the rock-fall"; "stone giants," "between stone and life," "stone-fleshed." But the human forms created by the artist seem always to conquer the natural stone—both in language and in reality—until the sculptured artforms take on a life of their own. And the identity of the human and the nonhuman, which the "Stone-Cutters" had only suggested, seems now to become reality.

But the transformation of stone and rock into the forms of human art is accomplished almost wholly by verbal means. The stones themselves seem to become active: a stone "torrent" in rock "fall." The stone "giants" become presences "growing" out of the rigid precipice, that "strive," "intense" to "cast" their chaos. The realistic description of nature becomes the narration of an interior action, leading to symbolic realization of pity and terror by means of art.

After this description of the "ravine of Titans," the artist appears in person: "I will not show you / More than the spalls you saw by accident." The unusual word "spalls" seems to express the artist's scorn for the imperfections of his art. But the dictionary defines "spalls" simply as "chips" or "fragments." No dictionary suggests the derogatory connotation implied by Jeffers' context. Once again the word means more than it says. The artist, meanwhile, explains the violence of his feeling:

> "What I see is the enormous beauty of things, but what I
>   attempt
> Is nothing to that. I am helpless toward that.
> It is only to form in stone the mould of some ideal humanity
>   that might be worthy to *be*
> Under that lightning. Animalcules that God (if he were given
>   to laughter) might omit to laugh at.
> Those children of my hands are tortured, because they feel,"
>   he said, "the storm of the outer magnificence.
> They are giants in agony. They have seen from my eyes
> The man-destroying beauty of the dawns over their notch
>   yonder, and all the obliterating stars.
> But in their eyes they have peace. . . ."

"The storm of the outer magnificence," leading to "some unbearable / Consummation of the ecstasy," has caused the passion of this artist. The language is extreme because the feeling that it describes is extreme. It is magnificent, but it also abstract and even a little magniloquent. What—in the words of T. S. Eliot—is its objective correlative? The extreme language of the next two lines seems to reinforce the question. In what possible sense are "the dawns over their notch yonder" "man-destroying" or "the stars" "obliterating"?

The language and the imagery both emphasize a shift from the human to the nonhuman: the "monstrous stone giants" that the poet-narrator saw are now replaced by the "enormous beauty of things" that the artist sees in the "outer" world "beyond the notch yonder." And it is this enormous beauty—not the dawns themselves—that is "man-destroying" in the sense that it destroys man's feeling of self-importance. "The storm of the outer magnificence" "obliterates" man's preoccupation with his own inner agonies. In this context, the word "obliterate" achieves a new perfection beyond simple meaning, for it is defined as "to remove from significance" or "to strike out." *Ob-* means "out" and *litera* means "letters." Not only will the "square-limbed letters" of "To the Stone-Cutters" be actually obliterated by time, but their narrow human meaning will be "obliterated" by the beauty of the stars. The single word, read in the full context of Jeffers' vocabulary, achieves a new level of signification.

What then is the objective correlative of all these words? To what actual experiences do they refer? Most obviously, they refer to the imagined experience of the artist in his desert valley, and more realistically to the experiences of the poet in his campouts under the stars, far from the little lights of civilization. More generally, they refer to the experiences of all those cattle-herders and sheep-herders who live and work in the wilderness, and particularly to those Greek and biblical shepherds who first named the stars and their constellations. But most of all, perhaps, to the primordial action of the Bushman mother described by the South African writer Laurens van der Post in *The Heart of the Hunter,* who holds her newborn baby above her head in dedication to the stars above her desert home. Ultimately the "enormous beauty" of the "obliterating stars" refers to the experiences of all those human beings who lived before civilization began and to all those in later times for whom the primitive awe aroused by the myriad stars still "obliterates" the literal patterns of civilization.

Finally, the brief poem "For Una" describes the poet's situation in his later years, using traditional rhythm and rhyme to emphasize its simple, autobiographical nature:

> I built her a tower when I was young—
> Sometime she will die—
> I built it with my hands, I hung
> Stones in the sky.
>
> Old but still strong I climb the stone—
> Sometime she will die—
> Climb the steep rough steps alone,
> And weep in the sky.

Never weep, never weep.

The first line describes the actual achievement of the young stonemason who built a tower for his young bride out of the most permanent material he knew. But "Sometime she will die": no longer "fighting time with marble," the poet recognizes and accepts the impermanence of life. His work, however, was not only actual, but devotional. "I built it with my hands," "For Una." The actual tower and the past action in building it are symbolic rather than practical. For this is, to borrow another Jeffers title, "the tower beyond tragedy." Its great value lies in the poet's transcendence, not only of the tragedy of life, but symbolically, of earth itself.

> . . . I hung
> Stones in the sky.

The single verb "hung" is perfect: it is symbolic but also factual. Although it is not humanly possible to "hang" stones in the sky, except momentarily, nevertheless the poet did actually hang stones for a moment from the top of his tower: having carried them up two flights of stone steps, he lifted them "with my hands" and momentarily hung them above the walls of the turret before lowering them to their place on the wall below. "Hung" emphasizes this momentary achievement of an actual position "in the sky," above and beyond the inevitable tragedy of life.

The moment has passed, however, and the stones have been set. The poet has grown old and the steps are steep. He can still climb them, but only to weep. But weeping is all too human, and so the last line breaks off with the exhortation: "Never weep, never weep." Now the tower beyond tragedy brings cold comfort.

Yet the tower still stands as the reminder of past accomplishment: "I hung / Stones in the sky." And the verb emphasizes the memory of a past transcendence, "in the sky." Once when the poet had stood at the top of the tower, it had seemed, symbolically, halfway to heaven. Now life's tragedy has come to its close.

Now, indeed, Una has died—and Jeffers too. The stones of the tower, viewed from a distance, seem to have become part of the low coastal hill. The traveler on the road below may look up at the strange architecture of stone above him and wonder. But the tower at the top still remembers the sky.

The Politics of Robinson Jeffers

Edward A. Nickerson

Ezra Pound broadcast for Italy during World War II, exalting the Fascist regime and blaming the war on Jewish bankers. Afterward, New Directions published Pound's *Pisan Cantos* without apology for his views. Various publishers also printed without disclaimers or apologies the writings of others who had remained indulgent of the Soviet Union long after there was massive public evidence of Stalinist tyranny. Yet Robinson Jeffers, who had endorsed democracy specifically and at some length in a talk at the Library of Congress in 1941, was subjected to the indignity of seeing *The Double Axe* appear in 1948, the same year as Pound's *Cantos*, bearing a publisher's disclaimer. The editors of Random House devoted an entire introductory page to announcing their disagreement with "some of the political views" Jeffers expressed in the book.

The incident, notorious among Jeffers readers, needs no elaboration here, but it is worth mention because it was symptomatic of public uneasiness about Jeffers' politics. Indeed, from a self-protective point of view Random House was correct in its nervousness. The views of a significant portion of readers were probably well represented by the reaction of the *St. Louis Post-Dispatch* to the book: "Only the most devout followers of the right-wing nationalists, the lunatic fringe, and the most ardent of Roosevelt haters could, after reading *The Double Axe*, welcome the return of Robinson Jeffers."[1]

The uneasiness about Jeffers went back to the growth of social protest writing during the Depression years and was doubtless fueled by fear and hatred of fascism, especially the German kind, whose power was on the rise at least into 1941. Yet less than a generation after *The Double Axe's* appearance, Jeffers' supposedly reactionary poetry caught on here and there with a curiously different audience. These new enthusiasts were typically students who had encountered Jeffers in college courses. Some were backpackers, climbers, or wilderness-lovers, and a great many of them were people opposed to the United States role in Vietnam. For these people Jeffers had two possible appeals. Poems like "Shine, Perishing Republic," which had warned that America was "heavily thickening to empire" in 1925, seemed extraordinarily prescient to war protestors watching the spread of American military bases through Southeast Asia and elsewhere. And for those primarily concerned with the environment, a cause that waxed as the Vietnam War waned, Jeffers provided hundreds of lines to conjure with. The Sierra Club, for instance, used Jeffers' lines to illustrate its popular book of photographs, *Not Man Apart.*

Thus Jeffers' political attitudes have been perceived in different ways over the years. To the casual reader they can seem somewhat contradictory. Some samples follow, drawn from the shorter poems. My labels are for convenience only.

Left Wing (In reference to Armistice Day, 1918)

> We were all glad a long while afterward,
> But still in dreary places of the earth
> A hundred hardly fed shall labor hard
> To clothe one belly and stuff it with soft meat,
> Blood paid for peace but those still poor shall buy it . . .
>
> "The Truce and the Peace"

Right Wing

> The proletariat for your Messiah, the poor and many are to seize
>   power and make the world new,
> They cannot even conduct a strike without cunning leaders: if they
>   make a revolution their leaders
> Must take power. The first duty of men in power: to defend their
>   power. What men defend
> To-day they will love to-morrow . . .
>
> "Blind Horses"

Environmentalist

> Oh, as a rich man eats a forest for profit and a field for vanity, so you
>   came west and raped
> The continent . . .
>
> "A Redeemer"

Antiactivist

> But most of us, one time or another

Have taken unhappy causes or hopes to heart, and gotten well burnt.
"Local Legend"

Isolationist and pacifist

I curse the war-makers, I curse
Those that run to the ends of the earth
To exalt a system or save
A foreign power or foreign trade
"Drunken Charlie"

It would be easy to go on, providing examples that seem to show
Jeffers as a Roosevelt-hater and even an advocate of violence and
of war as cleansing. But in the light of these apparent contradictions, what *were* his politics?

Jeffers is best characterized, I believe, as a radical conservative.
This term should not be taken to mean extremely conservative or
part "radical" (left-wing) and part conservative. Rather, his conservatism stemmed from the root, or *radix*, the original meaning
of radical. It was a conservatism of disbelief in the human capacity
for ameliorating society, at least within any period we think of as
historical. It was a conservatism that, unlike Eliot's, did not endorse any religion, and was especially suspicious of saviors and
Caesars. It believed, as the most casual of Jeffers' readers must
know, in conserving nature, although not necessarily in conserving particular human cultures or nations. Rather, it was coolly
neutral. It was also, interestingly enough, a conservatism that had
some sympathetic understanding of the left-wing or reformist
point of view and an affinity with Jeffersonian democracy. A
statement in a letter to Mark Van Doren and James Rorty in 1927
neatly capsulizes these seemingly conflicting attitudes. In the letter, which set out to explain *The Women at Point Sur*, Jeffers wrote:
"Some of you think that you can save society; I think it is impossible, and that you only hasten the process of decadence. Of course
as a matter of right and justice I sympathize with radicalism; any
way I don't oppose it; from an abstract viewpoint there is no
reason I know of for propping and prolonging the period of
decadence. Perhaps the more rapid it is, the sooner comes a new
start."[2]

Jeffers' attitudes were not, in fact, inconsistent unless one takes
a shallow view of what is conservative and liberal. Jeffers scorned
demonstrative patriotism in *The Double Axe* and elsewhere, but this
attitude hardly puts him in the liberal camp, for nationalism is a
development more associated with movements like the French

Revolution than with conservatism. Edmund Burke, Thomas Carlyle, and the Spanish philosopher Ortega y Gasset, all conservatives, associated patriotism with mob rule. Isolationism and a degree of pacifism used to be embraced in the years before World War II by many Republican conservatives. Conservation, now something of a liberal cause, was popularized by none other than a Republican superpatriot, President Theodore Roosevelt.

Some perceptions of Jeffers, moreover, were just factually wrong. The St. Louis newspaper critic who suggested that only "the most devout followers of the right-wing nationalists" could welcome Jeffers' return ignored the antinationalistic sentiments in "The Love and the Hate," the first poem of *The Double Axe*. As an ordinary soldier killed in battle, furthermore, Hoult Gore, the poem's protagonist, saw himself as a pawn sacrificed in someone else's game. This attitude is not right-wing, but typical of the proletarian views that became popular with some soldiers in World War I. A powerful example is Dalton Trumbo's *Johnny Got His Gun* (1939), the story of a World War I soldier who is blinded, deafened, and made a quadriplegic by his wounds—a living dead man. Its bitterness and horror precisely recall that of Hoult Gore. Trumbo was of the far left in politics.

If we are to understand Jeffers' politics thoroughly, however, it is necessary to do more than to search out his most representative statements and to note that his inconsistencies may be mostly in the eye of the beholder. It is instructive to consider his responses to the world of human institutions (a broad term for his political attitudes) as comprising three kinds. All such divisions are somewhat artificial, but these categories may help to illuminate the man and his art and explain his views.

The first kind represents a basically emotional response, visceral in the intensity of its anger and disgust. On this plane, despite his firm friendships with a few individuals and despite his happy marriage to Una, it is apparent that Jeffers did not enjoy people. In groups, he definitely disliked them. There may have been an aristocratic disdain for masses of chattering city-dwellers that stemmed from his isolated childhood and from an ineradicable shyness; in any case, he made his distaste for "the hive" of "communal people" repeatedly clear. He avoided cities whenever possible; he did not act as poet-in-residence in colleges, did not go to conferences, would not travel to accept awards, and made only one speaking tour, that being in 1941 to raise money to pay a special tax assessment on his increasingly valuable ocean-front property.

Jeffers asserted from time to time that he was neutral about the human race, and even that there was some virtue in humanity, but the emotional weight of his poetry was heavily on the negative side of the scale. Examples abound, especially in *Be Angry at the Sun* (1941) and *The Double Axe*. None is more powerful than "Original Sin" from the latter collection, especially the poem's first section:

> The man-brained and man-handed ground-ape, physically
> The most repulsive of all hot-blooded animals
> Up to that time of the world: they had dug a pitfall
> And caught a mammoth, but how could their sticks and stones
> Reach the life in that hide? They danced around the pit shrieking
> With ape excitement, flinging sharp flints in vain, and the stench of
>   their bodies
> Stained the white air of dawn; but presently one of them
> Remembered the yellow dancer, wood-eating fire
> That guards the cave-mouth: he ran and fetched him, and others
> Gathered sticks at the wood's edge; they made a blaze
> And pushed it into the pit, and they fed it high, around the mired
>   sides
> Of their huge prey. They watched a long hairy trunk
> Waver over the stifle-trumpeting pain,
> And they were happy.
>   Meanwhile the intense color and
>   nobility of sunrise,
> Rose and gold and amber, flowed up the sky. Wet rocks were shining,
>   a little wind
> Stirred the leaves of the forest and the marsh flag-flowers; the soft
>   valley between the low hills
> Became as beautiful as the sky; while in its midst, hour after hour,
>   the happy hunters
> Roasted their living meat slowly to death.

Robert Zaller has suggested that Jeffers' expressions of aversion to people function as poetic strategy, a way of dramatizing his points. I agree, and add that sometimes the disgust is more "used" for this purpose than fully felt, as in the famous line, "I'd sooner, except the penalties, kill a man than a hawk" ("Hurt Hawks"). In "Original Sin," however, the aversion is intense and is expressed in bitter, sarcastic outbursts as well as in the juxtaposition of noble nature to ignoble man: "And they were happy." The disgust precisely recalls Swift's king of Brobdingnag characterizing humans as the "most pernicious race of little odious vermin that nature ever suffered to crawl upon the surface of earth." Like the king, Jeffers describes humans in terms of unattractive creatures. In doing so, he violates the consistency of his own philosophy, for ordinarily he sees nothing evil in the nonhuman world, and he avoids negative animal characterizations like "bestial cruelty." Yet in this poem the hunters are compared to ground apes "shrieking with ape excitement." Such is the nature of Jeffers' anger.

In poems where he does assert that the human race has some value, the lines lack intensity. In "De Rerum Virtute," for example, Jeffers writes, "I believe that man too is beautiful, / But it is hard to see, and wrapped up in falsehoods." The "too" betrays his lack of enthusiasm, as does the "it," which indicates that the beauty of humanity is only a concept, not a feeling.

The second kind of response to the human world is the rational one. Jeffers was a wide reader of history as well as of literature, and was introduced by his father in early youth, as he noted in a letter to Hyatt Howe Waggoner, to "timely ideas about the origin of species, descent of man, astronomy, geology" (*Selected Letters,* 255). As an undergraduate in college, moreover, and in graduate schools, he had a broad education in both the humanities and the sciences, at one time working as a professor's assistant in physiology. His brother was an astronomer and this contact seems to have helped him to keep current with the latest cosmological theories. In his historical reading he was particularly intrigued by the cyclic theories of Giovanni Battista Vico and of Flinders Petrie. Jeffers' own observations, too, suggested that all things have a life cycle. He must have known the famous biological rule that ontogeny recapitulates phylogeny—the life of the individual reenacts that of the species or race. Jeffers was too careful a thinker to bind himself to any rigid theory that the cycles are of predictable length, but his poems (such as "At the Birth of an Age" and "At the Fall of an Age") repeatedly remind us of the rise and fall of old cultures and empires: Greek, Roman, pre-Christian Teutonic, Spanish, British. Poems like "Diagram" testify to his belief that the cycles are continuing:

> Look, there are two curves in the air: the air
> That man's fate breathes: there is the rise and fall of the Christian
>   culture-complex, that broke its dawn-cloud
> Fifteen centuries ago, and now past noon
> Drifts to decline; and there's the yet vaster curve, but mostly in the
>   future, of the age that began at Kittyhawk . . .

Perhaps the major conclusion Jeffers drew from his contemplation of history was that the human race, a species, does not fundamentally change any more than do other species—sharks, for instance, which have been unaltered for 350 million years. Why should man change, when his years were but a fraction of the short life of the planet earth in the universe? If Jeffers saw things this way, it was not surprising that he should be suspicious of those who would save humanity and those who would be saved by it: ". . . How many children / Run home to Mother Church, Father State / To find in their arms the delicious warmth and folding of souls." And later in the same poem: "Christ said, Marx wrote, Hitler says, / And though it seems absurd we believe" ("Thebaid"). Jeffers did not believe—not in the divinity of Christ, his father's lord and master all his life, and certainly not in secular saviors. In "Air-Raid Rehearsals" he coupled one of each kind of savior to give his opinion of their ultimate futility: "I see far fires and dim degradation / Under the war-planes and neither Christ nor Lenin will save you."

Jeffers did not believe, either, in dictators as a means of salvation from above. He feared, however, that prosperous, peaceful times led societies to forget their freedom and become ripe for Caesars. Hitler, he wrote, was a genius, "cored on a sick child's soul," a fanatic who knew how to appeal to tribal yearnings in the German psyche. He mentioned him, and Stalin, in repeatedly derogatory contexts, yet his characterizing word "genius" came back to haunt him, as did the masque, "The Bowl of Blood," which appeared in 1941 in *Be Angry at the Sun* with Hitler as the protagonist. As Frederic Carpenter observed, making Hitler a tragic hero, even if he was portrayed as an evildoer, was too much for many readers.[3] The public reaction to some extent recalls the criticism aimed at W. D. Snodgrass's poem-cycle *The Führer Bunker*, for "humanizing" the Nazis. "That's just the point," Snodgrass told this writer once: "they *were* human, and if we deny their humanity we do the same thing that they did to the Jews."

Jeffers was also suspicious of great men who were not Caesars but would-be saviors. Franklin D. Roosevelt, he wrote in "Great Men," a poem in which he spoke of Hitler's ruthless tactics, had gained his following through "grandiose good intentions, cajolery / And public funds." In one of the poems that Random House did not print in *The Double Axe*, Jeffers referred to the "cripple's power-need" of Roosevelt, although again, the words do not make the poet a Roosevelt-hater of the Union League Club variety: the context in "What Odd Expedients" shows this. Jeffers says first that the wild God of the world, his pantheistic God of eternal change and struggle, uses war to limit man's power. Then:

>   . . . and to promote war
> What odd expedients! The crackpot dreams of Jeanne d'Arc and
>   Hitler; the cripple's power-need of Roosevelt; the bombast
> Of Mussolini; the tinsel star of Napoleon . . .

In this view humans are actors playing out tragedy or comedy in a script they do not fully understand. Their flaws lead them and their followers into terrible fates, like the agonists in Jeffers' version of the Oresteia, "The Tower beyond Tragedy." Woodrow Wilson, who led Americans into a war that damaged American democracy and tolerance and laid the kindling for the 1939–45 war, had a tragic quality that required "the huge delusion of some major purpose to produce it" ("Woodrow Wilson"). Among Jeffer's "great men," only the quiet philosophers like Confucius or the artist Shakespeare escape censure. They did not lead nations or start religions.

If there was one area in which Jeffers, the former laboratory assistant in physiology, might see measurable progress, it was in science. In fact, as Hyatt H. Waggoner has pointed out,[4] the maturation of Jeffers as a poet coincided with the incorporation into his work of many references to scientific concepts and terms. He visited the Lick Observatory (where his brother, Hamilton, did his research) several times, and seemed particularly drawn to astronomy and to theories of the cosmos. The quiet concentration of scientists on nonhuman things attracted him, yet he did not trust what they would do with their discoveries: "Now he's bred knives on nature turns them also inward; they have thirsty points though. / His mind forebodes his own destruction." These lines from the relatively early poem "Science" are complemented by later poems, including Jeffers' expressed fear in "The Inhumanist" section of *The Double Axe* of scientists whose talents are at the disposal of the state.

After the development of the atomic bomb, Jeffers repeatedly mused on the possibilities of human self-annihilation through nuclear energy. In "Hungerfield," too, he presented the idea that every scientific bargain with nature, every cure, has its Faustian payback. The rancher Hungerfield wrestles with a death-angel and wins a stay in his mother's cancer; but strange deaths then occur to cattle and to people in the human household. The story seems a parable of scientific accomplishments in the field of medicine: chemotherapy can shrink a tumor but causes frightful nausea and can be fatal in itself; anabolic steroids build football

players with necks like Minotaurs, but subject them to early pros-
tate cancer and other diseases. The parallel in political life is clear:
when there is improvement of one kind, it is at the expense of
something else. "Men will fight through to the autumn flowering
and ordered prosperity. They will lift their heads in the great
cities / Of the empire and say: 'Freedom? Freedom was a fire. We
are well quit of freedom, we have found prosperity.'" After this,
however, "slowly the machines break down, slowly the wilderness
returns" ("Hellenistics"). In "The Purse-Seine," like "Hellenistics"
a poem of the 1930s, Jeffers presents the same idea.

Jeffers' views on specific political topics were not often expressed in poetry or in his letters, and there was no Boswell to
record his remarks—or, more precisely, to note the long silences
that he preferred to conversation. When he did express himself
on a current topic, however, his words make it clear that he had a
considerable factual familiarity with it. It is also certain that he
must have been exposed to the liberal and Marxist view of things,
for he had many left-wing or liberal friends: Charles Erskine Scott
Wood and his wife, Sara Bard Field, James Rorty, Louis Adamic,
George Sterling, Langston Hughes,[5] Ella Winter and her husband, Lincoln Steffens, and Albert Bender.

There are several examples of Jeffers' knowledgeability about
public issues. One appears in a letter to H. Arthur Klein of 4
October 1935. Klein, the author of a valuable but still unpublished
study of Jeffers' prosody, had suggested Georgi Dimitrov, the
Bulgarian Communist surprisingly acquitted in the famous Nazi
Reichstag fire trial, as a possible subject for a poem. Jeffers referred to the trail as "staged" and said, "I think it was not only
Communist morals that upheld Dimitrov—that was a factor, but
also Bulgarian toughness, and a power in the man himself" (Selected Letters, 230). Another example is Jeffers' response to a ques-
tionnaire from the League of American Writers that asked, "Are
you for, or are you against Franco and fascism?" and "Are you for,
or are you against the legal government and the people of Republican Spain?" Jeffers replied, in part, that "Great changes were
overdue in Spain, and the government's supporters are justified
in fighting for them. But Franco's people are justified in fighting
for the older Spain they are more or less loyal to, the religion they
believe in, and the rights they think are theirs, including the rights
to life and liberty. . . . As to fascism: I would fight it in this
country, but if the Italians want it that is their affair. The same
goes for Nazism. The same for communism, from which the
others learned their methods" (Selected Letters, 267). In "Going to

Horse Flats," Jeffers showed that Spain was still on his mind. Of the pro-Franco side he wrote: "They were proud and oppressed the poor and are punished for it; but those that punish them are full of envy and hatred / And are punished for it / and again the others; and again the others. / It is so forever, there is no way out."

One other example should suffice to show Jeffers' interest in and knowledge of public affairs. In an unfinished letter to the journalist Dorothy Thompson, who had written him in a moment of despair over the rise of Nazism in Germany and what she felt was the decay of decency in the world, he wrote:

> Germany has poetry on its side—race, blood, soil, the sword, sacrifice, vengeance,—are powerfully moving poetic conceptions (once the civilized insistence is broken down or avoided) even if they are false in fact or vicious in effect.
>
> Whereas democracy, fraternity, equality, civilization, humanitarianism, imagination, conversion, religion—are dangerous things. Christianity did not save the Roman civilization but presided over its destruction. (*Selected Letters*, 271)

What is significant here is Jeffers' understanding of official Nazi doctrine, an understanding not easily achieved by casual reading of the newspapers and newsmagazines. That doctrine, as developed by the "philosopher" Alfred Rosenberg, was built on four concepts: *blut, boden, ehre,* and *gemeinschaft.* Jeffers' terms essentially cover those: blood and race for *blut* and *gemeinschaft*, a misty term that in Nazi usage means fellowship or commonality; soil for *boden;* and, for honor, *ehre,* the combination of sword, sacrifice, and vengeance.

Granted that Jeffers thought there was "no way out" of the struggles of revolution and counterrevolution and that he believed that to say that civilizations rise and fall "is no more pessimistic than to say that men are born and die"—what were his specific preferences in politics? His wife described them in a letter to Fred B. Millett in 1937 as "Ideally, aristocratic and republican:—freedom for the responsible elements of society, and contentment for the less responsible. This idea being impractical for the present and conjecturable future, he is interested in politics but not inclined toward any party and votes in the sense of a choice of evils" (*Selected Letters*, 247). Una often masterfully summarized her husband's attitudes on many topics in her frequent role as amanuensis, but it looks in this case as if she has colored her interpretation of his views with her own, which seem to have been frequently reactionary. In his talk at the Library of Congress in early 1941, Jeffers sounded much more like a Jeffersonian democrat than someone with aristocratic views. He was the first speaker in the library's series entitled "The Poet in a Democracy," and so he began his talk with these remarks:

> . . . Our democracy has provided, and still provides, the greatest freedom for the greatest number of people. That is its special glory. It is a means of securing freedom, —the best and surest means, —but a means, to a purpose. Freedom is the purpose. Every decent government on earth aims at justice and public welfare, but ours is also aimed particularly at freedom; and that word, I think, best expresses our national ideal, the basic principle on which this republic was founded.

Then, after reading "Shine, Republic" to illustrate this view, he added:

> The word *democracy* means a system of government, the surest means towards freedom, and it has a secondary meaning in common usage. It means an attitude of mind, —tolerance, disregard of class-distinction, a recognition that each person, in certain rights and values, is equal to any other person. It means: no snobbery. And no flunkyism, no indecent humility.[6]

A society where class distinctions are disregarded, where there is no flunkyism or snobbery, and where equal rights are granted to all is not a place of "freedom for the responsible elements of society, and contentment for the less responsible." The statement just quoted, in conjunction with lines from many of Jeffers' poems, puts him squarely in the camp of Jefferson, and, perhaps, of some latter-day libertarian philosophers. Jeffers' words here, however, are often only a description of what democracy is supposed to be, not a song of praise. Democracy for Jeffers seems to have been the least of evils, with dictatorship ("I detest dictatorship, right, left, or center" he wrote Van Wyck Brooks in 1937) the greatest. It is interesting that the third president's preference for a society of small farmers matches the poet's frequently stated liking for a life close to nature (see "The Wind-Struck Music" and "Mara," especially.) This world of farmers and ranchers that Jeffers envied would be an uncrowded place. "Better for men to live far apart and be few," he advised in "Battle," though adding immediately, in parenthesis, "but that's a dream." Eliot expended considerable effort describing in his essays the ideal of a Christian, traditionalist, monarchist society. His contemporary Jeffers was more practical.

No lines are more fitting than the last six of "Original Sin" to conclude a discussion of the rational Jeffers, and to put his specific opinions in the context of his general concepts. For in these final words, he comments calmly on the events he has just described with anger (this sequence of emotional description and calm comment is a typical one in the lyrics):

> This is the human dawn. As for me, I would rather
> Be a worm in a wild apple than a son of man.
> But we are what we are, and we might remember
> Not to hate any person, for all are vicious;
> And not be astonished at any evil, all are deserved;
> And not fear death; it is the only way to be cleansed.

Jeffers' third kind of response to human affairs reconciles both thought to emotion and humanity to nature. In this view, the human race has two justifications for being present in the poet's beloved natural world. The first is simply that *genus humanae* is part of what Jeffers called in *Cawdor* the Great Life, the dynamic process of the growth, maturity, decay, death, and the reproduction of many lives, whether of mayflies, humans, planets, or solar systems. As he repeatedly stated in one way or another, Jeffers believed this process was divine; the human race must therefore be accepted as part of this whole. But the race had a second function in the poet's eyes: consciousness. Man, he wrote in "The Beginning and the End," is "one of God's sense-organs, / Immoderately alerted to feel good and evil." In scientific terms this translates into the concept that human beings are the only creatures capable of reflective thought and capable of communicating that reflection in written records, pictures, or music. Being conscious is a tragic condition because it means being aware of the terrible sufferings of humans through the centuries, even though some of these may be our own fault. Again and again Jeffers displays his own awareness of suffering, and nowhere more vividly than in "Passenger Pigeons," when he speaks of human bones:

> Bones that have been shaken with laughter and hung
>   slack in sorrow, coward bones
> Worn out with trembling, strong bones broken on the
>   rack, bones broken in battle,
> Broad bones gnarled with hard labor, and the little bones
>   of sweet young children. . . .

There is the evil, or a part of it, that the race is immoderately alerted to feel. The good, of course, is the "astonishing beauty of things," as when, in "The Great Explosion," dawn wanders "with wet feet down the Carmel Valley to meet the sea." Jeffers never ceased to celebrate this good.

Thus man has a role, as priest, in the function of exalting the beauty of things. And he has a role as sufferer, feeling the pain and the ugliness that he himself creates daily with his political behavior, which institutionalizes in different ways at different times greed, envy, power-hunger, and pride.

Jeffers himself, it seems clear, was a major sufferer. He was intensely interested in the doings of the human race, despite his call to his readers to turn outward toward nature; he kept up with current affairs and he read often of past ones. He was anything but the art-for-art's sake aesthete, contemplating a lily at a literary garden party. Nor could he deal in his writing with the political world as did his contemporary H. L. Mencken, who treated it as a grand, comic spectacle. Jeffers instead was a living refutation of Horace Walpole's epigram, "This world is a comedy to those that think, a tragedy to those that feel." Jeffers thought, and it was still a tragedy.

NOTES

1. R. I. Brigham, "Bitter and Skillful Treatise in Verse," *St. Louis Post-Dispatch*, 1 August 1948, sect. 6, 4f; quoted in Alex A. Vardamis, *The Critical Reputation of Robinson Jeffers* (Hamden, Conn.: Archon, 1972), 109.

2. Ann N. Ridgeway, ed., *The Selected Letters of Robinson Jeffers* (Baltimore: Johns Hopkins University Press, 1968), 117. Further references to the letters will be made in the text.

3. "Robinson Jeffers Today: Beyond Good and Beneath Evil," *American Literature* 10 (1977): 86.

4. "Science and the Poetry of Robinson Jeffers," *American Literature* 10 (1938): 275–88, passim.

5. One of the least known but most "political" of Jeffers' poems was a bit of light verse he wrote for his wife to read at the thirty-eighth birthday celebration of their friend Langston Hughes. In a letter of 1 February 1940, Una wrote her friend Maud (Mrs. Frederick Mortimer) Clapp that Jeffers had written a poem for her to read at the party. The title of the poem is a parody of the opening line ("Green as I would have you green") of Garcia Lorca's famous "Romance Sonambulo," which Hughes had translated. According to Una's letter, the poem read:

"Red as I wouldn't have you red."
       Una to Langston
"Red is a lovely color
Most pleasing to the eyes

But politically obnoxious
To me and Martin Dies.

Browder is red like a boil,
Stalin with red fire glows
But I am white like a lily
And Langston red like a rose.

Therefore as flower to flower
In spite of prejudices
I give him my affection
And birthday kisses.

Dies was then chirman of the House Un-American Activities Committee and
Earl Browder head of the Communist Party, U.S.A. Hughes was never actually a
member of the party. For a more complete account, see Edward A. Nickerson,
"An Unpublished Poem of Robinson Jeffers," *Yale University Library Gazette* 49
(1974): 231–33.
    6. Quoted in Melba Berry Bennett, *The Stone Mason of Tor House* (Los Angeles:
Ward Ritchie Press, 1966), 175.

Robinson Jeffers

Czeslaw Miłosz

Continent's End

At the equinox when the earth was veiled in a late rain,
   wreathed with wet poppies, waiting spring,
The ocean swelled for a far storm and beat its boundary,
   the ground-swell shook the beds of granite.

I gazing at the boundaries of granite and spray, the
   established sea-marks, felt behind me
Mountain and plain, the immense breadth of the continent,
   before me the mass and doubled stretch of water.

I said: You yoke the Aleutian seal-rocks with the lava and
   coral sowings that flower the south,
Over your flood the life that sought the sunrise faces ours
   that has followed the evening star.

The long migrations meet across you and it is nothing to
   you, you have forgotten us, mother.
You were much younger when we crawled out of the
   womb and lay in the sun's eye on the tideline.

It was long and long ago; we have grown proud since then
   and you have grown bitter; life retains
Your mobile soft unquiet strength; and envies hardness,
   the insolent quietness of stone.

The tides are in our veins, we still mirror the stars, life is
   your child, but there is in me
Older and harder than life and more impartial, the eye that
   watched before there was an ocean.

Previously published as "Carmel" in *Visions from San Francisco Bay* by Czeslaw Miłosz (New York: Farrar, Straus & Giroux, 1982), 87–94. Reprinted with permission of the publisher.

That watched you fill your beds out of the condensation of
 thin vapor and watched you change them,
That saw you soft and violent wear your boundaries
 down, eat rock, shift places with the continents.

Mother, though my song's measure is like your surf-beat's
 ancient rhythm I never learned it of you.
Before there was any water there were tides of fire, both
 our tones flow from the older fountain.

—Robinson Jeffers

Nor far from the steep coast of Big Sur, legendary as a hermitage
for hippie Buddhists, is the small town of Carmel with its mission,
the tomb of Father Junípero Serra, and another monument as
well—a little-remembered stone house by the water, built by the
poet Robinson Jeffers when today's elegant tourist and vacation
spot was only a fishing settlement. In that house Jeffers wrote
works dedicated to the contention that nature, perfectly beautiful,
perfectly cruel, and perfectly innocent, should be held in religious
veneration, whereas the human species was a sick excrescence, a
contamination of the universal order, and deserved only annihilation. One may suppose, however, that both his withdrawal into
seclusion (made possible by income received from relatives in
banking) and the direction his thoughts took were not without
their connection to World War I. The scorn shown mankind by
the creator of Inhumanism stemmed from an excess of compas-
sion, and many of his poems attest to his having read the newspapers with a sense of tragedy, wishing neither side victory. In his
mature years it was his fate to follow from his solitude the mas-
sacres of the thirties and forties, and what issued then from his
pen was laced with fury and sarcasm. To favor one side over
another, when he thought them both equally criminal monsters
tearing each other to pieces, was, in his eyes, a naïve submission to
propaganda.

I began to visit Carmel little more than two years after his death.
The cypress groves he planted to outlive his name had been cut
down because, in expanding, the little town had absorbed that
valuable property. Of the former wilderness there remained only
the crash of the waves spraying against the rocks, but the hill
where his house stands is separated from the sea by an asphalt
road hissing with tires. The gulls danced in the wind as they
always do, but a helicopter was flying above them, its rotor blades
clacking. The too-fertile humanity which Jeffers predicted would

suffocate on its own sinking excreta was now swarming in the deserts, on islands, and in the polar zones, and there was not much reason to believe that one could break free of its grasp.

We spent a long time walking around Jeffers' low granite house. Two large dogs were lying on the grass by the fence, a face appeared for a moment at the window. The tower standing a bit off to one side struck me most. It was there, I thought, that Jeffers would often go to meditate and write, listening to the ocean breathe, trying in his own words to be true to that single, age-old rhythm. Not to digress, I later learned that he had built the tower for his wife, Una, and so he must have only rarely worked there. The rough-hewn stones he fitted and joined made the building formless, and that worked well. Why didn't he maintain the stone's inherent modesty all the way through? But no, he stylized a bay window, an early medieval arch; denying history, taking refuge from it by communing with the body of a material God, in spite of everything he may still have seen himself as one of his own barbarian ancestors on the cliffs of Scotland and Ireland. That permanent oddity half-covered in ivy, that romantic monument raises various suspicions, even as far as Jeffers' poetry itself is concerned.

Who knows, he may have been just an aesthete. He needed to see himself as a being elevated above everything alive, contemplating vain passions and vain hopes, thereby rising above time as well. He seems to have been impressed at some point by tales of knights in their aeries, pirates in their lookouts by the sea. Even during my first visit to Carmel, I asked myself if I was like him, and, perhaps flattering myself, answered no. I was sufficiently like him to re-create his thoughts from within and to feel what had given rise to them. But I did not like my own regal soarings above the earth. That had been forced upon me and deserved to be called by its name, exile.

I also would have been unable to oppose eternal beauty to human chaos. The ocean, to him the fullest incarnation of harmony, was, I admit, horrifying for me. I even reproached Jeffers for his descriptive passages, too much those of the amateur painter who sets up his easel on a wild promontory. For me, the ocean was primarily an abyss where the nightmares located in the depths of hell by the medieval imagination came ceaselessly true, with endless variations. My kinship with the billions of monsters devouring each other was threatening because it reminded me who I was and their unconsciousness did not absolve me from sin.

Did Jeffers consider consciousness only an unforgivable flaw?

For him the nebulae, the sun, the rocks, the sea, sharks, crabs, were parts of an organism without beginning or end which eternally renews itself and which he called God. For he was a religious writer, though not in the sense that his father, a Calvinist pastor, would have approved. Jeffers studied biology as a young man, and once having accepted the mathematical system of cause and effect, he dethroned the Jehovah who makes incomprehensible demands of his subjects, who appears in a burning bush and makes a covenant with one tribe. Personal relations with a deity who graciously promises people that by remaining obedient to his commands they will escape the fate of all the rest of creation were, to his mind, only proof of what lengths human insolence and arrogance could reach. But Jeffers was even less able to reconcile himself to the scandalous figure of Jesus, which caused his stern and pious father to weigh all the more painfully on him; in rising from the dead, Jesus had broken a link in an infinite chain, thus making it known that the chosen would be wrested from the power of cause and effect, a power identified with hell. This was close to the claims of the modern revolutionaries who proclaimed universal happiness, but always for tomorrow, and Jeffers could not bear them. His God was pure movement pursuing no direction. Universes arose and died out in him, while he, indifferent to good and evil, maintained his round of eternal return, requiring nothing but praise for his continued existence.

This is very impressive even if Jeffers' attraction to piety and veneration was not unique among the anti-Christians of his time. He composed hymns of complete acceptance, and it is unclear whether he was more a stoic or the heir of his Calvinist father, who trembled before *Deus Terribilis*. Perhaps those were not hymns but psalms of penance. And it is because of his ardent bitterness that I acknowledge his superiority to his fellow citizens who sat down at the table, folded their hands in prayer, and said: "God is dead. Hurray! Let's eat!"

I have focused on his particular obsession. Whenever he wrote about people (usually dismal tales of fate, causing unbridled instincts to crush all the protagonists), they are reduced in size, tiny insects crawling along the piled furrows of the planet. He achieved that perspective by contrast with the background. Or, perhaps more important, his characters diminished as the action progressed, until finally the main hero, having committed murder, flees to the mountains, where his love, his hate, and the body with the knife in it now appeared ridiculous, inessential, pinpoints lost in infinity. What did that mean? Dimensions are a function of their distance from the eye. Like everyone else, Jeffers longed for a hierarchically ordered space divided into bottom, middle, and top, but an impersonal and immanent God could not serve as a keystone to a pyramid. Jeffers granted himself the superior position at the summit, he was a vulture, an eagle, the witness and judge of mortal men deserving of pity.

We used to walk the beach at Carmel fairly often, gathering pieces of wood, shells, and stones, smooth and pleasing to the touch. The cries of running children and the barking of their dogs vanished in the double roar of wind and surf. In the hollows shielded by the dunes, vacationers built fires, grilled frankfurters on sticks, took snapshots. Nearly all of them were unaware that Jeffers' house was nearby. Jeffers, if one overlooks a handful of admirers, has been almost completely forgotten. But, after all, whatever his faults, he was truly a great poet. Even in his own lifetime he did not have many readers, and before condemning his misanthropy, one must recall that he was neglected by people who placed great value on meat, alcohol, comfortable houses, and luxurious cars, and only tolerated words as if they were harmless hobbies. There was something paradoxical in my fascination with him; I was surprised that I, a newcomer from lands where everyone is burdened with history, where History is written with a capital H, was conducting a dialogue with his spirit though, had we met, we would not have been able to understand one another.

But I did conduct that dialogue. He was courageous, and so he broke through the spiderweb of invisible censorship as best he could, and compared with him, others were like dying flies utterly tangled in that web. They had lost the ability to be simple; they were afraid that if they called bread bread and wine wine they would be suspected of a lack of refinement, and the more caught they became in the perversions of their cultivation, the less sure they were of it. He bet everything, drew his own conclusions in voluntary isolation, making no attempt to please anyone, holding his own. Just as he appears, distinct, in photographs—the thin, proud face of a sailor, the narrow lips—Jeffers' work resembles nothing else produced in this century; it was not done for the cultural stock markets of the great capitals, and seemed intentionally to repel them by the violence of his tone, which is forgivable but only if the violence includes no preaching. His work is distorted, turn-of-the-century, tainted like that tower of his, but after all, he had to pay something too, like everyone else here. In contrast to the products of the jeweler's chisel to which we have become inadvertently accustomed, his work is striking in its simplicity, its roughness, but at the same time there was something sickly in his simplicity. The tasks he set himself no doubt exceeded his strength, and not his alone. In a time when no one knows what to believe in and what not to believe in, he studied himself and drew a distinct line expounding his image of God, the universe, and the human species, for which he foretold a quick finish. He understood the whole of his work as a new *De Rerum Natura,* and how could such ambition proceed without reversals?

I fumed at his naïveté and his errors, I saw him as an example of all the faults peculiar to prisoners, exiles, and hermits. But here in Carmel, where he had his body burned and his ashes strewn to the wind, his spirit, perhaps reincarnated in the gulls or pelicans flying over the beach in majestic formation, challenged me to wrestle and, through its courage, gave me courage.

Contributors

ROBERT BOYERS, Professor of English at Skidmore College, is the founder and editor of *Salmagundi* and editor of *The Bennington Review*. He has written studies of Lionel Trilling, F. R. Leavis, and R. P. Blackmur, and, most recently, *After the Avant-Garde* (1987).

ROBERT J. BROPHY has taught American literature at California State University, Long Beach, since 1968. He is the author of *Robinson Jeffers: Myth, Ritual, and Symbol in His Narrative Poems* (1973) and *Robinson Jeffers* (1975), and editor of Jeffers' *Dear Judas and Other Poems* (1977), *Whom Should I Write For* (1979), and *Songs and Heroes* (1988). He is currently engaged in editing the *Collected Letters of Robinson and Una Jeffers* for Stanford University Press with James Karman and Robb Kafka. Since 1968 he has been editor of the *Robinson Jeffers Newsletter*.

R. W. (HERBIE) BUTTERFIELD is Reader in Literature at the University of Essex. He is the author of *The Broken Arc: A Study of Hart Crane* (1969), an essay on Jeffers in *Modern American Poetry*, a volume edited by himself, and essays on Willa Cather, Ernest Hemingway, Herman Melville, Ambrose Bierce, and F. Scott Fitzgerald.

FREDERIC I. CARPENTER received his B.A. from Harvard in 1924 and his Ph.D. from the University of Chicago in 1929, and subsequently taught at Chicago, Harvard, and the University of California at Berkeley. He was the author of *Emerson and Asia* (1930), *American Literature and the Dream* (1955), and volumes in the Twayne Authors series on Jeffers (1962) and Eugene O'Neill. His essays on Jeffers appeared in *American Literature, Western American Literature,* and elsewhere. He died in 1991.

ARTHUR B. COFFIN is Professor of English and former department head at Montana State University. He received his Ph.D. from the University of Wisconsin in 1965 and is the author of *Robinson Jeffers: Poet of Inhumanism* (1971).

WILLIAM EVERSON, the distinguished American poet and printer, is the author of *Robinson Jeffers: Fragments of an Older Fury* (1968) and *The Excesses of God: Robinson Jeffers as a Religious Figure* (1988). He has edited Jeffers' *Californians* (1971), *The Alpine Christ and Other Poems* (1974), and *Brides of the South Wind* (1974), as well as *Cawdor and Medea* (1970).

HORACE GREGORY (1898–1982), the eminent poet, translator, critic, and biographer, received the Bollingen Prize in 1965 for his *Collected Poems.*

TIM HUNT is Associate Professor of English at Washington State University. He is the author of *Kerouac's Crooked Road: Development of a Fiction* (1981) and editor of *The Collected Poetry of Robinson Jeffers* (1988–   ). His essays on Jeffers have appeared in *American Literature*, the *Robinson Jeffers Newsletter*, and in *Critical Essays on Robinson Jeffers* (1990), edited by James Karman. He contributed the afterword to the Norton reissue of *The Women at Point Sur* (1977).

DELL HYMES has taught at Harvard, the University of California at Berkeley, and the University of Pennsylvania, and is currently Professor of Anthropology and English at the University of Virginia. His many books include *Language in Culture and Society* (1964), *Reinventing Anthropology* (1972), *"In Vain I Tried to Tell You": Studies in Native American Ethnopoetics* (1981), and *Essays in the History of Linguistic Anthropology* (1983). Most of his recent work has been concerned with the analysis of Native American myth and art.

CZESLAW MIŁOSZ received the Nobel Prize in literature in 1980. His *Collected Poems 1931–1987* appeared in 1988.

DAVID COPLAND MORRIS is Assistant Professor of English at Butler University. He holds master's degrees in English and in Regional Planning from the University of North Carolina, Chapel Hill, and received the Ph.D. from the University of Washington for his dissertation, "Literature and Environment: The Inhumanist Perspective and the Poetry of Robinson Jeffers" (1984).

EDWARD A. NICKERSON is Professor of English at the University of Delaware, where he directs the journalism program and teaches American literature. He has published a number of articles and reviews on Jeffers and has recently coedited an edition of Sheridan's translation of Guarini's *Il Pastor Fido*.

ALEX A. VARDAMIS teaches English at the University of Vermont. He received a B.S. from the United States Military Academy and his M.A. and Ph.D. degrees from Columbia University. He is the author of *The Critical Reputation of Robinson Jeffers* (1972).

ROBERT ZALLER is Professor of History at Drexel University. He is the author of *The Cliffs of Solitude: A Reading of Robinson Jeffers* (1983) and editor of *The Tribute of His Peers: Elegies for Robinson Jeffers* (1989), and has contributed to *Critical Essays on Robinson Jeffers*, edited by James Karman.

Index

"Adjustment," 180
"Age in Prospect," 90
"Air-Raid Rehearsals," 260
Alberts, S. S., 137 n.8, 141, 145, 153, 160 n.2, 162, 168
"Alpine Christ, The," 31, 140, 142–64, 166–67, 175, 177–78, 181
Alpine Christ and Other Poems, The, 137–61, 167, 180
Altieri, Charles, 91–94
Anderson, Dame Judith, 58
"Answer, The," 37, 108
"Ante Mortem," 72, 231, 232
Antoninus, Brother. *See* Everson, William
"Apology for Bad Dreams," 35, 38, 153
"Artist, An," 35, 125, 249, 250–52
"At the Birth of an Age," 145, 159–60, 222, 225 n.8, 259
"At the Fall of an Age," 25–26, 145, 259
"Ave Caesar," 23

"Barren Foreland, A," 181
Bartlett, Peter, 141
"Battle," 264
"Be Angry at the Sun," 43 n.24, 230, 233
Be Angry at the Sun and Other Poems, 22, 40, 47, 48, 49, 160 n.1, 184–85 n.21, 258
"Beginning and the End, The," 265
Beginning and the End and Other Poems, The, 53, 54
"Beginning of Decadence," 182
Bennett, Melba Berry, 57, 172
"Birds," 231, 232
"Bird with the Dark Plumes, The," 34–35
"Blind Horses," 23, 255
"Blood-Guilt, The," 41
"Bloody Sire, The," 230
"Boats in a Fog," 231, 232

Boswell, Jeanetta, 57, 61
"Bowl of Blood, The," 134, 145, 156, 260
Bricolage: concept of, 188–89; in Jeffers, 189, 195, 197–98
Brides of the South Wind, 31, 55, 140, 141, 142, 161–85
"Broadstone, The," 72
"Broken Balance, The," 35
Brophy, Robert, 56, 105 n.22, 106 n.29, 126, 237

Californians, 10, 31, 55, 86, 93, 123–37, 146, 147, 149–54, 162, 165
Carpenter, Frederic Ives, 156, 228
"Cassandra," 40, 232, 233
"Cawdor," 188, 196–97, 214–15, 217–18, 222, 223, 225 n.8, 265
Cawdor and Other Poems, 10
"Cloud, The," 148–49
"Coast-Range Christ, The": characters in, 214, 216–17, 222; and feminine archetype, 176–78; included with "Tamar," 99, 104 n.20; mentioned, 143; vista of, 238
"Come, Little Birds," 132–33, 134
"Compensation," 180
"Consciousness," 180
"Contemplation of the Sword," 49–50, 184–85 n.21
"Continent's End," 91, 92–93, 94, 99; metric of, 230, 234, 239; quoted, 268–69
Crabbe, George, 101–2
"Credo," 190
Cretan Woman, The, 16, 26
"Cruel Falcon, The," 72, 79–80, 234–35
"Crumbs or the Loaf," 40
"Cycle, The," 91

"Dance of the Banners, The," 100, 105–6 n.28

"Dead to Clemenceau, The," 39
"Dear Judas," 38, 50, 145, 148, 201, 208, 212
Dear Judas and Other Poems, 10, 46, 55, 62, 200–201, 208
De Casseres, Benjamin, 45, 50
De Man, Paul, 116
"De Rerum Virtute," 259
Derrida, Jacques, 111, 112, 114, 115, 188, 189, 198
Descent to the Dead, 10, 16, 23, 39, 42, 43 n.17
Deutsch, Babette, 32, 44, 48
"Diagram," 259
Dickey, James, 52, 60, 107, 109, 110
Dimitrov, Giorgi, 262
"Divinely Superfluous Beauty," 87, 178, 230, 232
Double Axe and Other Poems, The: attitudes toward humanity in, 258; censorship of, 260; controversy over, 40, 47–49, 254; politics of, 256–57; republication of, 55, 59; sales of, 62
"Drunken Charlie," 256

Eberhart, Richard, 52
Elder, Frederick, 109
Eliot, T. S., 11, 31, 36, 37, 52, 61, 69, 102, 104–5 n.22, 186, 187, 216, 256, 264
"Emilia," 125
Everson, William (Brother Antoninus), 54, 56–57, 70–71, 72, 80, 103 n.7, 107, 216, 217, 226, 245
"Excesses of God, The," 87–88, 104 n.8, 160 n.1, 178–79, 230, 233

Faulkner, William, 27, 34, 37–38
"Fauna," 143, 163, 168, 170–72, 173–74, 176–80
"Fire on the Hills," 72
Flagons and Apples, 17, 30, 55, 86, 123, 124, 173
"Fog," 231, 232
"For Una," 249, 252–53
Fox, C. J., 49, 54, 59, 60
Frazer, Sir James, 104–5 n.22, 224 n.6.
Freud, Sigmund, 17, 33, 130
Frost, Robert, 31, 50, 52, 61, 151–52

"Ghosts in England," 23, 24
"Give Your Heart to the Hawks," 18, 20, 21, 222, 223
Give Your Heart to the Hawks and Other Poems, 10, 142
"God's Peace in November," 179–80
Goethe, Johann Wolfgang von, 161 n.19
"Going to Horse Flats," 262–63
"Granite and Cypress," 231
"Great Explosion, The," 266
"Great Men," 260
"Great Sunset, The," 37
Greenan, Edith, 173, 184 n.15

Hardy, Thomas, 31, 156–60, 161 n.17, 167
Hartman, Geoffrey, 111–15
"Haunted Country," 72
"Hellenistics," 72, 262
Hemingway, Ernest, 215
Hitler, Adolf, 22–23, 39, 47, 260–61
Hotchkiss, Bill, 54, 61
Hughes, Langston, 266–67 n.5
"Humanist's Tragedy, The," 222
"Hungerfield," 18, 59, 221, 261–62
"Hurt Hawks," 29, 61, 72, 258

Inhumanism: Jeffers' concept of, 51, 57, 107–11, 118, 120, 187, 189, 197, 199 n.2, 211, 269
"Inhumanist, The," 159, 261
"Inscription for a Gravestone," 42
"In the Hill at New Grange," 23
In This Wild Water, 48
"Invasion," 106 n.32
"Invocation," 151
Irwin, John T., 34, 43 n.11

Jarrell, Randall, 53, 62, 68–69
Jeffers, Donnan, 9
Jeffers, Garth, 9
Jeffers, Hamilton, 184–85 n.21, 261
Jeffers, Robinson: accused of fascism, 48, 161 n.17; adultery of, 131, 133, 164, 170–73, 176, 184–85 n.21; aesthetic values of, 74–84; birth and education, 9, 17–18, 27 n.1, 259, 261; centenary of, 12 n.1, 58; classicism of, 24–27, 53, 159, 168, 196, 197, 214–15, 220–21, 223; coastal

setting of poems, 19, 25, 31, 127, 139, 151, 153, 162–63, 165, 202; concept of nature in, 86–103, 105 n.24, 117–18, 265; and consciousness, 108, 265; critical reception of, 10, 15, 29–43, 44–69, 101–2, 109, 254–55, 260; critical studies of, 54, 56–57; and culture cycles, 259, 263; death patterns of characters, 221–22; depression of, 163, 173, 180; dissertations on, 56; dramatic narratives of, 145–46, 154, 159–60, 167, 212; and ecology movement, 60, 62, 85, 255; and Eros-Thanatos archetype, 167–79, 184 n.20, 185 n.24; and Europe, 31, 38–39, 43 n.17, 49, 154–55, 163; and fascism, 262, 263; feminine archetypes of, 129–30, 134, 177, 184 n.20, 185 n.24; figure of Jesus in, 20, 38, 50, 145, 148, 208–9, 222, 225 n.8, 237–40, 242, 260, 271; Freudian elements in, 21, 104–5 n.22, 128, 130, 214–20, 227; and humanity, 35, 37, 76, 81, 82–83, 88–90, 93, 94–95, 194, 199 n.7; incest, theme of, 38, 126–29, 181–82, 191, 214–20, 245, 248; lyric poetry of, 93, 94, 95, 265; Marxist critics of, 45–46, 51, 262; maternal influence on, 129–32, 134–36, 153; metric of, 22, 103 n.5, 124, 137 n.8, 160, 175, 182, 226–47; and modernism, 10, 11, 85, 91–92, 101–2, 147; narrative poetry of, 18, 20, 27 n.1, 36, 70–72, 85, 93, 94–95, 96, 106 n.30, 146, 212, 243–44, 248–49; and Native American poetry, 245; and New Criticism, 29, 36, 52–53, 62, 101, 102, 109–10, 200; Nietzschean elements in, 18, 19, 22, 24, 45, 85, 130, 191–97; and occult experience, 132–36, 137 n.10; paternal influence on, 132–36, 148, 150, 151, 154, 163, 164, 167, 179, 216, 259; poetics of, 36–37, 41–42, 89, 100–3, 113, 115, 186–87; politics of, 10, 23, 37–38, 46, 47, 49–50, 98, 99, 254–67; posthumous editions of, 55, 57, 62; and poststructuralism, 109–17; productions abroad of, 59; and prophecy, 38, 39–41, 76; as prose stylist, 30; religious vision of, 57, 79, 142–43, 148–49, 159, 166, 178, 187, 190, 205, 211, 265, 271; ritual elements in, 220–24, 225 n.8; and romanticism, 57, 71, 91–92, 101–2, 147; and science, 27, 92, 117–18, 198, 261–62; sexuality in, 20, 21, 33–34, 36, 50, 71, 193, 248 (see also Eros-Thanatos archetype; Freudian elements; incest); sources of, 18–19, 24–25, 31, 91–92, 201–2, 212 n.9, 223, 259; and Spanish civil war, 38, 262–63; stone imagery in, 90–91, 115, 118–21, 130–31, 154, 181–82, 185 n.23, 233, 249–53; taught in universities, 61–62, 63; theater of, 10, 16, 58, 59, 146; and Tor House, 10, 31, 32, 131, 180–81, 182, 269–70; tragic vision of, 84, 253; translations of, 58–59; and Vietnam war, 59, 60, 261; violence in, 152–53, 161 n.17, 165, 175–80; and Western civilization, 18, 39, 79 (see also culture cycles; Europe); and World War I, 20, 31, 49, 98, 99, 131, 132, 139, 142, 145–47, 148, 151, 152–55, 157, 159, 163–80, 182, 184–85 n.21, 199 n.2, 261, 269; and World War II, 22, 39, 40, 47, 49–50, 98, 134, 146, 184–85 n.21, 199 n.2, 261; youth and marriage, 9, 17–18, 31–32 (see also adultery of; depression of; Jeffers, Una)

Jeffers, Una: addressed in "The Three Avilas," 127–28; on "The Alpine Christ," 141, 153; as amanuensis, 136 n.6, 263; confinement of, 153–54, 163–64; devotion of, 17; as guide to Jeffers, 180–81; letter to Lawrence Clark Powell, 130–31; marriage and marital difficulties of, 30, 164, 172–74, 184 n.15; mentioned, 257; poems about, 171–72, 252–53; and politics of Jeffers, 263–64; settles in Carmel, 151, 163; sociability of, 9; as student, 161 n.17; suicide attempt of, 184–85 n.21; and Tor House, 270. See also Hughes, Langston; Jeffers, Robinson

Jefferson, Thomas, 264
Jerome, Judson, 57, 61
"Joy," 58, 231, 232
Joyce, James, 33, 112–13

Karman, James, 57
Klein, H. Arthur, 226, 245–46 n.6, 262

Lawrence, D. H., 15–16, 17, 33, 36, 45, 71; on James Joyce, 112
Lechlitner, Ruth, 46–47
Levi-Strauss, Claude, 188, 197, 198, 245
Lewis, Sinclair, 9, 52
"Life from the Lifeless," 235–36, 248 n.14
"Little Scraping, A," 72
"Local Legend," 255–56
"Love and the Hate, The," 177, 215, 219, 221, 222, 257
"Loving Shepherdess, The," 18, 20– 21, 28 n.4, 201–13, 225 n.8
"Low Sky, The," 72
Lucretius, 189, 197
Luhan, Mabel Dodge, 45, 50, 184– 85 n.21

McGann, Jerome, 101–2
"Maid's Thought, The," 72, 87, 88, 99, 105 n.23, 178
"Maldrove," 125, 161 n.17, 165
Mallarmé, Stephane, 113
"Mal Paso Bridge," 131–32, 142, 152, 170–74, 175, 176, 180, 229
"Mara," 222, 264
"Margrave," 222
Marx, Leo, 107, 108, 111
Masters, Edgar Lee, 52
Medea: Jeffers' adaptation of, 10, 26, 53, 58, 146, 222
"Meditation on Saviors," 35, 38, 40, 43 n.22, 195
Mencken, H. L., 45, 266
Midgley, Mary, 109, 116
Millay, Edna St. Vincent, 50, 52
Miller, J. Hillis, 110, 114
"Moral Beauty," 150, 151, 166, 168
More, Paul Elmer, 51, 187
"Mountain Village, The," 154
Munthe, Axel, 169–70

"Murmansk Landing, The," 100, 105– 6 n.28

"Natural Music," 89, 90, 91, 98, 99, 104 n.10, 230, 232
Nietzsche, Friedrich, 11, 130, 190–91, 227
"Night," 237, 238, 239–43
Nolte, William, 49, 54, 57, 60, 61
Not Man Apart, 55, 255
"Not Our Good Luck," 91
"November Surf," 72, 81

"Ode on Human Destinies," 150, 151, 165–66
"Of Not Going to War," 182
"Oh, Lovely Rock," 118–21
O'Neill, Eugene, 34, 50, 248
"Original Sin," 258–59, 265
"Ossian's Grave," 39, 42, 72

"Passenger Pigeons," 265
"Peacock Ranch," 142–43, 174–76, 177, 181, 182
"People and a Heron," 231, 232
"Poetry, Gongorism and a Thousand Years," 41–42, 55
"Point Alma Venus," 105 n.22, 106 n.30
"Point Joe," 95–98, 230, 239
"Point Pinos and Point Lobos," 166, 230, 233, 234, 237–39, 240–42
"Post Mortem," 72, 231
Pound, Ezra, 11, 31, 36, 37, 38, 49, 69, 102, 254
"Practical People," 72
"Promise of Peace," 180
"Purse-Seine, The," 72, 73, 262

Ransom, John Crowe, 53, 74
"Rearmament," 43 n.15, 72, 83, 84
"Redeemer, A," 255
"Return," 72, 77–78, 80, 114, 115–17
"Return to Paradise," 151
Rexroth, Kenneth, 10, 69, 70
"Roan Stallion," 15, 32, 33, 45, 50, 57, 71, 187, 188, 192–94, 221–22, 225 n.8
Roan Stallion, Tamar and Other Poems, 10, 15, 16, 30, 44–45, 46, 100, 104 n.12, 186–87, 229–32

Robinson, Edward Arlington, 21, 22, 85
Robinson Jeffers Newsletter, 56
Rodman, Selden, 29, 52
Roosevelt, Franklin D., 47, 256, 260–61
Rorty, James, 16, 44, 47, 194, 195, 256, 262

Sade, Marquis de, 18–19, 21, 28 n.3
"Salmon Fishing," 89–90, 91, 93, 94, 231, 232
Schopenhauer, Friedrich, 85, 189–90
"Science," 231, 232, 261
Selected Poetry, 17, 23, 30–31, 34, 55, 103 n.5, 104 n.10, 134, 167
"Self-Criticism in February," 27 n.3, 37
"Shakespeare's Grave," 23, 42
Shelley, Percy Bysshe, 31, 32, 126, 144–45, 156–58
"Shine, Empire," 49
"Shine, Perishing Republic," 20, 29, 72, 76–77, 91, 99, 100, 230, 239, 255
"Shine, Republic," 58, 264
Snodgrass, W. D., 260
Solstice, 10, 48, 53
"So Many Blood-Lakes," 41
"Songs of the Dead Men to the Three Dancers, The," 164, 167, 168, 179
Starr, Kevin, 60
"Stars, The," 151
"Stephen Brown," 125
Sterling, George, 9, 17, 18, 44, 50, 137 n.9, 262
Stevens, Wallace, 61, 75, 101, 102, 187
"Subjected Earth," 39
"Such Counsels You Gave to Me," 20, 21, 47, 215, 218–19, 222
"Suicide's Stone," 90
"Summer Holiday," 231

"Tamar": characters of, 70, 216, 221 (*see also* "Tamar," victims in; Tamar, characters of); critical reception of, 15, 44, 52, 226; date of composition, 137 n.8, 182–83; discussion of, 191–92; fire as defining element of, 181; genesis of, 93–95, 135, 185 n.24; and incest, 33, 126–29, 191; and Jeffers' poetic development, 131,
132; mentioned, 187; metric of, 227, 237, 247 n.18; and Native American solar myth, 245; and Eugene O'Neill, 248; operatic version of, 58; source of, 18, 24; and *Tamar,* 106 n.30; and "Tower Beyond Tragedy," 146; victims in, 188, 214; and World War I, 20, 99–100
Tamar: character of, 125, 132–33, 135, 136, 177, 184 n.20, 185 n.24, 237
Tamar and Other Poems, 44, 86–101, 103 n.8, 104 n.20, 106 n.30, 131, 132, 162, 168, 229–32
Tennyson, Alfred Lord, 31, 175
"Thebaid," 23, 260
Themes in My Poems, 90, 198
"Theory of Truth," 43 n.16, 134, 137 n.10
"Three Avilas, The," 126–29, 130, 153
"Thurso's Landing," 10, 36, 215, 218, 222
Thurso's Landing and Other Poems, 45, 46
"To His Father," 180, 181
"To His Sons," 182
"To the House," 230, 232, 234
"To the Rock That Will Be a Cornerstone of the House," 90–91, 230, 231, 232, 234
"To the Stone-Cutters," 72, 88, 104 n.10, 231, 232, 249–50, 251
"To U.J.," 171–72
"Tower Beyond Tragedy, The," 25, 32, 33, 40, 140, 145, 146, 214, 217, 222–23, 261
"Trap, The," 40
"Treasure, The," 72
"Truce and the Peace, The," 255
Trumbo, Dalton, 257

"Unnatural Powers," 75–76

Van Doren, Mark, 29, 44, 69, 256
"Vardens, The," 126

Waggoner, Hyatt Howe, 259, 261
"What Odd Expedients," 260–61
Whitehead, Alfred North, 121
Williams, William Carlos, 61, 233, 236
"Wind-Struck Music, The," 264
Winters, Yvor, 46, 50, 74, 200–1

"Wise Men in Their Bad Hours," 230, 231, 232

"Woman Down the Coast, A," 150, 151, 180

"Women at Point Sur, The," 20, 35, 36, 70–71, 125–26, 152, 187–88, 194–96, 199 n.7, 205, 206, 222, 223, 248, 256

Women at Point Sur and Other Poems, The, 10, 34, 50, 52, 55, 62, 100, 106 n.30, 159. *See also* "Point Alma Venus"

"Woodrow Wilson," 22, 261

Wordsworth, William, 31, 91–92, 101

"Year of Mourning, The," 133, 134, 149, 151, 154, 165, 167

Yeats, William Butler, 24–25, 27, 43 n.24, 76, 81, 84, 135, 181

Young, Vernon, 48–49, 59

Zaller, Robert, 57, 226–27